LIBRARY, ST.PATRICK'S COLLEGE, DUBLIN 9
LEABHARLANN, COLÁISTE PHÁDRAIG, B.Á.C. 9

000159935

SUPPORTING THE FAMILIES OF
CHILDREN WITH

SUPPORTING THE FAMILIES OF CHILDREN WITH AUTISM

Peter Randall and Jonathan Parker

JOHN WILEY & SONS, LTD
Chichester • New York • Weinheim • Brisbane • Singapore • Toronto

Copyright © 1999 by John Wiley & Sons Ltd,
Baffins Lane, Chichester,
West Sussex PO19 1UD, England

National   01243 779777
International   (+44) 1243 779777
e-mail (for orders and customer service enquiries):
cs-books@wiley.co.uk
Visit our Home Page on http://www.wiley.co.uk
or http://www.wiley.com

All Rights Reserved. No part of this publication may be reproduced, stored in a retrieval
system, or transmitted, in any form or by any means, electronic, mechanical,
photocopying, recording, scanning or otherwise, except under the terms of the Copyright,
Designs and Patents Act 1988 or under the terms of a licence issued by the Copyright
Licensing Agency, 90 Tottenham Court Road, London, W1P 9HE, UK, without the
permission in writing of the Publisher.

Other Wiley Editorial Offices

John Wiley & Sons, Inc., 605 Third Avenue,
New York, NY 10158-0012, USA

WILEY-VCH Verlag GmbH, Pappelallee 3,
D-69469 Weinheim, Germany

Jacaranda Wiley Ltd, 33 Park Road, Milton,
Queensland 4064, Australia

John Wiley & Sons (Asia) Pte Ltd, 2 Clementi Loop #02-01,
Jin Xing Distripark, Singapore 129809

John Wiley & Sons (Canada) Ltd, 22 Worcester Road,
Rexdale, Ontario M9W 1L1, Canada

Leabharlann
MB
000159935
CLASS 616.85 882 RAN
18/8/04
ROI   ONRACH

Library of Congress Cataloging-in-Publication Data

Randall, Peter, 1948–
    Supporting the families of children with autism / Peter Randall
and Jonathan Parker.
        p.   cm.
    Includes bibliographical references and index.
    ISBN 0-471-97484-6 (cloth).—ISBN 0-471-98218-0 (paper)
    1. Autistic children—Family relationships.   2. Parents of
autistic children.   3. Autism—Patients—Family relationships.
4. Autism in children.   I. Parker, Jonathan, 1960– .   II. Title.
RJ506.A9R35   1999
649′. 154—dc21

                                                                    98-55962
                                                                    CIP

British Library Cataloguing in Publication Data

A catalogue record for this book is available from the British Library

ISBN 0-471-97484-6 (cloth)
1SBN 0-471-98218-0 (paper)

Typeset in 10/12 pt Palatino by Best-set Typesetter Ltd., Hong Kong
Printed and bound in Great Britain by Bookcraft (Bath) Ltd, Midsomer Norton, Somerset
This book is printed on acid-free paper responsibly manufactured from sustainable
forestry, in which at least two trees are planted for each one used for paper production.

For our families, colleagues and friends

ST. PATRICKS
COLLEGE
LIBRARY

CONTENTS

ABOUT THE AUTHORS

Peter Randall was the first Director and progenitor of the Family Assessment and Support Unit, at the University of Hull. His prior professional experience in educational psychology has led to the development of a specific interest in social, communication and developmental disorders of childhood. This is especially the case in respect of access to services which seemed to many people a complex, difficult and off-putting experience.

Jonathan Parker, current Director of the Family Assessment and Support Unit, comes from a professional background in mental health social work and cognitive-behavioural psychotherapy. His academic brief concerned the development of practitioner training and the establishment of a clinical research profile for the Unit.

PREFACE

The pressures, strains and, sometimes, joys of looking after a child with autism are increasingly recognised in professional and academic circles. This book presents key findings from our research study on the needs of the families of children with autism. Our intention is to provide clear understanding and practical advice arising from this study for practitioners working with families and children with autism and also, importantly, for those families themselves. The study, conducted at the Family Assessment and Support Unit, charts, for us, some of the developments that have taken place in our research and practice with families in which one child, or more, has autism. Moreover, it has crystallised our belief in the potential for greater development in the important marriage of practitioner training, and academic and clinical research throughout the helping professions.

Although it is becoming somewhat trite to say this, there are so many people to thank that we cannot mention everyone by name. We must mention, however, our immense gratitude to the National Autistic Society and their support for our research, and the invaluable help of the Humberside branch, especially Sally Stokes, the then chair of this group. Also, we could not have conducted such a widespread survey without the assistance of the trainee practitioners who learned the skills of the research interview so quickly and applied them so well. The importance of the University of Hull's support for the pioneering work which we have begun to develop at the Unit has been fundamental to our work with families where autism is an issue. Finally, of course, our thanks, appreciation and respect go to those families caring for a child or young person with autism and the person, him- or herself, who is struggling with a difficult and strange world.

To all those we cannot mention by name, we offer this book as a small token of thanks and hope that everyone has gained a little from the process and practice of this study.

Peter Randall and Jonathan Parker

August 1998

INTRODUCTION

The research study, of which this book is a product, stemmed from the recognition of a clear need for family services where autism is a feature. In 1994, the Family Assessment and Support Unit came into being. One of the first actions of the Unit was to set up local and national links to facilitate access to diagnostic assessment and to social and behavioural support for parents of children with autism. The nexus of client, support group and professionals, created by the work of the Unit, provided a standard to carry forward and explore. As members of Hull University, the authors shared a commitment to the training and development of practitioners and the production of high-quality clinical research. Our research study was greatly assisted by the constructive suggestions of the National Autistic Society.

One of the reasons for our continued interest in this field stems from the experience of families where there is a child with autism. Families often face enormous stress in having the disorder diagnosed. For many, there is the complex stress associated with increasing social and behavioural difficulties, there is guilt arising from others attributing these difficulties to the parents' 'mismanagement' of the children and there is the lack of willingness on the part of many professionals to acknowledge the likelihood or possibility of autism. It is in Chapter 1 that we outline some of the complex stressors affecting families. We draw on case-study material from the families we have seen at the Family Assessment and Support Unit and from many others that we have visited from it. This material is set in the context of previous research into the experiences of families with autism, unfortunately concluding that little has, in fact, changed.

The survey research we completed is described in Chapter 2. It builds on earlier research into needs (Liwag, 1989). Need is, of course, a notoriously difficult concept to define and can be 'hijacked' by interested parties and those in control of resources (Department of Health/Social Services Inspectorate, 1991). Rather than consider needs using a traditional hierarchical approach which may lend itself to resource-determined eligibility criteria, we chose to complement this with Bradshaw's (1992)

conceptualisation of the four elements of need. This allowed for normative, service definitions to be combined with the perceptual and attitudinal responses of individuals and families.

In the third chapter we outline the history of diagnosis and assessment
of autism from Kanner (1943) onwards, and we argue for the necessity
of multidisciplinary and in-depth assessment. It is in this chapter that
we present a picture of the main features associated with autism and the
core criteria for diagnosis, and consider questions relating to the fraught
area of aetiology. At the Family Assessment and Support Unit we offer
parents advice regarding assessment and diagnosis. People are told not
to accept a label but to ask questions and to insist on individually tailored
intervention.

Of course, autism is not always easy to diagnose and many confusions are possible. In Chapter 4 we delineate a range of possible
difficulties that can make diagnosis equivocal. Problems result from
many primary sources including a lack of knowledge amongst professionals and the need for funding authorities to restrict expenditure.
However, the importance for parents and children is clear and we
argue for an unequivocal diagnosis related to the diagnostic criteria
accepted.

The next two chapters focus in some detail on the profound and
significant effects that autism has on parents. This happens in two
discernible ways. The shock of something being wrong and, after time, a
diagnosis being given presents a situational crisis for parents. Also,
however, the long-term cumulative stress that builds up over time creates
enormous stressors, both on individual parents and between parents, and
affects the wider family unit and relationships within it.

The importance of social support in relation to coping is recognised
throughout the literature. It is also acknowledged that such support is
often lacking in families in which there are children with autism.

One of the major needs that is presented by families is to gain some
degree of understanding, control and management of behaviours that are
construed as challenging. Important in this regard, and much appreciated
by many of the families we have worked with in the Family Assessment
and Support Unit, are contingency management approaches derived from
operant and respondent conditioning. In Chapter 7 we demonstrate the
use of these interventions whilst acknowledging their clear limitations.
The importance of real participation with parents is emphasised, as we
have found time and again that parents 'know their own children best'.
Inclusion in the process of assessment, mediation and delivery of inter-
ventive programmes to replace challenging behaviours with more proso-
cial ones allows the parents to 'feel' involved and to be motivated, and it
ensures that they are comfortable with the strategies chosen. We consider

a range of techniques to help parents to tackle some of the more commonly experienced challenging behaviours.

Children and young people grow up, and autism itself does not remain static but changes and develops within children and their families. The needs of children with autism and their families cannot be addressed by contingency management programmes alone, and in the final two chapters we consider the range of educational and social needs of young people with autism, and also their changing needs as they experience puberty and young adulthood. These are fraught times for all parents and perhaps more so for the parents of children with autism.

Our intentions in this book are to promote sensitive and constructive approaches to the management of autism, to raise awareness of the needs of families and to offer a glimmer of hope for those living and working with individuals with autism and their families. It represents the product of four years of experience and research at the Family Assessment and Support Unit. Although the role of the Unit with regard to diagnostic assessment has changed there remains the commitment to provide behavioural and social support. In this way we hope to serve the families and individuals with autism that we have been privileged to meet and work with.

1

'SOMETHING IS WRONG WITH OUR CHILD'

John, a well-made 4-year-old, gyrated into the Family Room of the Family Assessment and Support Unit, his mother in tow. She was invisible to him as he tugged her away from a toy garage that caught his eye. He ran for it and knocked her aside again as she reached to pick him up. She tried to hold him and talk to him soothingly, but he refused her eye contact and deliberately moved his head and neck in desperate contortions to avoid looking at her. In desperation, she gave up and let him have his way; annoyed and humiliated she turned on me,[1] and said angrily 'And don't you tell me it's my fault he's like this'.

Later it became very clear that John was severely autistic, as indeed his presentation suggested. His mother had certainly picked up from the polite and platitudinous comments she had heard from several people that her management was responsible for the child's wilful and defiant behaviour. She had gone through a phase of feeling guilty before coming to accept that whatever she had done or failed to do as a parent, her child could not possibly behave in the way that he did simply because of her mismanagement.

There are few developmental disorders of childhood that create such complex stressors for families as autism. Not only is the disorder hidden behind a physical appearance of normality but also, for a variety of reasons, it creates enormous difficulties in terms of obtaining a diagnosis. Not only do the parents have to tolerate increasingly obsessive behaviour, destructive acts, failure to communicate, emotional rejection, aggression and tantrums, but also it appears that they have to cope with fragmentary professional services that are difficult to obtain and sometimes downright obstructive, from the time of seeking a diagnosis onward.

---

[1] The first author.

Perhaps due to the comparative rarity of autism, the range of professionals who are willing and able to make a diagnosis of autism is smaller than it should be. Although both authors have seen enormous improvements over the last decade in the ease with which parents may obtain a diagnosis, there are still too many barriers erected in front of them.

CASE STUDY 1.1

Michelle, single-parent mother of 6-year-old Lee, described the uphill struggle she had had with the practitioners from whom she had sought help. Her fears about Lee's development became acute from the age of 2.5 years onwards, by which time his social isolation and communication problems were obvious to her. 'The health visitor said it was probably because of my divorce that Lee had been very attached to his Dad and was feeling insecure and so anxious that he could not put effort into his own development.'

The fact that Lee's father had left the family when Lee was only 6 months old had not deterred this simplistic hypothesis, but it was sufficient to block further examination until the child was three.

'Lee started nursery school at three; the staff were on to me the first week saying that he was not talking, that he was aggressive with the other children and wouldn't do anything. They thought he had severe learning difficulties and wanted him referred to a clinical medical officer.' Michelle was pleased about this; she felt that something might come of it.

'In fact, it just started an obstacle course of different people. The CMO referred me to a speech and language therapist who referred me to a clinical psychologist who wanted a psychiatric opinion. All these people had their own waiting-lists. Lee was up and down waiting-lists like riding a roller coaster.' Finally, the psychiatrist entered Lee for a joint assessment with a paediatrician, and between them a diagnosis of autism was made. By this time Lee was over 4 years old.

'I was devastated by the diagnosis, although I was expecting it. When it came, the feeling was "At least we can move on from here". Then I discovered the local education authority wouldn't accept autism as a diagnosis'. Michelle's struggles with practitioners continued.

This parent had been passed from one professional to another as she sought help with Lee. Various and mixed messages had been given to her along the way, but mostly they could be summarised as 'Lee probably has a developmental delay and you aren't handling him properly'. This mother is not alone in the struggle to gain some clue as to the puzzling and stressful behaviour of her child. A survey currently being conducted by the authors has already found that 73% of the 212 families interviewed reported moderate to severe difficulty in obtaining a diagnosis of autism. Of these, nearly 60% complained that professionals either did not listen to them or did not attach much importance to what they said, appeared to have preconceived ideas and, in the worst cases, were inhibited by resource controllers from saying what they really felt.[2]

It is particularly saddening that, at the turn of the century, parents of children with autism are still experiencing these difficulties. Their problems resonate uncomfortably with research carried out by a number of clinicians in the 1970s (e.g. DeMyer, 1979), which found that parents experienced roughly the same level of difficulties 20 to 30 years ago as they experience today. At that time DeMyer reported that parents were well aware that there was something significantly wrong with their children even before their second birthday, and that they were confronted with tremendous difficulties when approaching doctors and others for an explanation of these difficulties.

The majority of parents with whom we have worked have acknowledged that their child was not developing as they had expected before the child was 2 years old. However, in common with the experiences of others who have worked with such parents (e.g. Gray, 1993), they have to wait for 2 years or more before they finally get a diagnosis. The intervening period brings with it enormous stress as their anxieties remain and the child seems to become more and more distant from the norms of their previous children, their relatives' children and those they see playing in the parks and streets around them. Despite their growing certainty and deepening anxiety, the majority of the parents we have spoken to experience what Gray describes as 'an emotionally difficult referral process' (Gray, 1993, p. 1040), a description which for many parents borders on understatement. In general, the parents contact their general practitioners or discuss matters with their health visitor if they have one. They are often told that their child is simply a late developer and will catch up, or that there may be a case of developmental delay to be investigated later. Over half of the parents we surveyed told us that they were sent away until their child was a little older and more easy to assess. In the meantime, they were told not to worry, as though that was a feasible option for parents who daily observe the growing differences between their own child and those of others around them.

In common with the individuals surveyed by Gray, the parents we have spoken to found little support when their fears were finally taken seri-

---

[2] One parent told us that an Educational Psychologist had said that she could put down that the child had 'autistic tendencies' but not 'autism', as that meant more money might have to be made available to support the Statement of Special Educational Needs.

ously. They were told either that their child had a developmental delay or that he or she was the product of their poor parenting or had some kind of language disorder. Thereafter would begin a long and dreary process of going to see first one professional and then another. Often the parents gained as much information from what was not said as from what was. Much of what was said to them was platitudinous and sometimes demeaning, particularly in cases where intelligent and well-educated parents were alert to the possible range of causes of their child's condition, including autism. What was not said to them was sufficiently informative to convince them that their fears about the possibility of autism were not groundless.

CASE STUDY 1.2

An appointment was made for us to take Mandy to see the educational psychologist and speech therapist together. They had their own records and all our observations and letters in front of them.

They were kind and told us how well we were doing with Mandy and what they thought was positive about her progress. This was very nice to hear but it didn't go anywhere. I asked 'Is Mandy autistic?' and they looked at each other and said something about her showing autistic features.

My wife asked 'Does that mean she is autistic?' and then we were told by the psychologist that it was not wise to look for labels; instead we must meet Mandy's needs. We felt insulted by this; we had felt we were meeting her needs as best we could.

Unfortunately, the child's condition does not remain static. During the time when the parents are struggling to transmit their anxieties effectively to professionals and so obtain a diagnosis, the child's 'condition' is often worsening (Gray, 1993). Under these circumstances, parents can become desperate. In fact, 23% of the population sampled in our survey used words like 'desperate' or 'terrified' to describe their feelings at this time.

CASE STUDY 1.3

The pressure on Stan and Mary, parents of Kris, became intense when he was three. Whereas his behaviour was becoming more challenging, the explanation for it seemed further away.

'We were told all children develop at different rates and had we heard of "the terrible twos". Mary's sister and my parents (paternal grandparents) told us firmly that if there was anything wrong the doctors would have said so—therefore it must be our fault.'

Stan began to be swayed by the forcefully expressed opinions of his parents, and Mary's confidence was undermined by her sisters. They became 'terrified' by the deterioration in Kris's behaviour and blamed each other for it. Fortunately, they were given an unequivocal diagnosis before their marriage was permanently damaged.

This last case study reveals another major and common source of stress, namely the response of other people close to the family, which can be less than supportive. In general terms the public is not aware of autism, although there have been an increasing number of documentary films made about it. Unfortunately, the film *Rainman* provides a picture of autism which many people now feel is representative, so they cannot equate the behaviour they see from the child next door with the high-functioning individual portrayed by Dustin Hoffman. The rejection of families by other members of the family is also a significant cause of stress, and frequently cuts the parents off from an important source of support.

CASE STUDY 1.4

We relied heavily upon my younger sister to provide us with childminding. It worked well at first, but as David grew more and more aggressive and almost spitefully detached from her, the unhappier she became. Eventually she told us that she didn't agree with parents being out at work when they had a handicapped kid and it was about time we looked after David properly. She said that he needed proper mothering and I would have to give up work. All the rest of our family agreed with her, and we were more or less sent to Coventry.

By this stage the parents may be weakened to the point of accepting advice from any apparently credible source. They are then most vulnerable to the suggestions of dominant people who, in our experience, have advocated severe punishments, drugs (for both parents and child), aromatherapy and even a boarding-school for under-fives. Many of the parents surveyed found that their doctors had little time for them because, in their opinion, there was nothing medically wrong with the child and therefore it was not their responsibility. These parents were naturally curious to know what, in the doctor's opinion, the source of the difficulties might be, and they were frequently told that their management was responsible for the failure of the child to progress normally. This simple statement, no matter how kindly expressed, immediately creates extreme levels of anxiety and causes great erosion of the parents' confidence in their abilities, as the next case study demonstrates.

CASE STUDY 1.5

Our autistic son, Phillip, is 19 now and everyone thinks he is doing really well. We know we can take pride in the fact that a lot of his progress is down to us and how hard we worked. But it took us over two wasted years to develop any confidence at all in being his parents after a paediatrician told us when he was three that we were simply too soft with him.

Unfortunately we were young at the time, Phil was our first child, and my parents agreed with the paediatrician. We believed them and tried to be firmer. Fortunately for Phil it wasn't in our nature to be 'firmer', otherwise he could have had worse problems than autism; tough-minded 'refrigerator parents' perhaps. But we felt that we were failing badly and couldn't raise our heads when the family was around.

I look back at that time and get angry thinking about what damage was done to our coping skills at a time when we really needed help.

The survey described in Chapter 2 found that approximately 60% of the parents reported that they had experienced difficulties within their extended family during the period leading up to the diagnosis. The findings were very similar to those reported by DeMyer (1979) in that the most awkward extended family members were likely to be grandparents. DeMyer reports that 33% of families experience problems with grandparents; our own survey figure is slightly lower, at 27%. The difficulty was invariably in the response of the grandparents to suggestions that their grandchild needed a medical examination and possibly help of a type that they associated with mental health problems. DeMyer (1979) suggested that some grandparents were mildly irritating (e.g. 'Oh, I think they try to look at it through rose-coloured glasses. It's pride but eventually they will accept it' (p. 174), and that was certainly true for some of the parents reporting in the present survey. They felt that grandparents were affronted by suggestions that their grandchild might have a difficulty, and that this was particularly acute in the case of boys who were later diagnosed as having autism.

Also consistent with DeMyer's findings was a much more serious type of problem with grandparents which, in some cases, caused such a rift in the extended family that the marriage of the parents itself was under threat. The following is a case in point.

CASE STUDY 1.6

It was his dad who first insisted there was something wrong with our Stevie. He was only a bairn then, not 2 years old. Rob said he was acting funny and not loving like he should have been. To be honest

I thought he was right, but my Mam blew her top. She went on about Rob being a perfectionist and that he wanted a plaster saint to make him look good.

Now my three sisters and I have always thought Mam was a wonder— she has done so much for us. I'm afraid we all ganged up on Rob and made his life hell for saying stuff about Stevie. He nearly left us, he was that fed up with us.

Of course, he was right. We got told Stevie was autistic 2 days after his fourth birthday. By then everyone agreed there was something wrong, even Mam.

But no one apologised to poor Rob; they just made out the autism had come on when Stevie was three.

Another significant stressor arises from the paradoxical feelings of hopelessness and hope produced in some parents by the delay in getting a positive diagnosis. Gray (1993) reported a similar finding. Essentially, the apparently worsening condition of the child causes many parents to believe that he or she has a serious and probably permanent disability, and this causes them acute anxiety. At this stage they do not of course know that they are right in this judgement because the diagnosis has not yet been made. On the other hand, the failure of those professionals with whom they have discussed the child (usually their general practitioner, health visitor and sometimes a speech and language therapist), has led them to believe that the problem may not be as serious as they suspect, and that it will either fade away in the manner of many 'late developers', or they will become more competent in dealing with it. As one mother remarked to the first author:

On Mondays, after a bad weekend, I would go back to work feeling dreadful and wondering if ever I would have a normal little boy. By Wednesday I was beginning to think 'Well, the doctor and the health visitor can't seem to say much about it; I'm probably worrying too much and it will all get better sooner or later'. By Friday, however, his nanna is telling me how awful he is to look after and how she can't take him shopping, get him to smile at her, let alone talk to her, and she keeps on about how he is spinning round and lining things up. So by Saturday I'm down in the pits again.

DIAGNOSTIC RED HERRINGS

The parents of children with overt disabilities such as severe cerebral palsy or Down's syndrome are confronted with obvious signs of the disabling condition. Although it is a tragic discovery that their child has a serious disability, they are left in no doubt almost from the moment of birth about its reality. This is not the case for the parents of children with autism, whose difficulties appear only slowly and who are often subject to 'red-herring' explanations such as 'deafness', late development, parental mismanagement or 'temperament'. Many parents would rather cling to these false explanations than face the possibility that their child has a life-long disability that will influence virtually every aspect of his or her development, create enormous problems with regard to education and personal/social growth, impact on siblings negatively, and make the transition into adulthood a time of great stress for the whole family.

WHAT PARENTS FEEL

On a number of occasions, in the preceding sections, an unfinished survey has been referred to. This survey is designed to assess the met and unmet needs both of people with autism and of their immediate family members. This survey will be published in the fullness of time, but meanwhile it has provided a great deal of information to guide services more effectively to families where autism is present. This will be described in the next chapter, but the following overview of stress on families is provided from the main findings to date.

Stressors Associated with Autism in Families
General effects

Autism is no different to any other disability in that the sooner it is identified, diagnosed and accepted, the better the outcome is for the child and his or her family. In this section the general stress effects of autism on family members will be considered briefly, and in subsequent chapters they will be expanded upon. As will be seen, these effects are profound and create circumstances unlike those of any other disability for families. The stress effects result mainly from the cognitive defects and the outcomes of these that are classically associated with autism. They include:

- impaired communication;
- dysfunctional social relations;
- self-injurious behaviour;
- tantrum behaviour;
- obsessive/compulsive behaviour; and
- a life-long dependency (Liwag, 1989).

Logically, the severity of the child's symptoms has much to do with the degree of stress experienced by their family (Bristol, 1984). DeMyer and Goldberg (1983) studied 23 families of children and adults with autism aged between 12 and 30 years. The associated stress effects impacted on most aspects of the families' lives, including family recreation, housekeeping, finances, emotional and mental health of parents, marital relationships, physical health of family members, limiting the response to the needs of other children within the family, poor sibling relationships, relationships with extended family, friends and neighbours, and the opportunities for the personal development of each family member.

Other studies have shown that autism creates more family stress than do other types of disabling conditions (Holroyd and McArthur, 1976; Bouma and Schweitzer, 1990; Bagenholm and Gillberg, 1991; Fisman and Wolf, 1991). For example, when compared with the mothers of Down's syndrome children and children without disabilities, the mothers of children with autism reported less parenting competence, less marital satisfaction and reduced family adaptability (Rodrigue et al., 1990). This comparative finding seems to move through the life course of the child with autism into adulthood. Hoppes and Harris (1990) studied 20 families with Down's syndrome adults and 19 families with autistic adults, and demonstrated that stress effects on the parents of the autistic adults cause them to capitulate to their autistic adult children, in contrast to the parents of the Down's syndrome adults. The general finding is that the mothers of children with autism report poor attachment and less gratification from their children with autism than do mothers of Down's syndrome children. This is associated with the autistic lack of interpersonal responsiveness, which may produce an increase in parental stress and a significant reduction in reinforcement of the parent by the child (Hoppes and Harris, 1990). In addition, children with autism are reported by their parents to have more difficult personality features and management problems. This leads to severe disruption of the integration of family members into the family unit in relation to participation in family activities such as mealtimes, holidays and day trips (Holroyd and McArthur, 1976).

Even before the diagnosis of autism has been made, research surveys appear to indicate that many parents use self-blame as a coping strategy ('It is our fault he/she is like this; we must try harder'). There is a greater burden on caretakers (usually the mother) and a higher probability of disruptive routines within the family than in the families of children with other disorders. Although some of the studies reported above show increased family cohesion, there is a belief that this is derived from the rigid structure which children with autism impose on other family members. Indeed there is evidence that the presence of children with autism may perpetuate some family difficulties by controlling the family's equilibrium and 'freezing' the conditions for positive change. Franko (1985) reports that where there is an absent or troubled father there is likely to be a more rigid family system.

Effects on parents

These effects will be examined in greater length in a subsequent chapter, and the following comments are intended only to portray the complexities of the impact of autism on parents. The variety of reactions that parents may experience when a child has a disability is very considerable. This is true irrespective of what the disability may be (Frude, 1992). Some parents experience helplessness, feelings of inadequacy, anger, shock and guilt (Frude, 1992), whereas others go through periods of deep sadness and depression (Liwag, 1989). These emotional responses are amplified by the fact that most children with autism are born apparently healthy and of normal physical appearance (Randall, 1995). In addition, because, as one parent said, 'autism creeps up on you', the period of experiencing the child as normal with an apparent potential to fulfil the parents' expectations makes the gradual realisation of his or her disability and acceptance of the diagnosis all the more difficult (Harris, 1984a) and anxiety-provoking. Some parents experience a paradoxical feeling, hoping for the best and then plunging into despair on receipt of the diagnosis (Harris et al., 1991) as they are forced to rethink their aspirations.

As devastating and disruptive to the parents as these realisations may be, they are frequently dwarfed in intensity by the growing awareness that the child with autism will always be autistic and therefore dependent to a greater or lesser extent. Even though many of the parents we have worked with have been quite young, they are brought face to face with their own mortality when they start to question what will happen to their child with autism when they are dead or too old to take adequate care of him or her. Tinged with these feelings may be a sensation of anger at being let down by their partner for their fate at having a child with a disability (Harris, 1983). In contrast, many parents, particularly mothers, experience guilt that they have failed to show enough positive emotional responses to the child (Tantum, 1993) and in relation to him or her (Harris and Powers, 1984). As we have shown, they may be encouraged in these inappropriate feelings by extended family members or friends who hint that the child might be normal were it not for their failure as parents to show adequate emotion (Liwag, 1989). Thus some parents may blame themselves for their child's condition (Rodrigue et al., 1990).

As will be discussed in Chapter 6, the parents of children with autism are vulnerable to the effects of long-term stress brought on by having to live with the condition. Mothers are generally at higher risk than fathers because of the greater amount of time that they spend with the child, but fathers are not immune to this stress, and may simply experience it differently (Liwag, 1989). Mothers tend to report more guilt, physical symptoms, feelings of inadequacy about their parenting ability, tension (DeMyer, 1979) and distress (Bristol, 1984) than do fathers. However, fathers may respond with higher level of depression, relationship difficulties and personality problems than do fathers of children who show normal development (Meyer, 1986; see also Burke and Cigno, 1996). A significant finding reported by DeMyer (1979) was that nearly half of the fathers she interviewed were significantly affected by their concern for their wife's distress and preoccupation with the autistic child's problem. Our own survey has also highlighted this concern of fathers, and the first author has noted that comments regarding this anxiety about the mother are often tinged with expressions of guilt about leaving the home to go out to work.

CASE STUDY 1.7

I have to work long hours as a regional manager—wherever I am seems not the right place to be and there are always staff and customers who think their problem is earth shattering and only I can save them.

Doreen works hard with Lesley, all the more so since we got the diagnosis, but she is pulled every which way by our other two children's needs and her disabled mother. I should be there to help her more.

Every time I drive away I feel more guilty. She (Doreen, his wife) never says anything, but each day she looks that bit more tired, that bit more 'down'. She hasn't got a life anymore and I know she hates me for just leaving her to it.

In the study by Rodrigue *et al.* (1990), it was stated that the mothers of children with autism reported less parenting competence, less marital satisfaction and less family adaptability compared to the mothers of Down's syndrome children and normal children. The fact that the mothers reported having lower parenting competence suggests that they may feel uncertain about whether they are good parents. Usually they doubt their parenting competence because their autistic child does not respond as expected (Bristol, 1984). Moreover, there appears to be increased self-blame as a coping strategy, greater caretaker burden, family burden and more disrupted planning reported by the mothers of children with autism. Hoppes and Harris (1990) have reported that mothers perceive lower responsiveness, less attachment and gain less gratification from their autistic child. It is probable that the autistic child's deficit in inter-personal responsiveness interferes with opportunities for reciprocity in the mother–child relationship, and may therefore cause an increase in parental stress. In addition, Bouma and Schweitzer (1990) believe that the deficit in emotional expressiveness of autistic children may lower empathy between mother and child, and so induce parental stress. On the other hand, parents may find it particularly difficult to juggle their dual roles of 'ordinary parent' to their non-disabled children and 'super-parent' to the child with learning disability (Newson and Hipgrave, 1982). They worry about how to apply principles of fairness and equal rights among siblings when the autistic child's needs have to be met first. They are concerned about not giving enough time and attention to the other children in the family because they are preoccupied with the needs of the autistic child. Parents also fear that their normal children may develop problems because of the autistic child's lack of social and com-municative skills and the imitation of their problem behaviours (Howlin, 1988).

It is not surprising that the marital relationship is affected when there is a child with a learning disability in the family (DeMyer and Goldberg, 1983). The autistic child typically requires very significant amounts of parental attention and energy, and the prolonged period of dependence may threaten the parental relationship. The child's extensive demands may be physically exhausting and reduce the free time and energy that can be devoted to the creation of intimacy (Kazak, 1987) and nurture that a relationship requires (Harris, 1984b). DeMyer (1979) suggested that the affectional bond between parents was weakened because of the presence of problems related to raising an autistic child. In addition, a couple's sexual relationship may suffer. This seems to be due both to the parents' anxiety and fear of conceiving another autistic child, and to the physical exhaustion caused by dealing with the child all day (Harris, 1983, 1984c). Furthermore, Trute and Hauch (1988) have suggested that raising a child with a developmental disorder causes some degree of social isolation. This may be more of a problem for the parents of an autistic child, as the child usually makes unexpected and prolonged demands on them, and other adults may not be sympathetic. It was reported that the mothers of children with autism were less involved with people and activities outside the home (Bristol, 1984). Moreover, because of the child's normal physi-cal appearance, the disruptive nature of autistic behaviour and the lack of public understanding about autism, most parents perceive themselves as being stigmatised by their child's disorder (Gray, 1993). This increases the parents' sense of social isolation.

Impact on siblings

A child with a learning disability may bring particular benefits for siblings personal/social development, but the siblings may also develop problems. Previous research findings have demonstrated that the consequences of having a sibling with a learning disability are not unequivocally positive or negative. Some research shows that the negative effects on the siblings include higher levels of distress, negative self-esteem, somatic complaints and behaviour problems (Tew and Laurence, 1973; Tew et al., 1974; Lavigne and Ryan, 1979; Tritt and Essess, 1988; Bagenholm and Gillberg, 1991).

On the other hand, there are studies which suggest that the siblings of children with learning disabilities do not experience greater difficulties and problems in behavioural or psychological adjustment than children without a sibling with a learning disability (Gath, 1972; Lonsdale, 1978; McHale et al., 1984, 1986). On the contrary, some siblings are reported to experience a sense of satisfaction in learning to live and cope with the demands of such a child. In addition, they showed more tolerance and empathy towards others with difficulties, higher levels of altruism and idealism (Grossman, 1972), and greater maturity and responsibility (Howlin, 1988). Thus living with children with learning disabilities does not necessarily have adverse effects on the siblings (Lobato, 1983). However, there are possible negative effects on siblings of autistic children which are specific. Indeed, the presence of a child with autism appears to have a significant influence on sibling development within the family (Morgan, 1988).

The child with autism usually requires a great deal of parental time, energy, attention and resources. DeMyer (1979) studied 59 brothers and sisters of autistic children and 67 siblings of normal children, and found that a greater proportion of siblings in the autistic group (30%) reported that they had feelings of being 'neglected'. In Howlin's (1988) study, many children also felt that they did not receive the same amount of parental attention as their autistic sibling. Because of the greater amount of parental time and attention required by the autistic child, siblings are expected to do more household chores and care physically for their autistic sibling. Sisters and siblings who are younger than the autistic child tend to be more at risk. This is probably the case because female siblings are frequently expected to take on the role of surrogate mother in caring for the child with a learning disability, and younger siblings assume a superordinate role (Farber, 1960, cited in Crynic and Leconte, 1986). In addition, they may lose some privileges arising from the exclusive caretaking that is usually reserved for the youngest child. Thus they may feel angry, resentful, guilty (Seligman, 1991) and burdened, and show more problems in adjustment (McHale *et al.*, 1984). There may also be a drop in the school achievement scores of older brothers and sisters, due to high levels of caretaking for their autistic sibling (Mates, 1982, cited in McHale *et al.*, 1984). Furthermore, such children report often feeling treated unfairly and according to a different standard, whereas their autistic sibling is able to 'get away with' certain behaviours (Howlin, 1988). They may feel obliged to compensate for the limitations of their sibling with a learning disability (Howlin, 1988), and they may also feel under pressure to meet their parents' high expectations (Seligman, 1991). Sometimes they may feel under a burden to offer extra emotional support to their parents (Howlin, 1988). Some experience doubt and uncertainty about their autistic sibling's disability, but do not ask their parents questions because they want to protect them from the need to talk about upsetting subjects. Thus some siblings may be forced into a sense of loneliness.

Feelings of guilt, fear, anxiety and embarrassment may also be experienced by normal siblings. Some children feel that they are responsible for the disability (Harris, 1983; Howlin, 1988; Seligman, 1991), while others fear that they may 'catch' or develop the condition (Featherstone, 1980; Crynic and Leconte, 1986). When children become more mature, they often fear that they might have a child with a learning disability because of genetic transmission (McHale *et al.*, 1984). Such children also show more concern about the future of their autistic sibling (Bagenholm and Gillberg, 1991) than do children with non-disabled siblings. It is understandable that they look anxiously to the future if their autistic sibling needs lifelong care or supervision.

In addition, many children feel ashamed to have an autistic sibling (Harris, 1983), particularly when they are embarrassed by that sibling's apparent rudeness, self-centredness and obsessional or other problem behaviours in front of others. They may also express feelings of resentment when their privacy or social lives are affected (Simeonsson and McHale, 1981), particularly when they enter adolescence. Indeed, research indicates that siblings of autistic children feel lonely more often, and many of them experience peer relationship problems. At a different level, many complain that they experience more problems with their autistic brother or sister disturbing them and breaking their possessions (Bagenholm and Gillberg, 1991). The development of an intimate relationship between the autistic child and his or her siblings is also hindered (Harris, 1984c) because of the autistic child's lack of social empathy and their impairment in reciprocal interaction. This is likely to produce stress in siblings. Finally, recent data suggests that the siblings of children with autism may themselves be at risk for some symptoms of cognitive dysfunction and learning problems (August *et al.*, 1983; Baird and August, 1985).

Families, needs and autism

When these specific stresses are examined closely, it appears that certain human needs appear to be threatened by the identified hardships of having a disabled child in the family. These range from basic needs (e.g. safety, financial security) to higher-level needs (e.g. the need for achievement). This suggests an alternative way of organising the existing stresses by utilising the basic human needs outlined by Maslow (1954). Briefly, according to Maslow, human nature consists of a number of innate needs that are arranged in a hierarchy according to their potency, i.e. some needs are more powerful than others. The lower the position of the need in the hierarchy, the more powerful it is.

Maslow identified seven needs ranging from the most to the least basic, namely physiological needs, safety needs, 'belongingness' and love needs, esteem needs, cognitive needs, aesthetic needs and the need for self-actualisation (Maslow, 1954). The definitions of Maslow's needs are outlined below.

1. Physiological needs—hunger, thirst, air, etc.
2. Safety needs—the need for freedom from threat or danger, and to ally oneself with the familiar and the secure.
3. Belongingness and love needs—the need for affiliation, 'belongingness' and acceptance.
4. Esteem needs—the need for achievement, strength, competence, reputation, status or prestige.
5. Cognitive needs—the need to know and understand, curiosity, the need to understand the mysterious and to tackle the unknown.
6. Aesthetic needs—the need for symmetry, order, system and structure.
7. The need for self-actualisation—the need for self-fulfilment, to realise potentialities, and to become what one is capable of becoming.

This model of needs can be used to help to illustrate the potential stressors in families with an autistic child. It is possible that this could be a first step in meeting those needs. Our survey results demonstrate the following outcomes in relation to Maslow's model.

Needs 1 and 2—physiological/safety/security/needs
- A potentially greater financial burden than a child without a disability.
- A higher probability of physical harm to the child and to other family members if the child with autism shows severely challenging behaviour.
- Constant uncertainty about the future.

Need 3—'belongingness' and love needs
- Reduced social interaction (both within and outside the family).
- Reduction of intimacy and recreation (both within and outside the family).
- Variable acceptance by people outside the family.
- Effects on acceptance by parents of each other, including blaming each other.

Need 4—esteem and achievement needs
- Reduced opportunities for parents' and siblings' career success and advancement.
- Decreased parental experiences of parenting competence.

Need 5—cognitive needs
- Reduced understanding of the child (often due to lack of knowledge and information from professionals).

Need 6—aesthetic needs
- Excessive rigidity of role definitions.
- Unequal balance of role demands (particularly in terms of the caretaking activities of the mother).
- Disorganisation in the family caused by behavioural difficulties and complex needs.
- Interference with family systems from outside the family.

Need 7—need for self-actualisation/self-fulfilment
- Reduced opportunities to follow individual pursuits.
- Greater blocks to opportunities for family members to fulfil ambitions.

Irrespective of the type and severity of the specific stressors caused by having a child with autism, coping with the general stress of a developmental disorder requires significant, long-term adaptation within the family, and these changes influence both individual family members and the family unit as a whole. Our experience suggests that the families of children with autism redefine their needs and their fulfilment such that their definitions will be significantly different to the definitions of families of children without a disability.

For example, it is a common finding that mothers of autistic children find it very difficult to pursue a career because of the excessive time and care demands of their autistic child and the frequent lack of available daycare services. Given these circumstances, many mothers of children with autism redefine the way in which they fulfil their achievement needs, and attempt to satisfy them through a greater emphasis on their parenting role. The importance of parenting their complex child becomes the primary means of meeting achievement needs.

As described previously, another specific stress experienced by the families of children with autism is the parents' feelings of rejection and social isolation (Intagliata and Doyle, 1984). Adaptations include the fulfilment of their love and 'belongingness' needs by increasingly looking inward to the core family. An emphasis on family-related values and activities (e.g. recreation, leisure time) and high levels of cohesiveness can be interpreted as indicators of this tendency. In addition, the parents of children with autism report a considerable amount of interference and disagreement from outside the family with regard to their parenting competence, the degree of the child's handicap and their probable future. In order to cope with these stressors, many parents assume a different set of standards to those externally imposed on childrearing and evaluating behaviour.

Finally, ambiguity is a stressor for these families, not only with regard to the nature and degree of the disorder, but also in relation to the prognosis, educational needs, expectations regarding the child's capabilities and potential, and the quality of available services. In order to cope with these uncertainties, many families of autistic children place a strong emphasis on organisation and control within daily life, often having a set of rules and procedures that govern the way in which the household is run. This need for order is often far greater than that found in families of children without disabilities.

STRESS ON SELF

No matter what impact autism may have on families, it is necessary to remember that it represents a huge and terrifying problem for those who suffer from it themselves, as they wrestle with the confusion of their minds and grapple with the buzzing, booming and incomprehensible social world around them. The following description given to those of us without autism by one who has the disorder (Brad Rand, 1996, personal story given within the pages of the website of the Autism Society of America; URL: www.autism-society.org.) provides an insight into this confusion, and perhaps helps us to cope better as a result.

> When I learned to do sign language and use the computer in 1992, I was surprised that other people wanted to know how I think. I always wanted to learn how everybody else thinks because there are so many of you, and I wanted to make myself like you so I could fit in your world.
>
> But I learned that people wanted to know about me too, and when they learned how I thought and why I did things, they did things that weren't

as confusing to me and I could understand them better. I learned that I could stay like me and still fit in your world, a little. So I decided it is better to stay like me and fit in a little, than become not like me and fit in a lot.

People who are different may not understand how to talk to other people, or how to act the right way at all the right times, or how to understand feelings, or how to sort out all the sights and sounds and smells in the world, but they are still special because there is just one of them, like there is just one of you.

Some people live in two different worlds. Some people who are different don't understand how to communicate very well with you and the outside world, which could be called the real world. Some people have a world inside their head, too, which is more peaceful and easier to understand than the real world.

The world inside my head is quiet and peaceful and there are no people inside and nothing hard to figure out. So it is a safe place when the real world gets too confusing.

So your world might be the one that most people know the best, but their world can mean a lot to them, too, when they need it. The world inside my head is not a bad place or a crazy place, it is just a quiet and peaceful place. Maybe it is like a quiet closet you used to sit in when you needed to be by yourself when you were little.

NEEDS OF PROFESSIONALS

From this brief overview and extracts from our survey, a number of clear needs stand out for professionals working with people with autism. Not only is it imperative for practitioners to gain a firm understanding and knowledge of the range of 'conditions' and disabilities affecting individuals and families, but also it is essential to obtain specific details. This will assist the professional in making his or her assessment. If the presenting problem appears to be the child's behaviour, then applied behavioural analysis may seem to be the best way to proceed. This is often the case and, whatever the outcome, such data is never redundant. However, a detailed and critical knowledge of the specific criteria for autism from DSM-IV (American Psychiatric Association, 1994), from case studies and training, will assist in a speedy consideration of autism.

Training for the helping professions draws from a range of disciplinary knowledge bases, one of which is social psychology. From social psychology derives labelling theory (Lemert, 1967; Scheff, 1974; Parker and Randall, 1997). This represents important knowledge, and warnings against the misattribution of diagnostic labels are well founded. However, it is important to have a full understanding of the process and to be aware that assumptions can be made and applied on the basis of what is not said, as well as on the basis of what is. Moreover, by refusing to diagnose autism, the label 'poor parent' is applied or assumed by default.

As we have seen many times, this can result in the assumption of guilt, poor parenting roles and a lack of motivation to continue fighting for one's child.

Professionals need to step back in order to see the effects of their conceptualisations and to work sensitively with parents and individuals to find ways of supporting constructively, using the knowledge at their disposal.

2

FAMILIES' NEEDS: MET AND UNMET

It has been said that autism is one of the most complex and intractable developmental disorders with which families may have to cope (Howlin and Rutter, 1987). The pain of discovering that one's longed-for child is afflicted with this cruel disorder has been discussed in the previous chapter. This pain is exacerbated as each new pervasive symptom of the disorder unfolds. Despite this, few studies have investigated the feelings, experiences, needs and stresses of families in which autism is present.

One study by Liwag (1989) did report on the stress and coping experiences of families of autistic children, and her work has contributed significantly to our own study. Liwag describes autism as 'one of childhood's most cruel diseases' and speaks of the children and their families as its 'victims' (p.3). The objectives of her study were to examine the impact of autism on families and to understand the 'depth and complexity of the stresses they undergo' (p.4). She also studied the strategies and styles of adaptation that parents adopted as the symptoms of autism unfolded.

Liwag was motivated to conduct this study by her experiences as a clinician, and she sought to reveal strengths of adaptation in parents as well as their suffering and weaknesses. Her research involved families of Filipino autistic children and addressed the following questions.

1. What stresses associated with the autistic child are experienced by these families?
2. What coping patterns are utilised by these families in living with their autistic child?
3. How are these stresses and coping patterns differentially experienced by the mothers and fathers of autistic children?

As is true for our own study, Liwag's research was broad and exploratory, rather than specifically targeted, and it was clinical-descriptive in nature. The research was restricted to a small number of families, and this has given rise to some criticism of its generalisation to families with autism, particularly those living in different cultures. Liwag made use of a projective questionnaire which was supplemented by semi-structured interviews. These methods yielded rich insights into not only the difficulties but also the triumphs experienced by these families. Liwag made no attempt to quantify the degree of stress. Her perspective from the family as a unit is that of a systemic model which emphasised the interactive nature of family stress.

In summary, Liwag's results reveal very complex effects on families of children with autism. She reported these effects and the strategies that had evolved to cope with them under a number of headings as follows.

Emotional concerns of parents

The majority of parents became distressed upon learning that their child had autism. Liwag reports that their predominant feelings were of depression and sadness, and that this was shared by both mothers and fathers. A similar mixture of feelings was reported to Liwag as in our own study. Predominant among these were sadness, feeling stunned/disbelief, feeling sorry for the child and, for some, a sense of guilt and blame.

Liwag's study revealed that fathers tended to experience less shock, pity and guilt, but were more concerned about seeking immediate help for the child and gaining as much information about autism and its course as possible.

For most of the parents in Liwag's study, some 3 or 4 years had elapsed from the time of the initial diagnosis to the investigation. Many of the parents, particularly the mothers, still felt emotional distress about the child rather than the diagnosis. Crying, feeling lonely, sad and depressed were common feelings but tinged with uncertainty and confusion about their child's behaviour.

More mothers than fathers kept questioning the reasons for their child developing autism and, despite the lack of knowledge about what causes autism, many parents had developed their own theories as to why their child had become autistic. Commonly the autism was attributed to events occurring during the pregnancy or the delivery of the child; other theories involved family dynamics or interactions with people from outside the family (e.g. childminders). Fortunately, few parents actually blamed themselves, but those who did suffered the greatest distress.

The stresses

Mothers and fathers were also differentiated according to the nature of the stresses that they experienced as a result of the autism. For the mothers, the behavioural outcomes of autism caused the greatest stress. This included temper tantrums, 'hyperactivity', speech and language problems, behaviour in public places, inability to socialise and enjoy friends, and challenging behaviour. However, fathers were stressed by the fact that their child would always remain autistic, that no matter how much care and education was given there was no 'cure', and in some cases there was a fear that the child's condition might worsen. Fathers were also more likely than mothers to be concerned about the level of dependence as their child grew older. Associated with this was a fear that there would come a time when the parents would be unable to cope with their child's needs, and uncertainty about what then might happen. The mothers interpreted this fear in a more personalised manner by worrying about what would happen to their child when they themselves were not around. This implied that the mothers saw themselves as having the primary care responsibility for their child with autism.

However, the biggest stressor for these parents was their level of concern about their child's ability to communicate, which they related to their perception of long-term problems with interpersonal relationships. The latter concern was both general, in terms of interpersonal relationships outside the family, and also specific to family members, particularly the siblings of the child with autism.

How do parents cope?

Liwag found that parents agreed upon two open-ended coping strategies. The first is that family life becomes centred on the child with autism, whose needs become the primary consideration in terms of time given, attention, effort and even expense. The fathers tended to think in terms of resources—of giving the child with autism the best they could afford—whereas the mothers took a more activity-based view and considered activities and a 'special time together'.

The second strategy concerned the behavioural and emotional adjustment of family members to the child with autism. This involved learning how to be more understanding and showing greater patience. It also included a need to 'accept the tragedy' and learning to accept the children as they are.

The differences found between the mothers and fathers of these children with autism were reflected in terms of effort and sacrifice. Thus many of the mothers felt that they had to make certain sacrifices, e.g. their careers and material pleasures. The fathers felt that their sacrifice was in having to work harder to order to find the money needed to resource whatever needs the family thought their child with autism might have. Caregiving tasks are often associated with the mothers of children (Ayer and Alaszewski, 1986). When fathers do report caring for children they are more likely to concentrate on the negative factors, and regret for what might have been (Hornby, 1992). Burke and Cigno (1996) concur with these gender differences in the perceptions of and participation in parenting. In their research study they describe the perceived lack of support from predominantly male partners. They also present evidence that fathers sometimes 'coped' by working away from home, leaving the relationship and, in one instance, gaining custody of the non-disabled child.

Perceptions of other family members

The sons and daughters of the autistic children in this study tended to be young, between 5 and 8 years of age. The parents of these children felt that, despite their young age, the siblings were aware that the child with autism was abnormal in some respect. Liwag quotes knowledge that the autistic sibling is 'sick somewhere inside of him'. Several parents tried to counter this impression by discussing the doctors and other professionals to whom they were taking their child with autism in the hope that 'he will soon catch up', or 'get well'. Some of the siblings were aware only that their brother or sister with autism could not talk, and they tended to use this as an explanation to their own friends.

Most of the families expected that the non-handicapped children should be made aware, even at their young age, of a responsibility to help the child with autism. The parents told these children that the child with autism is special and needs to be taken particular care of, and that he or she should be taught and played with often, defended against criticism, and treated very kindly.

Parents found that the attitude of extended family members was very important for them. The most common response to the child with autism made by relatives and close friends concerns a hope that greater professional help should be sought. Mingled with this is another concern about family attention concerning the child with autism. Many extended family members were not slow in stating opinions which could be interpreted as criticisms. Thus some parents were told to be more patient with their child and to give him or her more love and attention, and one mother is reported as having being told 'to stop working and concentrate more on my daughter'. Some fathers were particularly aware of criticism and reported various negative attributes in the statements of some family members, believing that they were suggesting that the child had been spoilt or neglected. The same findings were not reported in Burke and Cigno's study (1996). In fact they described fairly high levels of support from family members and also relatively high levels of appreciation.

Outside the family

There are also influences exerted from outside the family. Thus many parents favoured talking to the parents of other children with autism and found these conversations helpful, not only because of the support of being able to share experiences, but also because these conversations frequently provided strategies and advice on difficulties. Certainly the parents felt that they were not alone after having had this kind of contact.

The parents whom Liwag surveyed had some mixed opinions on the desirability of talking about their child with autism to people outside the family. Some felt that such conversations led to a greater awareness of their child in particular and autism in general, and helped them to feel that they had nothing to be ashamed of because they had a child with autism. Others disagreed with this view, believing that the inability of lay people to understand the complexities of autism would create problems.

This division of opinion was also evident in the way in which parents perceived that the general public reacted to them when their autistic child was with them. Thus about half of the parents felt that most people were ready to be sympathetic, or sometimes apologetic and pitying. Many of the others felt that the general public *en masse* did not seem to notice that their child was autistic unless the child did something that people recognised as abnormal or bizarre. Even then, parents noted that the response of people was not necessarily one of anger or dislike, but could be one of curiosity and a desire to understand more about the child.

Coping strategies

Liwag found that many coping strategies were used which parents had largely developed themselves, and that these tended to evolve from the general strategies of prioritising the needs of the autistic child and developing personal qualities of patience and understanding. Not surprisingly, parents found themselves making several mistakes as they developed their strategies within these two major adaptations. A common error identified was that parents felt that they had given up on the child too easily and that they had been 'leaving matters as is without seeking help' or giving in to a depressing thought that 'nothing can be done'. Some parents experienced a belief that it was too easy to allow professionals to try to assist the child in preference to active involvement with those professionals.

The theme of working with people at the level of service provision was extended into the belief that it was a mistake to try and hide the truth of their child's condition.

Some parents believed that they had also been mistaken in trying to confine their autistic child's activities such that the nature of his or her difficulties would not become apparent to others in the community. A similar number of parents felt that it was a mistake to spoil the child or to expect too little, such that the effects of the autism were magnified by a consistent underestimate of what might be achieved.

Thinking about the future

Parents considered the future in a variety of ways, and there were differences between the fathers and mothers. For example, more fathers than mothers were optimistic and positive, whereas the mothers were concerned about the uncertainty of what the future would bring. They experienced hopelessness and insecurity, and more mothers than fathers were likely to feel scared and anxious about obstacles that they might face. Many parents tried not to think too hard about the future, preferring to tackle autism day by day.

Most of the parents were able to articulate one or more objectives that they would like their child with autism to achieve. For some this was a wide range of self-help skills, so that they could learn to take care of themselves and yet still appear acceptable to the community. Others wanted more abstract successes, such as the acquisition of a career or 'to be successful like an ordinary human being'.

Mothers were apt to dwell on emotional and relationship objectives. Some wanted their child with autism to feel that he or she was loved and 'treasured as any other child in the family'. One mother articulated a desire for her child to become aware that 'he matters, not only to his family, but to the rest of humanity' (Liwag, 1989, p.12). Most mothers wanted their children to be happy in the future.

NEEDS

When attempting to conceptualise the 'needs' of families with one or more members with autism, it is helpful to ponder Liwag's summary of her findings. Many of the experiences and stresses of her families can be converted directly into needs statements. For example, 'I wish I could understand what is really wrong with him' is a needs statement for information. Similarly, 'I wish we could get on top of her terrible tantrums' is a needs statement for the provision of successful strategies for managing challenging behaviour.

Our survey identified a whole series of consistently unmet needs. These will be described in greater detail in later chapters, but the close similarities between our survey and that of Liwag justify a brief summary of what was uncovered.

It is abundantly clear that parents can have an extremely fraught time while trying to obtain a diagnosis, and that, when they do, both surveys indicate that they understand little more than that autism is something that will affect them for the rest of their lives. Lack of information and lack of support lead to emotional distress characterised as anger and disbelief, depression and hopelessness, guilt and great sorrow for the child. A sensation of bereavement and loss is common, and in most cases the parents are not helped to find their way through this. Mothers bear the greatest brunt, and frequently demonstrate overt depression, appetite problems and sleeplessness, spasmodic crying and an overwhelming sense of deep sorrow. Fathers become distracted, anxious and unable to function well in their work. Liwag refers to this period as the mourning phase, and she states that each family grieves at its own pace. This is true in our experience as well, and we have noted that a protective factor which helps to alleviate this process is the opportunity to talk to trusted extended family or friends. If social support has waned because of the demands of caring or the negative attitudes of others (Burke and Cigno, 1996), there can be a major problem. The buffering hypothesis suggests that social support is mobilised when it is needed and when there is stress. In fact, stress appears to affect health adversely when there is little social support, and social support affects health positively when there are high levels of stress. Ill health can perhaps be seen as a combination of high stress and low social support. The negative side is that too much support reduces self-reliance and creates more tensions and worries. Nolan *et al.* (1996) suggest a complex perspective in which beneficial effects of support are evident up to a certain level, after which stress is exacerbated.

Ell (1996) indicates that family support is important to the seriously ill patient, but also that the impact upon those family members who may also need support can be great. One study indicates that family and social support can act as a buffer against stress for the chronically ill male patient and the male carer (Unger *et al.*, 1996). In another study, social support was indicated in recovery from serious illness (Keeling *et al.*, 1996). This highlights the need for information about social support systems, and the encouragement and opportunity to develop these.

A further protective factor which helps to alleviate this phase is the provision of information, as the parents discover that increasing their knowledge of autism gives them a clearer idea of what they have to cope with. Nevertheless, this mourning stage may go on for 2 or more years, with one and sometimes both parents experiencing hopelessness and depression.

Both surveys also reveal that there are strong needs associated with the stress caused by the gradually unfolding symptoms of autism. Liwag describes parallels in this to the findings of Gallagher *et al.* (1983) in a study where level and type of parental stress were found to be associated with child characteristics such as 'difficult personality' or degree of physical incapacitation.

Liwag reports that her parents then question whether their children will ever be normal. This differs slightly from our own findings where parents who are probably better informed understand that there is no future possibility of normality, but still find it almost impossible to accept that they should be experiencing such difficulties with *their* child.

Many parents understand that autism cannot be cured and that their future is to a greater or lesser extent going to be dictated by the problems that they experience with their child with autism. They hear the message from professionals that autism cannot be cured although the condition of their child can be improved through education and other relevant experiences, but they have no real understanding of what this means. Once again they have a need for information that will give meaning to this statement and help them to understand how their child may have potential which can be unlocked from the grip of autism. Without this understanding they can have no real concept of how their own efforts and the consistency of their care and attention may be of direct benefit to their child.

Both surveys identify how, in many cases, this lack of understanding creates a significant tendency to deny in various subtle ways the extent of the disorder. Thus many parents try to reconceptualise autism as deafness, a less severe difficulty causing lack of speech, or simply a phase that the child may work through. Such cognitive dissonance is perfectly understandable, but in itself constitutes a need for therapeutic intervention without which the aspirations and expectations of the parents may become even more adrift from reality and eventually lead to greater pain.

A related need concerns those parents experiencing eternal optimism about a cure. This can give rise to unrealistic optimism and a tendency to be overly susceptible to success stories heard from other parents and indeed portrayed by purveyors of different schemes. This translates into a need not only for information about autism but also for an appreciation of how best to judge the validity of claims made for intervention strategies.

Liwag states that financial concerns were not a significant source of anxiety for the parents she had studied. She felt that this was due to the fact that the majority of them were fairly high-income, middle-class people. The parents in her study spoke mainly of child-centred stressors, whereas the parents of handicapped children in other surveys (e.g.

Farber, 1963) have expressed dominant anxieties related to expense, child-care arrangements and the general cost of resources for the special needs of their child. Our survey has involved a far wider range of parents with regard to income, and many of them expressed the need for more financial assistance from the state or the Local Authority to help supplement their own resources. In general terms, the lower the income of the family, the more likely such needs were to be identified and reports of shared responsibility with statutory agencies be given.

Our survey also revealed the two general styles of coping, namely making the autistic child the centre of the family's efforts and attention, and secondly the learning by parents and, in many instances, siblings to subjugate natural and spontaneous emotional expression in order to show greater patience and understanding towards the child with autism. Liwag describes this process as 'truly child-centred with the autistic child as the centre around which the wheel of family life revolves' (Liwag, 1989, p.13).

Although these strategies may be helpful in the short to medium term, many families experience a need to express their family life and individual lives differently. Many parents state that they feel they have no individuality left, that they are merely sitters to their children with autism. As one mother put it, 'I feel I must get a life'. Despite the fact that many individuals within families, particularly mothers, experienced this need, most of them have received little or no help in accepting the expression of it without guilt. This represents a significant need, and one which is seldom met.

As children with autism grow older, so their families have to make significant adaptations to the changes in the pattern of autism that their children manifest. Often these changes occur more quickly than the families can adapt, leaving one or more members struggling to cope with strategies that are no longer suitable. Their need is for greater support at these points of transition, and an understanding that it is often necessary for the families to distance themselves slightly from the immediacy of the autistic child's desires. Families need help in understanding that this process of withdrawal is not just good for them, in that parents and siblings may have more time for their own activities undiluted by almost constant attention to the child with autism, but that this is also developmentally necessary for their child with autism and will help him or her to develop independence.

These are just some of the major stressors associated with autism that can be reinterpreted as largely unmet needs. They become needs which should be met, sometimes through within-family support, sometimes from external agencies, and often by a combination of both. Perhaps, therefore, families should be asked what these needs are and the agencies of society should then endeavour to find the resources to meet them. Many responses to autism and other complex disorders have been based on such a simplistic notion.

Parents report to us that they are often asked 'What do you need?', and some feel embarrassed when they find the question too complex to answer coherently. Part of this problem is that it is difficult to differentiate needs from wishes—what is required from what is simply desired.

Defining Needs Assessment

Non-physical needs such as social and educational requirements are notoriously difficult to pin down, and constitute a topic about which people from every walk of life and from many different professions all have differing opinions. Service-users (or clients) will tell researchers what their problems are and what type of help they want, and service-providers may share these views, but sometimes differ on what is best for the clients, and they also have their own needs. Finance managers argue from the viewpoint of vested interest and are unwilling to define needs in a manner that threatens to tie up a large amount of capital. In addition, it has been argued that the caring professionals tell clients what their problems are and what they need without seeking an opinion from the clients themselves.

Bradshaw (1993) states:

> the concept of needs has always been too imprecise, too complex, too contentious to be a useful target for policy and also (and therefore) leaves a lot to be desired both as an epidemiological identifier and also as a basis for evaluating the performance of policies.

It is not surprising, therefore, that social and educational needs, like health care, are now a firmly established political problem at both national and local level, and the way in which they are defined has repercussions both for those who need help and for those who fund and provide that help. It is as a consequence of this that arguments rage between politicians, providers and clients about the concept of 'unmet need', which is precisely the type of need that many parents of children and young people with autism are loudly expressing throughout the world.

Concept of Needs

Need cannot be determined by opinions or epidemiology alone. In its guidance to managers, the then Department of Health/Social Services

Inspectorate (1991) defined need in terms of 'the requirements of individuals to enable them to achieve, maintain or resource an acceptable level of social independence or quality of life'. This definition looks at needs in terms of outcomes, although it also begs the question 'what is an acceptable level?'. Any attempt to identify the needs of the population of families with autism should be based on a paradigm that is sufficiently robust to deal with these problems.

It would be overly simplistic to try to apply a Maslow-type structured hierarchy of needs to this situation. Although there are clear requirements concerning physiological, safety and security needs, the higher-level needs, such as social activity, esteem and self-realisation, defy agreed definition. One finds reference to these higher-level needs in the mission statements of providers and in many local authority policy statements, but in actuality providers are required by law to satisfy the lowest levels of Maslow's hierarchy.

Bradshaw (1993) has subdivided social need into four elements as follows:

1. *Normative*—a standard laid down by professional expertise.
2. *Felt*—a subjective 'want' of a service that is unstated.
3. *Expressed*—a stated 'want', in which the felt need is turned into action.
4. *Comparative*—the difference between those who qualify for and receive services and those who qualify but do not receive them.

Although this subdivision of need does not help to prioritise in the same way as a hierarchical structure, it does help us to understand how the social/educational need is being defined. There is an argument that a 'real' need would only exist if all four elements were present, but in certain circumstances a 'real' need may not always be felt or expressed by the subject (e.g. an elderly person with advanced senile dementia). There is also scope for a dynamic interplay between professional 'normative' definitions of need and subjective 'felt' and 'expressed' definitions of need given by clients.

Putting together these hierarchical and conceptual classifications leads to a more balanced approach for the purposes of assessment and survey. A purely epidemiological analysis would yield only a comparative element. Measurement to a professionally set standard would give a purely normative view, and reacting only to clients' views would give only a subjective 'want' list. None of these would be politically or socially satisfactory. To obtain a more comprehensive view it is necessary to take each into account and then, when planning a response to those needs (or recommending a response to them), to prioritise them according to a hierarchical model which is defensible.

The survey carried out by the Family Assessment and Support Unit began this process by dealing first with the perceptions and wishes of the families. It also related what family members had to say to the current diagnostic status of the individual with autism. In this way it would be possible to determine which factors that define the response of individual families are dependent upon the severity of the autism present, and which factors are independent of this. Among the latter are those attitudinal facets of response which are intrinsic to the individuals' perceptions and stress tolerance.

THE SURVEY

These concepts were placed centrally in the design of the survey, still ongoing, which is being conducted by the Family Assessment and Support Unit. The earliest experiences of families seeking a diagnosis are investigated, as well as their experiences in finding resources and information. The present-day presentation of their children with autism is also examined and related to current stressors. In between the earliest fears and the present-day stressors of each family there is a complex array of factors which impacts differentially on families to stimulate their highly individual responses to the disorder.

However, as we have seen, the stresses are not just products of the nature of the disorder, but they are also products of the agency systems for dealing with it, the responses of siblings and extended family, the idiosyncratic responses of the parents themselves, and the frustrations of trying to cope in as normal a manner as possible. Family 'feelings' and beliefs can therefore also become 'needs' rather than 'wants', and these too, were examined. The result of these considerations was a single, lengthy questionnaire administered by interview over a period of 2 to 3 hours divided into as many sessions as the family require. This is shown as Appendix A.

APPENDIX A

[1]SURVEY OF MET AND UNMET NEEDS

In respect of

FAMILIES AND AUTISM

THE FAMILY ASSESSMENT AND SUPPORT UNIT

THE UNIVERSITY OF HULL

Family name: Code number:

Name of the person with autism: Date of birth:

Address:

Telephone number:

Date(s) of interview(s):

Name of respondent: Date of birth:

Relationship to the person with autism:

Name of interviewer:

The material contained in this document is confidential to the respondent and the Unit. It will not be passed to any other person or agency unless disclosures concerning Child Protection are made.

---

[1] © Pete Randall, Family Assessment and Support Unit, The University of Hull, 1996.

1.0 FAMILY COMPOSITION

1.1   Record details of family composition here: (names and ages/dates of birth if known)

Nuclear family   Extended family

1.2   Details of second family or reconstituted family (if relevant):

1.3   Draw genogram here:

1.4   Employment of parents:

Mother:

Father:

1.5   Age of parents at time of diagnosis:

Mother:

Father:

2.0 DIAGNOSIS OF AUTISM OR RELATED DISORDER

2.1 Has your child/young person had a diagnosis of autism from the following? (Get names if possible)

    2.1.1 Child/adolescent psychiatrist   (Yes/No) Date:

    2.1.2 Paediatrician   (Yes/No) Date:

    2.1.3 General practitioner   (Yes/No) Date:

    2.1.4 Clinical psychologist   (Yes/No) Date:

    2.1.5 Educational psychologist   (Yes/No) Date:

    2.1.6 Specialist assessment centre   (Yes/No) Date:

    2.1.7 Family Assessment and Support Unit   (Yes/No) Date:

    2.1.8 Other centre (specify which below)   (Yes/No) Date:

2.2 Has your child/young person had a diagnosis of autism from the following?

    2.2.1 Speech and language therapists   (Yes/No) Date:

    2.2.2 Health visitor   (Yes/No) Date:

    2.2.3 Teacher   (Yes/No) Date:

    2.2.4 Voluntary agency   (Yes/No) Date:

    2.2.5 Other (specify which below)   (Yes/No) Date:

2.3 Has your child/young person had a diagnosis of Asperger's syndrome from the following?

    2.3.1 Child/adolescent psychiatrist   (Yes/No) Date:

    2.3.2 Paediatrician   (Yes/No) Date:

    2.3.3 General practitioner   (Yes/No) Date:

    2.3.4 Clinical psychologist   (Yes/No) Date:

    2.3.5 Educational psychologist   (Yes/No) Date:

    2.3.6 Specialist assessment centre (specify)   (Yes/No) Date:

    2.3.7 Other centre (specify which below)   (Yes/No) Date:

2.4 Has your child/young person had a diagnosis of Asperger's syndrome from the following?

    2.4.1 Speech and language therapists   (Yes/No) Date:

    2.4.2 Health visitor   (Yes/No) Date:

    2.4.3 Teacher   (Yes/No) Date:

    2.4.4 Voluntary agency   (Yes/No) Date:

    2.4.5 Other (specify which below)   (Yes/No) Date:

2.5 Has your child/young person had any other diagnosis, such as the following?

    2.5.1 Attention deficit disorder   (Yes/No) Who by: When:

    2.5.2 Pervasive developmental disorder (Yes/No) Who by: When:

    2.5.3 Semantic pragmatic disorder   (Yes/No) Who by: When:

    2.5.4 Childhood schizophrenia   (Yes/No) Who by: When:

    2.5.5 Severe language/communication disorder   (Yes/No) Who by: When:

    2.5.6 Pathological demand avoidance syndrome   (Yes/No) Who by: When:

    2.5.7 Other (specify below)   (Yes/No) Who by: When:

2.6 Prediagnosis: Who first suspected that your child had autism/special needs? (Please circle)

GP   Health visitor   Speech therapist   Teacher   Social worker

Playgroup leader   Yourself

Other (please specify)

2.7 How knowledgeable did they seem to be about autism? (Please circle)

Extremely knowledgeable   Very knowledgeable   Quite knowledgeable

Fairly knowledgeable Not very knowledgeable   Not at all knowledgeable

Why do you think this?

2.8 Please describe how you felt when you got a diagnosis of autism/(other diagnosis). (Prompts: relief, sadness, grief)

2.9 What sort of support or other help did you feel you needed when you got that diagnosis? (Prompts: more information, counselling, etc.)

2.10 Did you get that help? If not, why not?

2.11   Have you any comments to make about the time before you received the
        diagnosis and the difficulties you experienced?

2.12   Have you any comments to make about the time when you received the
        diagnosis? (Prompt: happy, sad, relieved, etc.)

2.13   Has your son/daughter had any further diagnosis or diagnoses?   (Yes/No)
        If yes, what was it/were they?

2.14   Around the time of the first diagnosis, did you receive the following?

    2.14.1   Explanations of the condition   (Yes/No)

             If yes, from whom?

    2.14.2   Opportunity to discuss the diagnosis   (Yes/No)

             If yes, with whom?

    2.14.3   Advice on reading or other guidance material   (Yes/No)

    2.14.4   Advice on schooling   (Yes/No)

    2.14.5   Attendance allowance   (Yes/No)

    2.14.6   Respite care   (Yes/No)

             State where and how much:

    2.14.7   Advice on behaviour management   (Yes/No)

    2.14.8   Advice on helping your other children   (Yes/No)

    2.14.9   Other (please specify)   (Yes/No)

2.15   Who did you see around the time of the diagnosis?[1]

      2.15.1   Psychiatrist   (Yes/No)

      2.15.2   Clinical psychologist   (Yes/No)

      2.15.3   Educational psychologist   (Yes/No)

      2.15.4   Health visitor   (Yes/No)

      2.15.5   Community nurse   (Yes/No)

      2.15.6   Speech and language therapist   (Yes/No)

      2.15.7   Occupational therapist   (Yes/No)

      2.15.8   Teacher   (Yes/No)

      2.15.9   Social worker   (Yes/No)

      2.15.10 Voluntary agency worker   (Yes/No)

      2.15.11 Pre-school special needs adviser   (Yes/No)

      2.15.12 Portage worker   (Yes/No)

      2.15.13 Support group   (Yes/No)

      2.15.14 Other (please specify)   (Yes/No)

2.16   Please give any comments you wish about the diagnostic procedures and your experience of this.

---

[1] Get the parents to rate these people's value on a 1–5 scale where 1 is Awful and 5 is Very Good for (i) support and (ii) information. Put the ratings beside each.

2.17 Do you belong to a support group? (Yes/No)

(If yes, specify which, where they meet, how many there are, how often, etc. If yes, please rate how useful attendance is to you (1 = not at all, 5 = very useful)

1   2   3   4   5

If not, why not?

2.18 Do you have much family support? (Yes/No)

If yes, who from?

If no, why not?

Please rate the support you get from family.   1   2   3   4   5

2.19 Do you have much support from friends?   (Yes/No)

If yes, please describe.

Please rate the support you get from friends.   1   2   3   4   5

2.20 Do you have much support from professionals?   (Yes/No)

If yes, please describe.

Please rate the support you get from professionals.   1   2   3   4   5

2.21   Do you get much support from other parents? (Yes/No)

Are you a member of a parent support group? (Yes/No)

If yes, give details.

If no, why not?

Please rate the support you get from other parents.   1   2   3   4   5

3.0   THE PRESENT CLINICAL PROFILE

3.1   The diagnostic criteria of autism and Asperger's syndrome are taken from DSM-IV. The following items in this section relate to these criteria.

To gain a diagnosis of autism, an individual should show a total of six (or more) items from section A (1), (2) and (3), with at least two from (1) and one each from (2) and (3).

The child should also show at least one item from section B.

The child should not have Rett's disorder or childhood disintegrative disorder (see Appendix A).

SECTION A

(1)   Qualitative impairment in social interaction, as manifested by at least two of the following:

(a)   Marked impairment in the use of multiple non-verbal behaviours such as eye-to-eye gaze, facial expressions, body posture and gestures to regulate social interaction.

ASSESSMENT ITEMS 1a

Please ask the parents to indicate whether any of the following is true NOW or IN THE PAST; tick according to whether this was minor or severe.

	NOW		IN THE PAST	
	Minor	Severe	Minor	Severe

Marked impairment in:

Eye-to-eye contact

Facial expressions

Poor gestures

Body posture

Understanding of parental facial expression

(b) Failure to develop peer/other relationships to appropriate developmental level.

ASSESSMENT ITEMS 1b

Please ask the parents to indicate whether any of the following is true NOW or IN THE PAST; tick according to whether this was minor or severe.

	NOW		IN THE PAST	
	Minor	Severe	Minor	Severe

Marked impairment in development:

Eye-to-eye contact

Contact with adults

Contact with peers

Clinging to parents

Aloofness

Quality of attention to others

Level of contact initiated by
  the child

Level of response to contact

Behaves to avoid contact

(c) A lack of spontaneous seeking to share enjoyment, interests or achievements
     with other people.

ASSESSMENT ITEMS 1c

Please ask the parents to indicate whether any of the following is true NOW
or IN THE PAST; tick according to whether this was minor or severe.

	NOW		IN THE PAST	
	Minor	Severe	Minor	Severe

Lack of:

Showing objects/toys/etc.

Bringing objects/toys/etc.

Pointing out objects of interest
  to other people

Spontaneous speech/other
  communication

(d) A lack of social or emotional reciprocity.

ASSESSMENT ITEMS 1d

Please ask the parents to indicate whether any of the following is true NOW
or IN THE PAST; tick according to whether this was minor or severe.

	NOW		IN THE PAST	
	Minor	Severe	Minor	Severe

Not participating in simple
  social play or games

Preference for solitary play or
  activities

Only involves others as
  mechanical 'tools'

(2) Qualitative impairments in communication as manifested by at least one of
the following:

(a) Delay in or total lack of development of spoken language (not accompanied
by an attempt to compensate through alternative modes of communication
such as gesture or mime).

ASSESSMENT ITEMS 2a

The subject has no meaningful speech   (Yes/No)

Speech shows delay but is meaningful   (Yes/No)

Bizarre sounds (e.g. 'animal noises', squeals)   (Yes/No)

(b) In subjects with adequate speech, marked impairment in the ability to
initiate or sustain a conversation with others.

ASSESSMENT ITEMS 2b

Excessive questioning   (Yes/No)
Preoccupation with particular topics   (Yes/No)
Poor use of voice pitch/tone   (Yes/No)
Inability to let others have a turn   (Yes/No)
Refusal to let others select the conversation   (Yes/No)

(c)   Stereotyped and repetitive use of language or idiosyncractic language.

ASSESSMENT ITEMS 2c

	NOW	IN THE PAST
Echolalia	(Yes/No)	(Yes/No)
Pronoun reversal	(Yes/No)	(Yes/No)
Use of peculiar words or jargon	(Yes/No)	(Yes/No)
Repetitive saying of words or phrases	(Yes/No)	(Yes/No)

(d)   Lack of varied, spontaneous make-believe play or social-initiative play appropriate to developmental level.

ASSESSMENT ITEMS 2d

Atypical use of toys (e.g. banging, sucking)	(Yes/No)
Atypical orientation of toys (e.g. repetitive lining up of toys, making repetitive patterns out of them)	(Yes/No)
Focusing on insignificant parts of toys/objects (e.g. watching light following them, repetitive movement of parts)	(Yes/No)
Excessive attachment to one toy/object, obsessive interest in it	(Yes/No)
Lack of 'pretend' quality to play	(Yes/No)
Gets distressed if the pattern of toys/objects is changed	(Yes/No)

(3)   Restricted, repetitive and stereotyped patterns of behaviour, interests and activities, as manifested by at least two of the following:

(a)   All-encompassing preoccupation with one or more stereotyped and restricted patterns of interest that is abnormal in either intensity or focus.

ASSESSMENT ITEMS 3a

Putting objects repeatedly into mouth beyond normal developmental age	(Yes/No)
Sniffing objects repeatedly	(Yes/No)
Ignoring pain	(Yes/No)
Reacting very strongly to even slight discomfort	(Yes/No)
Repetitive ordering of objects/toys	(Yes/No)
Obsessive about topics of conversation	(Yes/No)

(b) Apparently inflexible adherence to specific, non-functional routines or rituals.

ASSESSMENT ITEMS 3b

Accepts change to routines without complaint/distress	(Yes/No)
Resists change, particularly to activities or outcome, and tries to continue as before the change	(Yes/No)
Resists changes and becomes unhappy/angry	(Yes/No)
Cannot accept change without severe emotional outbursts (e.g. screaming, tantrums)	(Yes/No)

(c) Stereotyped and repetitive motor mannerisms.

ASSESSMENT ITEMS 3c

	MINOR	SEVERE
Hand flapping	(Yes/No)	(Yes/No)
Face fanning	(Yes/No)	(Yes/No)
Finger twirling	(Yes/No)	(Yes/No)
Twisting/twirling whole body	(Yes/No)	(Yes/No)

Repetitive head banging, face slapping or self-abuse (specify)	(Yes/No)	(Yes/No)
Pacing vigorously	(Yes/No)	(Yes/No)
Rocking on balls of feet	(Yes/No)	(Yes/No)
Other	(Yes/No)	(Yes/No)

(d) Persistent preoccupation with parts of objects   (Yes/No)

   If yes, please specify.

SECTION B

Delays or abnormal function in at least one of the following areas with onset prior to 3 years of age.

Ask the parents to confirm that their child's functioning in at least one of the following was delayed or abnormal before the age of 3 years.

(1) Social interaction (specify)

(2) Language as used in social communication

(3) Symbolic or imaginative play

3.2 Interviewer: does the subject show sufficient indicators to confirm autism? (Yes/No)

3.3 If no, does the subject have some other autistic-like condition (e.g. Asperger's syndrome, semantic pragmatic disorder, other; please specify). If so, use the diagnostic criteria in Appendix A.

4.0   EDUCATIONAL AND EDUCATION-RELATED PROVISION

4.1   Which school does your child attend?

What type of school is it?

Mainstream school and support	(Yes/No)
Mainstream school and unit (specify type)	(Yes/No)
Special day school for children with SLD	(Yes/No)
Special day school for children with MLD	(Yes/No)
Special day school for children with autism	(Yes/No)
Special residential school for children with SLD	(Yes/No)
Special residential school for children with MLD	(Yes/No)
Special residential school for children with autism	(Yes/No)

4.2   Does your child have a Statement of Special Needs?   (Yes/No)

If yes, when did you receive it?   Date:

May we have a copy please?   (Yes/No)

4.3   Are you satisfied with this Statement?   (Yes/No)

If not, why not?

4.4   Have you received all of the services that the Statement lists?   (Yes/No)

4.5 Was/is there a co-ordinator available to your family to improve the joint assessment procedures?

(Yes/No/Don't know)

4.6 How helpful would you consider it to be to have a co-ordinator to improve the joint assessment procedures? (Please circle)

Very helpful   Quite helpful   Helpful   Of some help
Not particularly helpful   Not helpful

4.7 How smooth was the transition from preschool to full-time education? (Please circle)

Very smooth   Smooth   Fairly smooth   Acceptable
Some minor delays   Had to wait for a place

4.8 Did you have a choice of primary schools?

(Yes/No/Don't know)

4.9 How wide a range of provision is/was there from which to choose? (Please circle)

Very wide   Wide   Quite wide   Not very wide   Quite narrow   Narrow

4.10 Were the choices offered applicable to the needs of your child? That is, was it a fair choice, based on real options? (Please circle)

Yes   Yes, to a degree   Not really   No   Don't know

4.11 How easy is/was it for your child to travel to school? (Please circle)

Very difficult   Difficult   A little difficult   Fair easy   Easy   Very easy

4.12 Was there a waiting-list?

(Yes/No/Don't know)

4.13 How much experience or knowledge do you think that the school have/had of autism? (Please circle)

None   Not very much   A little   Some   Quite a lot   A great deal

4.14 How much peripatetic help is there in the classrooms? (Please circle)

A great deal   Quite a lot   Some   A little   Not very much   None

4.15 Did/does your child attend as follows? (Please circle)

Daily   Weekly boarder   Termly boarder   52-week placement

4.16 What would have/does suit your child's needs best? (Please circle)

Daily   Weekly boarder   Termly boarder   52-week placement

4.17 How satisfied were/are you with the provision? (Please circle)

Very satisfied   Quite satisfied   Satisfied   A little dissatisfied
Not at all satisfied   Dissatisfied

4.18 How satisfied are you that your child receives an appropriate special education programme? (Please circle)

Dissatisfied   Not at all satisfied   A little dissatisfied   Satisfied
Quite satisfied   Very satisfied

4.19 How much advice and support have you received/do you receive at this stage in your son's/daughter's life? (Please circle)

Plenty   Quite a lot   Enough   Not enough   Hardly any   None

4.20　Have you been offered access to other services?

Please tick any that might apply:

Speech therapy

Educational psychologist

Behavioural advice

Portage worker

Respite

Play-scheme

Befriending

Domiciliary help

Clinical psychologist

Occupational therapist

Other (please specify)

Now please indicate which services you would like to have access to.
Please tick any or all that might apply:

Speech therapy

Educational psychologist

Behavioural advice

Portage worker

Respite

Play-scheme

Befriending

Domiciliary help

Clinical psychologist

Occupational therapist

Other (please specify)

Which were most helpful?
Why?

Which were least helpful?

Why?

4.21 How much practical help were you/have you been offered in the school holidays? (Please circle)

None   Hardly any   Not enough   Enough   Quite a lot   Plenty

Who by?

4.22 How much practical help were you/have you been offered after school? (Please circle)

Plenty   Quite a lot   Enough   Not enough   Hardly any   None

Who by?

4.23 How satisfied do you feel with the practical support you have been offered? (Please circle)

Very dissatisfied   Quite dissatisfied   A little dissatisfied
Fairly satisfied   Satisfied   Very satisfied

For young people aged 11 years or over

Was the transition from primary to secondary school managed well?

If not, why not?

5.0 ADVOCACY

5.1 How much of a say in the present choice of nursery/playgroup/school did your son/daughter have? (Please circle)

None at all   Not much   A little   Quite a say   A big say

As much say as anyone else

5.2 How wide and how real a choice would you say there was of nursery/play group/school for your son/daughter? (Please circle)

Very wide and real   Quite wide and real   Fairly wide and real   Limited

Quite narrow and not particularly real   Narrow and not very real

5.3 To what extent do you feel that your son/daughter is represented in any forum where decisions are made about him/her? (Please circle)

Not represented   No real representation   Hardly represented
Some representation   Definitely represented   Very much represented

5.4 Please read the following statements concerning your son's/daughter's nursery/playgroup/school and score them from –3 to +3 on the scale beside each.

My son/daughter is treated with dignity and respect: –3 –2 –1 0 +1 +2 +3

His/her individual needs, wishes and opinions are sought, and he/she is helped to express and action these where possible: –3 –2 –1 0 +1 +2 +3

My son's/daughter's right to religious and cultural freedom and practice is respected: –3 –2 –1 0 +1 +2 +3

My son's/daughter's right to his/her own possessions, clothing, etc. is respected: –3 –2 –1 0 +1 +2 +3

Again, we very much value your views and comments about your experiences. Have you anything that you would like to add regarding advocacy?

6.0 FAMILY SERVICES

6.1 Were you allocated a community nurse?

(Yes/No/Don't know)

If so, when?

6.2 How much experience does he/she seem to have in the area of special need experienced by your son/daughter? (Please circle)

Not experienced at all   Not very experienced

Seems to have some experience   Quite experienced

Very experienced   Extremely experienced

6.3 Were you allocated a contact for family services?

(Yes/No/Don't know)

If so, who?

6.4 Were they effectual?

(Yes/No/Don't know)

6.5 How experienced does he/she seem in autism? (Please circle)

Extremely experienced   Very experienced   Quite experienced

Seems to have some experience   Not very experienced

Not experienced at all

6.6 How much information and support do you feel you have received from the statutory services? (Please circle)

Plenty   Quite a lot   Enough   Not enough   Hardly any   None

6.7 How much information do you feel you have received from voluntary groups? (Please circle)

None   Hardly any   Not enough   Enough   Quite a lot   Plenty

6.8 How much information do you feel you have received regarding benefits? (Please circle)

Plenty   Quite a lot   Enough   Not enough   Hardly any   None

6.9 How much support have you received regarding behaviour management? (Please circle)

None   Hardly any   Not enough   Enough   Quite a lot   Plenty

Again, we very much value your views and comments about your experiences. Have you anything that you would like to add regarding Family Services?

7.0 RESPITE CARE

7.1 Has your family been offered respite care? If so, on what basis is it available to you? (Please circle)

Whenever you want it   1 week in 4   1 week in 8   Other, please specify

7.2 How often does your family use it? (Please circle)

In an emergency only   1 week in 4   1 week in 8   Occasionally
Other, please specify

7.3 Is the respite care offered to your family residential, or is it assistance in the home? (Please circle)

Residential respite   Assistance in the home

7.4   Is it voluntary or statutory? (Please circle)

Voluntary   Statutory

Which would you like?

7.5   Is there a facility available to you whereby somebody will come to your home
      to help with your son/daughter (e.g. sitting with him/her whilst you go out;
      or domiciliary help in general)?

      (Yes/No/Don't know)

7.6   How much do you feel that your family needs a facility of this kind?
      (Please circle)

      Very great need   Great need   Some need   A little need
      No great need   Do not need

7.7   If respite care is available to your family, how suitable is it? (Please circle)

      Not at all suitable   Not very suitable   Not particularly suitable
      Satisfactory   Fairly   suitable   Very suitable

7.8   If it was completely suitable, how much more would you use it? (Please
      circle)

      Much more   Considerably more   Somewhat more   A little more
      Not much more   No more

7.9   Which establishment provides the respite care for your family?

7.10   Is there an age limit to the respite care your family receive?

(Yes/No/Don't know)

If yes, what is it?

7.11   If you do/did get respite care, who pays/paid for it?

8.0   ADULT SERVICES

8.1   How smoothly was the transition made by the services, for the young person, from school to adult services? (Please circle)

Very smooth   Smooth   Fairly smooth   Acceptable

Some minor problems   Not smooth at all

8.2   How smoothly was the transition made by the services, for you and the rest of the family, in terms of preparation, from this son/daughter/relative attending school to attending adult services? (Please circle)

Not smooth at all   Some minor problems   Acceptable

Fairly smooth   Smooth   Very smooth

8.3   Does your relative/son/daughter have access to independent housing? Please tick one or more of the following:

No, and I/we prefer that he/she lives with me/us

No, and he/she prefers to live with me/us

No

Yes, but I/we prefer that he/she lives with me/us

Yes, but he/she prefers to live with me/us

Yes

Don't know

8.4   Thinking about these arrangements, how satisfactory are they? (Please circle)

      Very satisfactory   Quite satisfactory   Satisfactory
      Not quite satisfactory   Not at all satisfactory   Most unsatisfactory

8.5   Where does your relative/son/daughter live?

8.6   If your relative/son/daughter has a residential placement, how experienced
      are the staff there in the special need that your relative has? (Please circle)

      Extremely experienced   Very experienced   Quite experienced
      Seem to have some experience   Not very experienced
      Not experienced at all

8.7   What kind of day care is available for your relative/son/daughter?

8.8   Does your relative/son/daughter receive a day service that is separate from
      his/her residential care?

      (Yes/No/Don't know)

8.9   Did you have a choice of day service?

      (Yes/No/Don't know)

8.10 Was your relative/son/daughter given a choice of day service?

      (Yes/No/Don't know)

8.11 How wide a range of provision was there from which to choose? (Please circle)

Very wide choice   Wide choice   Quite a wide choice   Some choice
Little choice   No choice

8.12 Were the choices offered applicable to the needs of your relative/son/daughter? That is, was it a fair choice, based on real options?

(Yes/No/Don't know)

8.13 How easy is it for your relative/son/daughter to travel to the day service? (Please circle)

Very difficult   Difficult   A little difficult   Easy   Quite easy
Very easy

8.14 How experienced are the staff at the day placement in the special need experienced by your relative/son/daughter? (Please circle)

Not at all experienced   Not very experienced   Hardly experienced at all
Experienced   Quite experienced   Very experienced

8.15 How great are the opportunities to attend social and leisure activities at the day service? (Please circle)

Many opportunities   A lot of opportunities
Quite a number of opportunities   Not many opportunities
No opportunities

8.16 Are further education or training opportunities offered at the residential service (if applicable)?

(Yes/No/Don't know)

8.17 How great are the opportunities to attend social and leisure activities at the residential service (if applicable)? (Please circle)

Many opportunities   A lot of opportunities

Quite a number of opportunities   Not many opportunities

No opportunities

8.18 Does your relative/son/daughter have employment opportunities?

(Yes/No/Don't know)

8.19 How meaningful a programme do you consider that your relative/son/ daughter enjoys at his/her day Service? (Please circle)

Not very meaningful   A little meaningful   Fairly meaningful

Quite meaningful   Very meaningful   Extremely meaningful

8.20 Are individuals offered an assessment in accordance with the Community Care Act?

(Yes/No/Don't know)

8.21 How satisfied are you with Adult Services? (Please circle)

Very satisfied   Quite satisfied   Satisfied   Dissatisfied

Quite dissatisfied   Very dissatisfied

8.22 How fully are the person's needs met by the day service? (Please circle)

Entirely met   Almost fully met   Some way towards being met

Not fully met   Hardly met at all   Not met at all

8.23 To what extent would you say that your son/daughter absorbs staff time compared to other clients in the day service? (Please circle)

Absorbs much more   Absorbs more   Absorbs not much more

Absorbs no more   Absorbs less   Absorbs far less

8.24 Is specialist support provided?

(Yes/No/Don't know)

8.25 What is the ratio of staff to members at the day service? For example; 1 member of staff to 2 members. If you don't know please say so.

8.26 To what extent would you say that your son/daughter/relative challenges the present-day service? (Please circle)

Does not challenge at all   Presents no great challenge

Challenges occasionally   Challenges it a little

Challenges it a lot   Challenges it to a great extent

8.27 Is your relative/son/daughter unsettled by the population or environment in the service? (Please circle)

Very unsettled   Unsettled   A little unsettled

Occasionally unsettled   Hardly ever unsettled

Not at all unsettled

Have you any other comments regarding your experience of day services? Please feel free to add them below.

PARENTS' INDIVIDUAL EXPERIENCES

(data collected through conversation and incidental discussion)

(1) Reaction to diagnosis

(2) How parents presently feel about autism

'How do you now feel about your son/daughter having a diagnosis of autism/
Asperger's syndrome?'

Sample responses with frequency rates expressed as a percentage (no limit on
response number):

I am emotionally upset (depressed/lonely/guilty)	36%
I pray that he/she will be normal one day	24%
I worry about the future	24%
I am puzzled about the condition	56%
I want to know the cause	36%
I cry a lot	16%
Others	

(5) The uncertainty of parents about the cause

Pregnancy/birth	28%
Child's early traumatic experiences	32%
Genetic factors	8%
'My fault' in handling/postnatal depression	24%
Don't know	12%

(6) What do the parents find hardest to accept?

Will never be normal	37%
Lack of speech/communication	33%
'Ignore' behaviours	28%
Lack of affection	39%
Fears about dependency/what will happen when I'm gone	57%

Special education	35%
Reaction of others	23%

(7)   How families cope with the child

Learn to be extra patient/understanding/accepting/love him/ her as he/she is	30%
Adjust, making autistic child the centre/first priority	32%
Make sacrifices, give up career/holidays/material objects	12%
Make family co-operate/communicate	4%
Others	10%

(8)   'How do your other children accept (CHILD'S NAME) with autism?'

They think he/she is sick/ill/mentally ill	14%
They know that X will never talk/play	21%
They think he/she will get better	9%
They know to give way/be patient/accept the difficult behaviour	22%
They try and teach him/her	23%
They fight/argue/say 'Its unfair'	21%
Others	7%

(9)   'What do your relatives think of (CHILD'S NAME) with autism?'

Won't accept it	8%
Think he/she will catch up	8%
Blame parents	30%
'Tell us to relax'	4%
'Tell us to do more'	6%
Say child needs better professional help	30%
Say child is spoilt/was neglected when younger	8%
Say child is sad/unfortunate, to be pitied	8%
Others	8%

(NB Relatives can and do hold paradoxical positions)

(10) 'How do people react to (CHILD'S NAME) in public?'

Unsympathetic/disapproving/irritated	15%
Sympathetic/pitying/helpful	18%
Often just don't notice	16%
Don't understand/confused/puzzled/enquiring/interested to learn	12%
Others	12%
Don't know, don't take him/her out	14%

(13) 'What mistakes do you feel you have made?'

Hide child away/hide the truth	12%
Giving up/not doing much about it/'what will be will be'	20%
Leaving treatment to the experts/not getting actively involved/giving simple care only	16%
Spoiling/indulging/giving in	12%
Losing patience/anger/punishing	12%
Others	12%

(14) 'What thoughts have you had about the future?'

Optimistic/positive	4%
Hoping for the best	28%
The future is black—very worried/scared/frightened	22%
'I live from day to day'	10%
Others	8%

(15) 'What are your wishes for (CHILD'S NAME) with autism?'

To get well/become normal	43%
For him/her to become independent of me	40%
For him/her to feel our love/accepted/wanted/valued	7%
To be as happy as possible	59%
To have a satisfactory job/life/time at school	61%
Others	10%

Please use this space to add any further comments:

3

DIAGNOSIS AND AUTISM

The diagnosis of autism is a complex process and is not one that can be accomplished in a single assessment by just one profession.[1] When this happens, all parents actually get is an opinion that can easily be challenged by any other professional who chooses to disagree. Many of the parents who responded to the survey experienced this problem when, after the event, they sought to use the 'diagnosis' to impress on resource controllers in Local Education Authorities or Social Services Departments the needs of their child with autism.

In addition, such one-off assessments frequently lead to parents coming away with a label but no solid information, and often also with no real idea where to go next to get help or guidance. Again the survey data on this was very clear. Parents often went long distances to have an assessment lasting one day or less, and came away with a diagnosis but no clear idea as to what they should do next. Many complained that they then had to wait for months to receive a report which made unrealistic recommendations about resources that were simply not available.

Exactly why the diagnostic process should be intricate and multidisciplinary may be deduced from even a brief overview of the nature of autism. The section which follows provides such an overview.

It is over 50 years since Dr Leo Kanner, a psychiatrist at Johns Hopkins University, wrote the first paper applying the term 'autism' to a group of self-centred children with severe social, communication and behavioural problems. Here we provide a general overview of the complexity of this developmental disability by summarising many of the major topics in autism. We have found that parents have appreciated and benefited from this information, and we now routinely supply it.

---

[1] Although it is sometimes possible to clarify points of diagnosis for parents on the basis of psychological assessment.

Frequency of Autism

Many parents whom we interviewed knew that autism was rare but still wanted to know how unlucky their child was. Autism occurs in 4.5 in 10 000 live births, a debatable figure based on large-scale surveys conducted in America and the UK. Many more have autistic-like behaviours—about 15 to 20 in 10 000. Throughout the world, estimates of the prevalence of autism vary considerably, ranging from only 2 in 10 000 in Germany to as many as 16 in 10 000 in Japan. Probable causes of the discrepancy in prevalence rates could include differing diagnostic criteria, genetic factors and/or environmental influences.

Males are three times more likely to be affected than females, and this imbalance is found throughout the range of developmental disorders.

What to Expect from Autism

Many autistic children are clearly different even as babies. Some bend their backs away from their parents to avoid touching and do not like being picked up, so they become floppy. As infants they are often passive or overly fractious babies in that many may make few, if any, demands on their parents, whereas others tend to cry during their waking hours and refuse to be calmed. During infancy, many begin to rock or head-bang on the cot side, and many parents have told us how distressing this is as it occurs night after night.

Many autistic infants reach their developmental milestones, such as talking, crawling and walking, earlier than is the norm, but most are considerably delayed. Approximately one-third of autistic children appear to develop normally until between 18 and 36 months of age, when autistic symptoms then become evident. A variety of causes may be at work, including the effects of vaccinations, exposure to a brain virus or the onset of epilepsy.

During childhood, autistic children generally fall behind their same-age peers in the areas of communication, social skills and cognition. In addition, the classic dysfunctional behaviours, such as self-stimulatory behaviours (i.e. repetitive, non-goal-directed behaviour such as rocking and hand-flapping), self-injury (e.g. hand-biting, head-banging), sleeping and eating problems, poor eye contact, insensitivity to pain, and attention deficits, may start to appear.

Most of the parents surveyed experienced their child's insistence on sameness or perseverative behaviour. Many children became overly insistent on routines, and became distressed and angry if there were even slight changes. Some common examples include drinking and/or eating the same food items at every meal, wearing certain clothing or insisting that others wear the same clothes, and going to school using the same route. Parents understood intuitively that a possible reason for 'insistence on sameness' may be the child's inability to cope with new experiences.

As will be described later, most of the older children had experienced difficulty with the transition to puberty. Seizure disorder onset during puberty, which may be due to hormonal changes, was evident in some families. In addition, behaviour problems became more frequent and more intense during this period. Few individuals experienced puberty without significant problems.

The parents whom we surveyed were keenly interested in the future. They were aware that many autistic people live in institutions, and were pleased to learn that some people with autism live at home with their parents. Others may live in residential facilities, while some live semi-independently (e.g. in a group home) and some live independently. Parents liked to know that there are autistic adults who go to university and obtain degrees, and that some develop adult relationships and may marry. Parents also liked to know that many autistic adults can be reliable and conscientious workers and hold down jobs, albeit with difficulty.

Causes

Although there is no known single cause of autism, there is growing evidence that it can be caused by a range of problems. There are certainly indications of a genetic influence in autism. For example, there is a higher probability that identical twins will have autism than that non-identical twins will do so.

In a survey conducted in America, researchers identified 11 families in which the father had autism. Of the 11 families, there was a total of 44 off-spring, of whom 25 individuals were diagnosed as having autism. Other difficulties may also be present, and some research has shown that depression, dyslexia and language disorders are quite common in one or both sides of families in which autism is present.

Some evidence suggests that viral infections can cause autism. There is an increased risk of autism after exposure to rubella during the first trimester of pregnancy. In addition, there is speculation that viruses associated with vaccinations, such as the rubella vaccine, may be linked to autism.

Physical Abnormalities

Researchers have identified a variety of brain abnormalities in individuals with autism. The reasons for these are not yet known, nor is the influence that they have on behaviour. There are two major types, namely dysfunctions in the neural structure of the brain and abnormal biochemistry of the brain. Future research will need to examine the relationship between these two types of abnormality.

With regard to brain structure, post-mortem studies located two areas in the limbic system which are underdeveloped, namely the amygdala and the hippocampus (Bauman *et al.*, 1991). These two areas have been shown to be responsible for emotions (including anger), sensory input and some learning. Courchesne (1989) has identified two areas in the cerebellum which are significantly smaller or larger than normal in autistic individuals. These areas of the cerebellum are believed to be responsible for attention.

With regard to biochemistry, many autistic people have increased levels of serotonin in their blood and cerebrospinal fluid, whereas others have relatively low levels of serotonin. It should be mentioned that other disorders, such as Down's syndrome, attention deficit/hyperactivity disorder and unipolar depression, are also associated with abnormal levels of serotonin. Some autistic individuals have been found to have elevated levels of beta-endorphins, which are endogenous opiate-like substances, in the body. It has been noted that those individuals who have elevated levels of beta-endorphins also have a higher-than-normal pain tolerance.

Finally, some studies have indicated that dysfunctional immune systems have also been associated with autism. Possibly a viral infection or an environmental toxin may be responsible for damaging the immune system.

Sensory Impairments

Some autistic people show impairment of one or more of their senses. This impairment may involve the auditory, visual, tactile, taste, vestibular, olfactory (smell) and proprioceptive senses, which may become hypersensitive or hyposensitive, or it may result in sensory interference. These effects make it difficult for individuals with autism to process incoming sensory information accurately.

The existence of sensory impairments may also explain why some individuals with autism may only be able to withstand normal stimulation with difficulty. For example, some autistic individuals are 'tactilely defensive' and try to avoid all forms of body contact. Others, by contrast, have little or no tactile or pain sensitivity. A common example of sensory abnormalities is hypersensitive hearing. Almost 40% of individuals with autism experience some discomfort when exposed to certain sounds. As children they generally cover their ears and may become aggressive after hearing sounds such as a vacuum cleaner or bus engine. In contrast, some parents suspect that their children have a hearing impairment because they appear to be unresponsive to sounds.

Deficits of Thinking and Reasoning

'Theory of mind' is the term given to our ability to understand that other people have their own unique point of view about the world. Many autistic individuals do not possess 'theory of mind', and so do not understand that others may have different thoughts, plans and beliefs to their own. In one example, a child may be asked to show a photograph of an animal to another child. Instead of turning the picture to face the other child, the child with autism may instead show them the back of the photograph. The autistic child can view the picture but, lacking 'theory of mind', does not realise that the other child has a different perspective and does not share the same information.

About 10% of autistic individuals have savant skills, and have an ability which is exceptionally well developed by normal standards. These abilities are often found in music and art, but some individuals have incredible mathematical ability and can multiply large numbers rapidly by mental arithmetic, while others can give the correct day of the week for any future date.

Less dramatic but no less abnormal are those with a focused attention span, referred to as 'stimulus overselectivity'. Their attention is focused on only one (often irrelevant) aspect of objects. For example, they may focus on colour and ignore shape. In this case, it may be difficult for them to discriminate between completely different objects if their colour is the same. Since attention is the first stage in processing information, failure to attend to the relevant aspects of an object or person destroys the ability to learn.

Diagnostic Criteria

From this brief overview of autism, it is possible to begin a process whereby the incredible variety of the characteristics of autism can be placed within a systematised framework of diagnostic criteria.

The majority of parents in our survey complained that few professionals had been able or willing to do this for them. The minority of 15% had been taken through a well-structured process and found that it gave them considerable understanding of how their child functioned. They found this both reassuring and confidence-boosting.

The diagnostic criteria for autism have changed considerably over time (Rutter and Schopler, 1987) to become defined as a constellation of mainly behavioural symptoms (Frith, 1989). Two similar, detailed and internationally accepted diagnostic systems are used to classify autistic children. These are the Diagnostic and Statistical Manual (DSM-IV) of the American Psychiatric Association (1994) and the International Classification of Diseases (ICD-10) of the World Health Organisation (1993). Both systems class autism as a 'Pervasive Developmental Disorder' (PDD). This emphasises the developmental origins of the condition and so distinguishes it from other mental disorders.

The core criteria for diagnosing autism from both DSM-IV and ICD-10 incorporate Wing's triad of impairments (Wing and Gould, 1979; Wing, 1988, 1995). These are as follows: (1) impairment of social relationships affecting social contact with others, with lack of understanding of the sometimes subtle rules of social behaviour; (2) impairment of social communication, ranging from a total absence of desire to communicate with others through to poor reciprocal conversation; and (3) impairment of social understanding and imagination, ranging from a total absence of pretend play to repetitive play without imagination or creativity. Consequently, the diagnosis of autistic disorder in DSM-IV and ICD-10 focuses on three main groups of symptoms: (1) qualitative impairment in reciprocal social interaction; (2) qualitative impairment in verbal and non-verbal communication, and in imaginative activity; and (3) a markedly restricted repertoire of activities and interests. In addition, this impaired development must be observable before 3 years of age. We shall now consider these three areas in turn.

Impairment of social interaction

The major problems of social interaction in autism centre on a characteristic lack of reciprocity (Rutter, 1978; Gillberg, 1993). Although children with autism can demonstrate emotional attachments to their parents or other primary caregivers (Sigman and Mundy, 1989), they do not respond appropriately to love and affection in the way in which those people expect (Attwood, 1993). Parents tell us that these children are less likely to open their arms for a cuddle and to seek comfort from their parents when they are in distress. In addition, they seem to ignore or misinterpret people's emotional behaviour (Sigman et al., 1992), and so show lack of awareness of the feelings of others. This creates inappropriate social behaviour and an obvious lack of empathy. Children with autism also show lack of joint attention and affective sharing (Volkmar and Mayes, 1990; Kasari *et al.*, 1993), which means that they cannot develop parallel or social play. Their capacity for pointing and other gestures is absent or severely impoverished (Baron-Cohen, 1989), such that they rarely point at objects in order to direct people's attention to them. By the same token, they fail to interpret the gestures of others. In addition, children with autism tend to use others mechanically to obtain what they want, making 'machines' out of people in the process (Richman, 1988). This was found to be particularly wounding by many of the parents who spoke to us.

Eye contact is frequently abnormal, and facial expressions are not often used as a means of non-verbal communication. Parents told us that they often feel 'dehumanised' or 'rejected' by the stare they receive from their children with autism. Many children with autism find eye contact and facial expressions perplexing and difficult to understand (Wimpory, 1991), thereby restricting their social interactions with other people. This difficulty is one of many problems they experience as they approach others, and their inability to understand basic social rules of greeting and interaction affect their peer relationships greatly (Richman, 1988). Furthermore, some children with autism may put themselves at risk by treating strangers and familiar adults alike, approaching both without caution.

Impairment of language and social communication

Children with autism often fail to understand the purpose and meaning of language, and so cannot use it as a tool for communicative purposes (Gillberg, 1993). Few are capable of using language adequately to exchange thoughts, ideas and feelings with others. Indeed, approximately 30% of children with autism fail to develop effective speech. Moreover, they do not use gesture or mime to compensate for this, and the remainder show either delays or deviance in language. Grammatical problems, stereotyped phrases, abnormalities in rhythm and pitch, and semantic or conceptual difficulties are common (Happe, 1994). Immediate or delayed echolalia is common (Attwood, 1993), and was particularly distressing to many parents to whom we spoke. Children with autism may echo other people's utterances, or even whole conversations, without understanding or taking account of the listener's needs. Even those children with autism who acquire reasonable speech still have difficulties in reciprocal conversation, and their topics are generally restricted. Their comprehension is limited and very literal, with understanding of abstract concepts being particularly impaired. In addition, most find it difficult to talk about feelings or thoughts (Wing, 1995), and thus they have no vehicle for ventilating their emotions through language.

Impairment of imagination

Children with autism also show abnormality in play and imaginative skills (Wing *et al.*, 1977; Riguet *et al.*, 1981), and this is an important area for assessment. They are impaired in their ability to play symbolically (Harrold, *et al.*, 1993), and so most fail to play imaginative/pretend games by themselves or with other children. As a result of their poor imaginative ability, children with autism have difficulty in utilising models of other people's actions and using imitation in a creative way (Wing, 1976). They rarely imitate their parents' routine domestic behaviour or the play of other children, and this is a source of great distress to parents. Their play tends to be repetitive, stereotyped, uncreative and non-social. Their failure to play imaginatively and socially also impacts on their language development (Howlin and Rutter, 1987), not least because the opportunities to 'hear' language and practise it are greatly reduced.

Repetitive stereotyped activities and interests

'Stereotyped body movements, adherence to strict routines and various other ritualistic phenomena are part and parcel of the autistic syndrome' (Gillberg, 1993, p. 347). Parents tell us that their children with autism tend to engage frequently in repetitive stereotyped movements such as rocking, tapping, flicking and twirling, moving around in circles, head-banging, face-fanning, or flapping their hands and fingers. These actions are thought to provide sensory stimulation, but are not necessarily enjoyable. In fact, many parents tell us that their children are distressed as they go through these behaviours. One told us that his son '. . . seems almost driven to rock back and forth and he cries all the time. If I stop him he seems genuinely pleased.' In some cases these movements may be a response to stress (Attwood, 1993). Children with autism often exhibit a fascination with particular objects that borders on obsessive attachment, and they may have an obsessional interest in collecting those objects. If the objects are removed or lost, the children may be profoundly distressed and have severe temper tantrums.[2] They may also exhibit all-consuming

---

[2] Child with plastic lemons—Asperger's differentiation.

preoccupations with bus routes, railway timetables or numbers. Others may engage in verbal stereotypes, and may talk incessantly about very restricted topics that are of narrow-focused interest only to them. Many children with autism repeat questions in an identical manner and demand standard answers. They seldom notice the boredom and intolerance of people around them and cannot understand why people become impatient with them. Over 60% of the parents we interviewed had autistic children who resist changes in daily routines and rituals. These may include lengthy bedtime rituals, going to local shops in the same order, or following identical routes to certain places—all demands that make life predictable (Attwood, 1993). Their children show great distress if these daily routines and rituals are altered. Parents also report that their child's obsessional activities cause great disruption, as they interfere with other family activities, and siblings are particularly irritated as their preferences are often negated.

CASE STUDY 3.1

James, aged twelve, attended the special needs unit of his local school. Each day he took the same route past the local park, at the same time, and made the same comments about the park keepers and emptying the bins. At home time he walked on the other side of the road and waited each day by the launderette to watch the machines spinning around. If, as had happened on occasions, his mother was in a rush and he was hurried away, James would scream, shout and run back to the launderette until it was his time to go.

Other problem behaviours

Apart from having problems of social interaction, communication, play and stereotyped behaviour, many autistic children commonly display less specific emotional and behaviour problems. Parents complain of sleeping and feeding problems, marked food fads, temper tantrums, aggression, destructiveness, hyperactivity, running away, screaming in public, short attention span, fears and panic reactions, and self-injury. Although such problems are not specific to autism, they may cause further difficulties for parents to manage at home, and they heighten family stress.

These characteristics of autism have been encapsulated in the diagnostic criteria used for formal diagnosis. It is our experience that parents who need clarification of a diagnosis that has not been fully explained to them benefit from an assessment process targeted specifically at these criteria. The following is a hypothetical example that is fairly typical of the kind of report that parents find useful when it is worked through carefully with them.

PSYCHOLOGICAL REPORT

CONFIDENTIAL

NAME: Sally Smith

ADDRESS: XXXX

DATE OF BIRTH: 10/05/93

AGE AT ASSESSMENT: 4 years 6 months

A: REASON FOR ASSESSMENT

Mrs Smith (Sally's mother) contacted the Family Assessment and Support Unit (FASU) requesting the department's involvement in the assessment of her daughter, Sally. Mrs Smith expressed her concern that Sally has been increasingly displaying symptoms similar to those exhibited by a cousin, William, who was previously assessed by the department and was subsequently diagnosed as having Asperger's syndrome. A comprehensive assessment of Sally was conducted in order to ascertain the information required to confirm or refute Mrs Smith's concerns regarding Sally's behaviour.

I undertook a psychometric assessment with Sally, using the Vineland Adaptive Behaviour Scales, the Symbolic Play Test and the British Ability Scales—revised edition (BAS-II). In addition, a history and clinical profile was completed with Mrs Smith by a social worker in training who used the Unit's questionnaire for the purpose.

B: PROCESS OF ASSESSMENT

Sally was assessed at the family home over three sessions. Present at both sessions were myself, Mrs Smith and Sally.

C: PRESENTATION DURING ASSESSMENT

Sally presented as a friendly yet shy little girl. Despite this she made frequent eye contact with both myself and others present throughout the assessment procedure. Sally separated from her mother without difficulty, and was easily engaged in the majority of tasks presented. However, Sally's level of verbal interaction during the assessment was minimal—that is, she rarely entered into any dialogue initiated by others, although she did verbalise spontaneously during administration of certain BAS-II subtests, these articulations usually taking the form of short (4- or 5-word) sentences ('I want the video') or single words used to name items ('car, Sooty, drink').

Sally was co-operative and focused well during administration of the Symbolic Play Test.

Sally was easily engaged in all of the BAS-II subtests, with the exception of the Recall of Objects subtest. She attempted the majority of items presented to her enthusiastically and confidently. For the most part, Sally focused well on the items presented to her and was able to concentrate on tasks of short duration. She appeared to understand the requests, questions and instructions directed to her without difficulty. In addition, I observed Sally as demonstrating a right-handed typical tripod grip.

D: ASSESSMENT RESULTS

D1: Vineland Adaptive Behaviour Scales

The Vineland Adaptive Behaviour Scales consist of a structured interview investigating an individual's 'life skills', which is completed by an informant who knows the child well, in this case Sally's mother. The test is employed in conjunction with various other psychological and psychometric measures of an individual's level of functioning, and the results may be integrated to produce a comprehensive individual profile. The Vineland Adaptive Behaviour Scales assess many aspects of behaviour, and are organised according to four distinct domains/dimensions of overall adaptive functioning. These are the Communication, Daily Living Skills, Socialisation and Motor Skills domains, performance in which is used to estimate an individual's Global Adaptive Behaviour. The content of each domain may be best understood in terms of its constituent subdomains, a summary of which is provided in Appendix A. An individual's performance, i.e. the scores attained, may be compared to the population of individuals of the same age.

The age equivalent represents the age at which Sally's performance would be average. As indicated in Table D1.1, for the most part Sally is between 3 years 7 months and 1 year 3 months behind her chronological age in the

Table D1.1: Vineland Adaptive Behaviour Scales

Domain adaptive level	Raw score	Age equivalent	
Communication			
Receptive	44	4 years 8 months	Adequate
Expressive	113	3 years 0 months	Low
Written	13	4 years 11 months	Adequate
Daily living skills			
Personal	112	3 years 5 months	Moderately low
Domestic	12	2 years 6 months	Moderately low
Community	16	2 years 11 months	Low
Socialisation			
Interpersonal	34	1 year 1 month	Low
Play and leisure	29	1 year 7 months	Low
Coping skills	15	2 years 8 months	Moderately low
Motor skills			
Gross	62	2 years 2 months	Low
Fine	58	5 years 2 months	Low

behaviour domains assessed. It should also be noted, however, that Sally's score on the receptive communication domain matches what would be expected of a child of her age, while her scores on the written communication and fine motor skills subdomains exceed those expected in accordance with her chronological age. That is, Sally's skills in these subdomains are marginally advanced (i.e. by approximately 3 and 6 months, respectively). Due to their limitations ('one year's growth' has a very different meaning at different points on the age continuum and for different areas of adaptive behaviour), age equivalents should be interpreted with caution. However, such scores do provide readily understandable guidelines regarding Sally's level of adaptive functioning in the specific areas assessed.

The age equivalents presented above indicate that Sally's life skills, in certain subdomains of each of the behaviour domains assessed, are significantly behind her chronological age. Her main areas of weakness are associated with her expressive communication skills, her domestic and community daily living skills, her gross motor skills and her socialisation skills. As indicated by the age equivalents above, Sally's receptive and written communication skills, together with her fine motor skills, are relative individual strengths. Table D1.2 summarises Sally's level of functioning in the broader domains of communication, daily living, socialisation, motor skills and global adaptive behaviour.

The age-equivalent data presented in the Table D1.2 demonstrates that Sally's life skills in each of the behaviour domains assessed are delayed to varying degrees. A score indicative of a marked delay may be observed in the socialisation and adaptive behaviour domains, while scores in the other domains indicate a moderate level of delay. Reflective of this is the fact that Sally's scores for all of the domains fall into the category designated 'moderately low', with the exception of her socialisation and adaptive behaviour scores, which fall into the category designated 'low adaptive level—mild deficit'.

The percentile rank indicates how Sally performed in relation to other children of her age. That is, it indicates the number of children in every hundred who would be expected to score lower than Sally in each behaviour domain, with a percentile rank of 50 being regarded as average. The delay with which Sally presents in the communication, daily living and motor skills domains is exhibited by less than 14 in 100 children, less than 4 in 100 children and less than 5 in 100 children, respectively. More importantly, the marked delay with which Sally presents in the socialisation and adaptive behaviour domains is exhibited by less than 2 in 1000 children and less than 1 in 100 children, respectively. This means that Sally will need considerable assistance in developing these skills in the future.

Table D1.2: Vineland Adaptive Behaviour Scales—Domains

Domain	Standard score	Percentile	Age equivalent
Communication	84	14	3 years 8 months
Daily living	74	4	3 years 2 months
Socialisation	57	0.2	1 year 8 months
Motor skills	75	5	3 years 4 months
Adaptive behaviour	65	1	2 years 11 months

D2: Symbolic Play Test

The Symbolic Play Test is a set of materials designed to elicit symbolic play, which is a precursor to imaginative play. The test is designed to evaluate the language potential of children who for some reason display a lack of, or delay in, the development of receptive or expressive language. It fulfils this function via administration in conjunction with other selected tests.

For the most part, Sally played appropriately with the materials presented to her and scored at a level expected of children 33.7 months old, which is 12 months behind her chronological age.

D3: British Ability Scales (Revised Edition)—Early Years, Upper Level

The BAS-II is a set of individually administered standardised questions and tasks designed to assess different aspects of a child's current intellectual functioning and, in comparison with these, their basic educational progress. Comparison can be made of a child's subtest scores, allowing identification of areas of relative strength and weakness.

T-scores of 45 to 50 are considered average for a child of Sally's age. As can be seen from Table D3.1 below, Sally's scores on verbal comprehension and pattern construction are above average (T-scores of 67 and 53, respectively), while her remaining scores are all marginally below average.

The percentiles show how Sally's scores compare with those of other children of her age. They show the number of children in every hundred who would achieve lower scores than Sally on a specific subtest. For example, 96 in 100 children would score lower than Sally on the verbal comprehension subtest, and 4 in 100 children would score higher. As indicated in the table, therefore, Sally's performance on matching letter-like forms puts her in the bottom 4% of the population on these items. However, these data must be interpreted with caution due to the fact that this subtest was the last one administered in the first assessment session, during which Sally appeared to become tired and lose her previously exhibited enthusiasm for answering items presented to her. In addition, Sally's scores on the picture similarities and recognition of pictures subtests place her in the bottom 18% of the population, while her scores on the early number concepts and copying subtests put her in the bottom 24% of the population. In contrast, Sally's performance on the verbal comprehension subtest was exceptional for a child of her age, placing her in the top 4% of the population. Her score on the

Table D3.1: British Ability Scales—Subtest Scores

Subtest equivalent	T-score	Percentile
Verbal comprehension	67	96
Picture similarities	41	18
Naming vocabulary	45	31
Pattern construction	53	62
Early number concepts	43	24
Copying	43	24
Recall of objects	45	31
Recall of digits forward	49	46
Matching letter-like forms	33	4
Recognition of pictures	41	18

Table D3.2: British Ability Scales—Cluster Scores

Cluster	Standard score	Confidence interval	Percentile
Verbal ability	110	99–120	75
Pictorial reasoning	86	77–96	18
Spatial ability	96	85–108	39

pattern construction subtest also indicates a relative strength in Sally's profile, placing her in the top 38% of the population.

The age equivalent represents the age at which Sally's performance would be average. As can be seen from Table D3.1, Sally is between 1 year 6 months and 3 months behind her chronological age, except in the verbal comprehension domain, where she is 2 years 9 months ahead of her chronological age, and in the area of pattern construction, where she performs at the level expected of a child of her age.

Standard scores of 90 to 110 are considered average for a child of Sally's age. As indicated in Table D3.2 above, her strongest skill is verbal ability, which requires understanding and use of speech. Her weakest skills are in the area of pictorial reasoning, i.e. tasks which require counting and matching graphically presented information. Sally's standard score for the pictorial reasoning cluster is below average, indicating the presence of a moderate learning difficulty with pictorial reasoning tasks.

Tests are only estimates of a child's ability, and therefore confidence intervals are provided. These provide estimated ranges within which the child's score is likely to fall. That is, if Sally was to be retested, this score would fall within the range(s) shown for 95% of the time.

The percentiles indicated in Table D3.2 above show how Sally's scores relate to the population of children of her age. The overall level of difficulty that Sally showed in the area of pictorial reasoning is only experienced by 18 in every 100 children.

D4: Present Clinical Profile
In order to address Mrs Smith's concerns that Sally may be displaying behaviour commonly observed in those children diagnosed as having Asperger's syndrome, Sally's behaviour was checked against the diagnostic criteria (as specified in DSM-IV) for Asperger's syndrome together with those for autism. A social worker in training from the Unit conducted a structured interview with the informant, Mrs Smith, using the Unit's clinical profile format.

Diagnostic criteria for autistic disorder: the following is taken from the Diagnostic and Statistical Manual of Mental Disorders, Fourth Edition (DSM-IV)

A. A total of six (or more) items from (1), (2) and (3), with at least two from (1) and one each from (2) and (3).

(1) Qualitative impairment in social interaction, as manifested by at least two of the following:

(a) marked impairments in the use of multiple non-verbal behaviours such as eye-to-eye gaze, facial expression, body posture and gestures to regulate social interaction

(b) failure to develop peer relationships appropriate to developmental level

(c) a lack of spontaneous seeking to share enjoyment, interests, or achievements with other people (e.g. by a lack of showing, bringing or pointing out objects of interest to others)

(d) lack of social or emotional reciprocity (e.g. not actively participating in simple social play or games, preferring solitary activities, or involving others in activities only as 'mechanical aids')

(2) Qualitative impairments in communication as manifested by at least one of the following:

(a) delay in, or total lack of, the development of spoken language (not accompanied by an attempt to compensate through alternative modes of communication such as gesture or mime)

(b) in individuals with adequate speech, marked impairment in the ability to initiate or sustain a conversation with others

(c) stereotyped and repetitive use of language or idiosyncratic language

(d) lack of varied, spontaneous make-believe play or social imitative play appropriate to developmental level

(3) Restricted repetitive and stereotyped patterns of behaviour, interests and activities, as manifested by at least two of the following:

(a) encompassing preoccupation with one or more stereotyped and restricted patterns of interest that is abnormal in intensity of focus

(b) apparently inflexible adherence to specific, non-functional routines or rituals

(c) stereotyped and repetitive motor mannerisms (e.g. hand or finger flapping or twisting, or complex whole-body movements)

(d) persistent preoccupation with parts of objects

B. Delays or abnormal functioning in at least one of the following areas, with onset prior to age 3 years:

(1) Social interaction

(2) Language as used in social communication

(3) Symbolic or imaginative play

It is now possible to compare Sally's presenting characteristics with the diagnostic criteria detailed above. Sally clearly presents as having certain indicators which suggest the presence of some autistic features, although these do not necessarily confirm a diagnosis of autism. In respect of the criteria for (A) she shows some evidence of each of 1a, 1b, 1c and 1d. Also in respect of (A), Sally shows some evidence of 2b, 2c and 2d, together with 3a, 3b and 3c, as reported by her mother.

In respect of those items under (B), it may be noted that prior to the age of 3 years Sally has shown a limited degree of abnormal functioning in the area of social interaction. However, no such abnormality/delay is reported for her functioning in the areas of language as used in social communication or in imaginative and symbolic play.

As mentioned in section A above, her mother's concern is focused on Sally's presentation of symptoms similar to those which occur as Asperger syndrome. There is therefore a need to consider her presenting clinical profile in the light of the current diagnostic criteria for this developmental disorder. DSM-IV documents the following criteria.

(1) Qualitative impairment in social interaction, as manifested by at least two of the following:

(a) marked impairments in the use of multiple non-verbal behaviours such as eye-to-eye gaze, facial expression, body posture and gestures to regulate social interaction

(b) failure to develop peer relationships appropriate to developmental level

(c) a lack of spontaneous seeking to share enjoyment, interests or achievements with other people (e.g. by a lack of showing, bringing or pointing out objects of interest to others)

(d) lack of social or emotional reciprocity

(2) Restricted repetitive and stereotyped patterns of behaviour, interests and activities, as manifested by at least two of the following:

(a) encompassing preoccupation with one or more stereotyped and restricted patterns of interest that is abnormal in intensity of focus

(b) apparently inflexible adherence to specific, non-functional routines or rituals

(c) stereotyped and repetitive motor mannerisms (e.g. hand or finger flapping or twisting, or complex whole-body movements)

(d) persistent preoccupation with parts of objects

(3) The disturbance causes clinically significant impairments in social, occupational or other important areas of functioning

(4) There is no clinically significant general delay in language (e.g. single words used by age 2 years, communicative phrases by age 3 years)

(5) There is no clinically significant delay in cognitive development or in the development of age-appropriate self-help skills, adaptive behaviour (other than social interaction) and curiosity about the environment in childhood

(6) Criteria are not met for another Pervasive Developmental Disorder

It is obvious that the diagnostic criteria for Asperger syndrome are very similar to those for autism given above. However, there are significant differences pertaining to language and cognitive skills. That is, with respect to the former, language should not show a clinically significant general delay. In Sally's case, evidence of such a language delay is not well documented and, as such, indicator (4) may be confirmed. In addition, however, indicator (5) requires that the child should show no clinically significant delay in cognitive development. Given the moderate delay in development indicated above, Sally's cognitive skills cannot be judged to have developed normally. As indicator (5) is not appropriate to define Sally's clinical presentation, it is possible to conclude that a diagnosis of autism may be retained as that most fitting to her current presentation.

E. SUMMARY

In summary, therefore, it is possible to conclude that the clinical and psychometric results presented above yield sufficient evidence to sustain a diagnosis of autism at this time. It is in this context that Sally's future needs should now be assessed, since a comprehensive understanding of the core difficulties associated with this developmental disorder must guide both planning of current educational provision and long-term care.

Signed   Date

Causes

Many psychologists, psychiatrists and biologists have tried to use different theories to explain possible causes of autism. This is made difficult because autism is a condition that changes with age (Trevarthen *et al.*, 1996). Whereas it is a specific behavioural syndrome, it is not a disease (Bauman *et al.*, 1991) or a condition with a single aetiology (Le Couteur, 1990). Goodman (1989) describes a coexistence of distinct constellations of functional impairments in general intelligence, social interaction, play, non-verbal communication and mechanical language skills.

One of the earliest explanations of autism focused on psychodynamic processes. Kanner (1943) suggested that children with autism 'come into the world with innate inability to form the usual biologically provided affective contact with people, just as other children come into the world with innate physical or intellectual handicaps' (p. 250). This implies that a disturbance in the biological systems, or more likely a deficiency in the growth of brain (Trevarthen *et al.*, 1996), is responsible. Kanner (1943, 1949) also believed that the innate nature of autism was confounded by 'refrigerator' parents who were intelligent and highly educated, but who were also cold, obsessive, lived in an emotionally detached manner and so could not form normal bonds of attachment with their children and provide them with nurturing warmth and affection. Bettelheim (1967) and O'Gorman (1967) also stated that the cause of autism was a failure to establish a normal emotional bond between infants and their parents, and inadequate mothering. This theory has caused great distress to many of the parents we interviewed, who had heard of 'refrigerator parents' even if they did not know the name Bettelheim. Fortunately, several studies have failed to support this psychogenic theory of autism (McAdoo and DeMyer, 1978; Cantwell *et al.*, 1979), and parents can be reassured that they are not to blame.

More recently, several studies have demonstrated that autistic children experience difficulty in entering into emotional relationships with others because they have difficulties in recognising and understanding emotional expressions (Hobson, 1986a, 1986b; Hobson *et al.*, 1988; Capps *et al.*, 1992). Hobson (1989) states that autism is a social and emotional dysfunction originating from an incapacity to respond and relate emotionally to others (Hobson, 1989, 1993). He also suggests that autistic children's disabilities in cognition and language are the product of dysfunctional interpersonal relatedness (Hobson, 1993).

Alternative explanations veer away from the emotional. In the mid-1960s, psychologists had shifted to cognitive explanations of autism. Hermelin and O'Connor (1970) were among the pioneers of autism as a set of cognitive deficits. They suggested that the social impairment of autistic children stemmed from their inability to encode stimuli meaningfully. Rutter (1983) argued that the cognitive deficits of autism are closely linked to its social and behavioural features, and that they are fundamental to the disorder, not simply secondary to other autistic features.

According to Leslie (1987), children possess two types of representations, namely 'primary representations' of things and people as they really are in the world, and 'metarepresentations' which are then formed and used to structure pretence and understanding that other people have minds like their own. Autistic children are postulated to have a specific impairment in forming metarepresentations, and thus they are unable to understand other mental states. The developmental ability to attribute independent mental states with content to oneself and others in order to explain behaviour is known as 'theory of mind'. These mental states must be independent both of reality (as people can believe things which are not true) and of other people's mental states (as we believe, want and pretend different things to one another) (Happe, 1994, pp. 39–40). Baron-Cohen et al. (1985) were the first to demonstrate that autistic children lack a 'theory of mind'. That is, autistic children have problems in differentiating between what is in their own minds and what is in others' minds, and they fail to recognise that other people have independent minds. Thus they cannot understand what other people might be thinking that is different (Baron-Cohen et al., 1985; Baron-Cohen, 1986b; Leslie and Frith, 1988; Frith, 1989). Consequently, they have difficulties in understanding other people's 'true beliefs' (Leslie and Frith, 1988), 'false beliefs' (Baron-Cohen et al., 1985; Frith, 1989) and 'desires' (Harris, 1989). This would produce difficulties in comprehending emotion caused by false beliefs (Baron-Cohen, 1989) Furthermore, the same cognitive ability is also important for intentional communication (Frith, 1989) through which meaning is shared and understood. Consequently, the intentional communication of autistic children is also impaired.

However, it is also the case that autism may exist at the level of organic dysfunction (Steffenburg and Gillberg, 1989). Steffenburg (1991) found that about 90% of her study sample of autistic and autistic-like children showed some evidence of brain damage or dysfunction. Courchesne (1989) provides evidence that autism may be related to specific abnormal development in the cerebellum. Further evidence in support of brain damage as a cause of autism comes from the high incidence of epilepsy (about 35–40%) in autistic children (Olsson et al., 1988; Volkmar and Nelson, 1990), and about 75% of people with autism also have learning disabilities (Smalley et al., 1988).

Working with Parents

In order to work with these parents we must remember that all of the usual problems of infant behaviour may also arise, including sleep difficulties, food fads, toileting problems, and so on. Despite those difficulties, however, it is clear that constructive task-centred work carried out by parents after training not only has direct benefits for the further development of their child, particularly in relation to the reduction of challenging behaviour (e.g. Robbins and Dunlap, 1992), but is also associated with improved psychological well-being of the parents. In one study (Bristol *et al.*, 1993), mothers were asked to complete a depression scale at the time of their child's diagnosis and again 6 months and 18 months later. Mothers who participated showed a decrease in their depressive symptoms over time, whereas the non-participants showed no change.

Our own experience of parents referred to the Unit confirms these findings. Success in improving one or both of two main areas of concern is positively associated with an increase in optimism and a strengthening of relationships.

The first of these areas concerns challenging behaviour, where training in the STAR strategy (Zarkowska and Clements, 1989) has led to reassertion of control for many parents. The second is the area of communication, where training in the use of a behavioural approach to simple communication and other skills (Gibb and Randall, 1989) has been greeted with relief by parents who had previously felt disempowered by their inability to encourage two-way conversation with their autistic child. This experience is particularly marked when the child has used them to serve basic needs (e.g. fetching drinks or snacks, playing in ritualistic ways) rather as though they were objects instead of people. Under these circumstances the communication of need has been one-way and parents feel used and rejected. We know that many educationalists will shudder at the thought of non-concept-based training, but think of this. Even the simplest communication in response to the parents can be greeted with joy. This mother's own words describe this very clearly:

> After two years of being pulled and pulled around we both felt used like robots. We certainly had no sense of being loved by Robbie, who seemed not to notice us when were weren't useful to him. It feels great now that we have simple but reliable communication with him, such as him turning to his name or getting his shoes when we ask. We feel that we are members of **his** family again.

The earlier co-operative work with parents starts the better. There is then likely to be more rapid developmental progress, and there is less time for the parents to suffer the negative effects of struggling to cope without professional advice. Working within the home on a multidisciplinary basis is particularly strongly associated with positive outcomes with very young children (Prizant and Wetherby, 1988) and, in our experience, has a greater chance of success than clinic- or classroom-based work. It is clearly reflected, too, in the research study undertaken by Burke and Cigno (1996).

Management at School

This is not an area that will be covered in any depth at this point, because this book is not about educational practice, but this is of course one of the greatest worries that parents have, so the following represent some general ideas which have more to do with advocacy than curriculum issues. The worries are becoming more frequent in our experience because many more high-functioning children with autism, particularly those with Asperger's syndrome, are finding their way into mainstream schools. We provide a number of set-piece tips for parents to pass on to teachers and other school staff. A few of them are given below.

The most important starting point in helping a pupil with autism to function effectively in school is for all of the staff who will come into contact with the child to understand that he or she has an inherent developmental disorder which causes him or her to behave and respond in a different way to other pupils. Too often, behaviours in these children are interpreted as 'emotional', 'manipulative', or some other term is used that misses the point that they respond differently to the world and its stimuli. It follows from this that school staff must carefully individualise their approach for each of these children. They cannot be treated just the same as other pupils.

Asperger understood the central importance of teachers' attitudes from his own work. In 1944 he wrote, 'These children often show a surprising sensitivity to the personality of the teacher. . . . They can be taught, but only by those who give them true understanding and affection, people who show kindness towards them and, yes, humour. . . . The teacher's underlying emotional attitude influences, involuntarily and unconsciously, the mood and behaviour of the child.'

It is also necessary for teachers to avoid escalating power struggles. These children do not understand displays of authority or anger, and will themselves become more rigid and stubborn if forcefully confronted. Their behaviour can then rapidly escalate out of control, and at that point it is often better for the member of staff to 'damp down' the situation and allow it to dissipate. It is always preferable to try to anticipate such situations and to take preventative action to avoid confrontation through calmness, presentation of choices or diversion of attention elsewhere.

A major activity as the child progresses through school is the promotion of more appropriate social interactions aimed at helping him or her to fit in better socially. Formal, didactic social skills training can take place both in the classroom and in more individualised settings. Approaches that have been most successful utilise direct modelling and role play at a concrete level. By rehearsing, overlearning and practising how to handle various social situations, the child may learn to generalise the skills to naturalistic settings.

It is often useful to adopt a paired approach in which the child is put with another to carry out such structured activities. The use of a peer support can be very successful, since autistic children relate best one to one. Careful selection of a non-autistic peer for the child can be a tool to help build social skills, encourage friendships and reduce stigmatisation.

Care should be taken, particularly in the upper years, to protect the child from teasing both in and out of the classroom, since it is one of the greatest sources of anxiety for older children with autism. Efforts should be made to help other pupils to reach a better understanding of the child with autism in a way that will promote tolerance and acceptance. Teachers can take advantage of the strong academic skills that many autistic children have, in order to help them to gain acceptance by peers. It is very helpful if the autistic child can sometimes be given opportunities to help other children.

Partnership and Families

In attempting to put a comprehensive teaching and management plan in place at school, it is necessary for staff and parents to work closely together, since the parents are often most familiar with what has worked in the past for a given child. It is also wise to put as many details of the plan as possible into an Individual Educational Plan, so that progress can be monitored and carried over from year to year. Finally, in devising such plans it can sometimes be helpful to enlist the aid of other professionals who are familiar with the management of children with autism, such as psychologists. In complex cases a team orientation is always advisable.

Working with families

The Family Assessment and Support Unit at the University of Hull adopted such an approach, and there are practical and organisational factors which govern what it provides. The team structure is as follows.

- The multidisciplinary team consists of a psychiatrist, clinical and educational psychologists, a specialist speech and language therapist and a specialist senior practitioner social worker,
- Assessments by the team follow home visits and possibly the videotaping of the child/young person in everyday life settings.
- Reviews take place annually, and the family receives support with emotional difficulties, challenging behaviour, explaining the syndrome to relatives and friends, advocacy with statutory agencies, etc.

Any treatment and intervention programme must start with a thorough assessment of the child's deficits and assets in the context of the multidisciplinary evaluation, including assessments of behavioural (or psychiatric) history and current presentation, neuropsychological functioning, communication patterns (particularly the use of language for the purpose of social interaction, or pragmatics) and adaptive functioning (the individual's ability to translate potential into competence in meeting the demands of everyday life). The final formulation should include a characterisation of the child's deficits and abilities in these various areas.

The actual diagnostic assignment is the final step in the evaluation. We recognise that labels are often necessary in order to secure services and guarantee a certain level of sophistication in addressing the child's needs. However, the assignment of a label should be done in a thoughtful way, so as to minimise stigmatisation and avoid unwarranted assumptions. Every child is different. If someone was to observe a group of individuals with autism, he or she would probably be more impressed by how they differ than by how they resemble each other. It is therefore absolutely crucial that intervention programmes derived from comprehensive assessments are individualised to ensure that they address the unique profile of needs and strengths exhibited by the child.

The diagnostic label should never be assumed to convey a precise preconceived set of behaviours and needs. Its most important function is to convey an overall sense of the pattern of difficulties present. Professionals should never start a discussion of the child's needs by evoking the label. Rather, they should provide a detailed description of assessment findings that resulted in the diagnosis of autism. A discussion of any inconsistency with the diagnosis, as well as of the clinicians' level of confidence in giving that diagnosis, should also be provided.

The following comments reflect our clinical experience with autism. The label should not be applied in specific cases without a thoughtful discussion of the individual child's profile. The specific guidelines should be seen as a series of suggestions to be considered when planning for the individual's educational, treatment and vocational programme. Parents are given the following advice.

- Do not take the diagnosis of autism for granted. Ask for details and for the individualised profile of your child.
- Do not accept a discussion of your child's profile that does not include strengths that may be utilised in an intervention programme.
- Do not accept an intervention programme that is based solely on the diagnosis.
- Ask for the development of an appropriate programme on the basis of your child's profile, his or her educational setting or living conditions, and realistic short-term and long-term goals.
- Do not assume that the best learning environment for your child is necessarily a specialist school for children with autism.

Helping Parents to Understand and Evaluate New Methods

It has been our experience that parents can become vulnerable to new programme ideas that emerge without the benefit of effective scientific scrutiny.

Tens of thousands of pounds are raised for very dubious 'treatments', and the public, and therefore other parents, seldom get to hear the outcomes. We have seen a lot of disasters, including the breakup of families, because of the money and effort that have been invested in some inappropriate interventions.

Parents need help, support and guidance. Here are some of the issues which they need to explore or of which they should at least be aware.

GUIDELINES TO PARENTS

1. Programme Description

- What is the intervention programme? Who does what, and how?
- Is there written information, a programme description, a detailed brochure, etc.?
- Exactly what is involved for the child and the family?
- What is the length of the intervention?
- What is the frequency of sessions?
- How much parent time is required?
- What are the financial costs?
- Does the intervention programme focus on one particular skill, or is it a general, comprehensive approach?
- Do parents, care-providers, teachers and others need to be trained in the intervention technique?

- Is there co-ordination between the intervention programme and other individuals/services working with the family (e.g. teachers, therapists, doctors)?
- Are the intervention programme goals individualised for each person and his or her family?
- Is there follow-up and/or support after intervention termination?

2. Rationale and Purpose of the Intervention

- What is the rationale, philosophy or purpose underlying the intervention programme?
- How is the philosophy tied to the specific intervention techniques?
- How were the philosophy and intervention methods developed (e.g. by scientific research, clinical experience, application or extension from a related field such as learning disabilities or mental retardation)?
- Are you comfortable or do you agree with the philosophy of the programme?

3. Credentials of the Intervention Programme Director and Staff

- What is the background of the programme staff?
- What are their training and professional credentials?
- What is the staff's training and experience in autism?
- What is their understanding of the nature of the disorder?
- How much experience have they had in providing this type of intervention?
- Are the programme staff open to questions and input from the family or other professionals involved with the child?

4. Effectiveness of the Intervention

- What is the supporting evidence for the effectiveness of the programme? Are there publications about it in appropriate journals?
- Is there any independent confirmation of the effectiveness of the intervention programme?
- What are the possible negative effects or side-effects of the intervention?
- What impact might the programme have on the family's lifestyle?

4

DIAGNOSTIC CONFUSIONS AND DISORDERS PRESENTING LIKE AUTISM

As we have seen, the whole process whereby parents eventually obtain an unequivocal diagnosis of autism can be fraught with many sources of stress. The combination of poor resource availability, professional scepticism, indifferent awareness and subsequent lack of information has been shown to distress even the strongest families. Regrettably, as our survey has shown, these difficulties are magnified greatly by the receipt of an equivocal diagnosis. This was reported by 32% of our sample who met with varying degrees of professional uncertainty.

Among the many confusing diagnoses that parents in our survey have received were 'autistic tendencies', 'partial autism', 'pathological demand avoidance with a dash of autism', 'severe autistic learning difficulties' and 'autistic-like developmental delay'. Not surprisingly, a common question put by this group of parents was 'What does it mean?'

Unfortunately such equivocation and diagnostic confusion are frequently masked behind a display of professional certainty and confidence which implies that the clinician concerned really does know what he or she is talking about. Most parents in the survey took note of the diagnoses that they had worked hard to acquire, but left the consultation even more confused than before.

Sometimes there are reasons other than professional uncertainty for the failure to give an adequate and supportable diagnosis. One educational psychologist told the first author that his Local Education Authority (LEA) would not allow 'autism' to go on a Statement of Special Educational Needs, and that the only way to get the higher banding (i.e. more cash value on the Statement) was to use the term 'autistic tendencies' because, for some unknown and probably illogical reason, this was permitted. Presumably the officers holding the purse-strings of that LEA thought that parents might be more vociferous about out-of-county expensive placements if children were described as 'autistic' rather than as having mere 'autistic tendencies'.

There is, of course, no justification for referring to 'autistic tendencies' or 'partial autism'. Autism is reasonably clearly defined by DSM-IV, and either there is enough evidence to sustain the diagnosis or there is not. The core impairments of autism, referred to as the Triad, are either to be found or they are not. If not, then the diagnosis should not be given, and another explanation or explanations for the child's presenting problems should be sought. Lack of awareness of what the continuum of autism actually is means that some professionals consider it appropriate to describe those who are at the shallow end as having autistic tendencies rather than the full-bodied disorder.

There may be many reasons for the failure to give an unequivocal diagnosis, as our survey has shown. Some of these reasons will be considered within the context of representative case studies.

Severe learning difficulties with autistic features

This is a common example of diagnostic confusion experienced by parents who have children with significant intellectual impairments as well as autism. In view of the high proportion of children with autism who have an IQ of 70 or below, then it is clearly the case that many such parents will find themselves receiving this mix of diagnostic labels. The term 'severe learning difficulties' is one used by educationalists, particularly educational psychologists, and frequently Statements of Special Educational Needs are written in such a way as to reflect the learning difficulties as the primary presenting problem. The Statement then comments at length on the child's needs as an individual with severe learning difficulties, and the provision section of the Statement reflects this consideration of the primary difficulty. The reference to 'autistic features' or 'tendencies' is seldom given as great an emphasis.

The parents in our survey who had such Statements then found it extremely difficult to persuade the LEA to name a provision other than that within the authority for children with severe learning difficulties. Whereas some of the parents were satisfied with the provision that their child received, the majority (76%) were not. Their dissatisfactions ranged from a sense of vague unease that possibly the school was not meeting the totality of their children's needs, to complete dissatisfaction when it became obvious that their children were being treated no differently to those other pupils of the school who had severe learning difficulties only. These parents believe the severe learning difficulty provision made for their children is completely unsuitable because it fails to take into account the needs associated with autism and, in many cases, the staff openly report to the parents that they have no particular training or skill in dealing with autistic children. The result of this is great stress for the parents during the years of their children's education in the severe learning difficulty schools. The following case study illustrates a typical example.

CASE STUDY 4.1

We had to move heaven and earth to get the diagnosis of autism, but it didn't result in anything because all Rob got was the local school for severely retarded children. We knew he had learning difficulties, but we noticed that he learned more during the holidays than he did at school.

In fact the diagnosis was a curse because the staff kept using it as the reason why they were making no progress with him. We kept hearing 'well, we're doing our best but we don't know anything much about autism'.

It took us three years to get him into the proper school, and that meant him being in residence—now all we hear from the Local Authority is how much it is costing.

Poor understanding of the triad of impairments

In other cases revealed by the survey, the clinicians making the diagnosis respond to only a part of the triad of impairment. Thus, for example, the presence of ritualistic hoarding or 'evening out' and sorting behaviour, which is common to children with obsessive-compulsive disorder, may be viewed as essentially autistic. In the absence of communication or social impairments then autism is not a viable diagnosis. However, this does not prevent it from being made, as the following case studies reveal.

CASE STUDY 4.2

From as young as five years old, Sharon suffered very intrusive fears that something terrible was going to happen to her family. She found relief through cleanliness, structure and perfection. She couldn't speak about her fears much, and tended to look away when her parents tried to speak to her about the compulsive behaviours. Later Sharon was able to tell a psychologist she believed that if she could keep everything about her clean and germ free, then the people she loved would be safe from harm. Eventually she was sedated because her insistence on scrubbing the entrance to the house left her hands seriously distorted and bleeding.

Sharon was given a series of assessments and the first diagnosis was autism; only further investigation by a clinical psychologist revealed the exact nature of her problem.

Sharon suffered from obsessive-compulsive disorder (OCD). Current theories indicate that OCD is a biological disease involving an imbalance of a chemical called serotonin in the brain. Serotonin is a naturally occurring chemical that transmits impulses from one nerve cell to another. Medication may help to correct this imbalance. Although stress does not cause OCD, a stressful event such as death of a loved one, birth of a child or divorce can trigger the onset of the disorder. There is little similarity with autism in terms of treatment and prognosis.

The following case study demonstrates an even closer example of OCD in relation to autism; one can easily understand how the first diagnosis of autism was made by the child psychiatrist who saw the boy at the height of his difficulties.

CASE STUDY 4.3

As a 4-year-old boy, Paul would continually repeat certain words and actions. His toys were kept in perfect order, and the slightest change in their location sent him into a tantrum. Clinicians thought his need for endless repetition was a severely autistic trait, but for Paul it was a strenuous battle to discharge anxiety.

Autistic traits

Probably one of the saddest confusions arises when a child is labelled as having 'autistic traits' because he or she has a personality structure that is markedly introvert. In failing to recognise that individuals do vary widely across the normal range, and in being intolerant of children as quiet people who prefer their own company and the content of their own minds to the babble of the herd and the activities of the crowd, some professionals have used this term to imply a pathological condition. It appears that they are unable to distinguish the child who prefers to be quiet and engaged in solitary activities from one who is withdrawn, aloof and unable to engage in such activities. After creating this basic confusion the professionals involved then seek an explanation and, believing that autism is only about social aloofness and withdrawal, decide that the problem must be of that type. Receiving such an opinion about their child is devastating to parents, as the following case study reveals.

CASE STUDY 4.4

We always knew Don was a quiet child who preferred to play by himself. His organisation was excellent and he could entertain himself for hours. We also know he is a shy boy, possibly because both of us are. When he started school the reception teacher was worried because he wouldn't stay to dinner and she thought he didn't mix enough. She, at least, was prepared to let him develop in his own way. His next teacher, though, kept trying to thrust him into friendships, and pressured other children to let him join in their games and sit on their tables. One of them actually said 'But he doesn't like what we like—why should we make him?'

That child obviously had more insight than the teacher did because she told us in the second term that she thought he seemed 'a bit autistic' and we ought to take him to a specialist.

We were very upset and it caused ructions in the family—people didn't talk to us; they thought it was our fault. We finally got to see a paediatrician and a clinical psychologist who more or less said we were wasting their time and please could we just accept our little boy simply had the great gift of liking his own company.

The particular confusion and diagnostic misapplication revealed in the last case study may also be apparent in other situations when children with autism show a less marked impairment on one or other of the facets of the triad. In expecting to find all three facets to be equally impaired and ignoring the fact that none of the clinical instruments available has such a degree of accuracy anyway, diagnosis is marginalised by the suggestion that the disorder is, for that child, in some way incomplete. The real danger of this bad practice is that resource controllers may then assume that the child is less needy.

The named officer read all the reports and casually told us that since Jimmy had some symbolic play, he could probably get away with an MLD school[1]. He thought we would be pleased because that would be more 'normal' than a specialist school.

The marginalisation of autism

Overwhelmingly, however, the marginalisation of the diagnosis of autism occurs when the child being assessed is found to have normal or better intellectual skills. High-functioning children with autism are wrongly assumed to have fewer problems than children with attendant learning difficulties. It is our experience that this is not the case. Examination of clinical narratives provided by parents and the young people themselves clearly reveals that such children and their families have very severe difficulties to face and overcome, albeit of a rather different nature to those found among the group where learning difficulties are also present.

Among this group of poorly diagnosed children are to be found many

---

[1] A school for children with moderate (general) learning difficulties.

with Asperger syndrome, and whose complex difficulties are definitely not best assessed as 'autistic tendencies'. The next section of this chapter will consider this disorder and the complex needs associated with it that should be properly assessed and reflected in the diagnosis.

ASPERGER SYNDROME (AS)

Asperger syndrome (also called Asperger disorder) is a relatively new diagnostic label, having only come into use from about the mid-1980s. Children with this clinical picture were originally and accurately described in the 1940s by a Viennese paediatrician, Hans Asperger. Despite this, Asperger syndrome (AS) was only 'officially' recognised in the Diagnostic and Statistical Manual of Mental Disorders for the first time in the fourth edition, published in 1994.

Asperger syndrome is the proper diagnosis applied to the mildest and most functional end of the autism spectrum. Like all levels along that spectrum, it is a neurologically based disorder of development, most often of unknown cause, in which there are the typically autistic deviations or abnormalities of social relatedness and social skills, the use of language for communicative purposes, and behavioural and stylistic characteristics involving repetitive or perseverative features and a limited but intense range of interests. The same three categories of dysfunction, which can range from relatively mild to severe, clinically define all of the spectrum, from AS through to classic autism. Although the concept of a continuum along a single dimension is helpful for understanding the clinical similarities of presentations along the spectrum, it is not clear that Asperger syndrome is just a milder form of autism, or that the conditions are linked by anything other than their broad clinical similarities.

Asperger syndrome represents that part of the spectrum which is characterised by higher cognitive abilities (at least normal IQ, reaching and up into the very superior range), and by more normal language function compared to other levels along the spectrum. In fact, the presence of normal basic language skills is one of the criteria for the diagnosis of AS, although there are nearly always subtle difficulties with pragmatic/social language. It is these two areas of relative strength that distinguish AS from other forms of autism, and so account for its better prognosis. Some clinicians, particularly in North America, distinguish between AS and what is referred to as high-functioning autism (HFA). There have been suggestions that the basic neuropsychological deficit is different for the two conditions, but others do not consider that any meaningful distinction can be made between them. Uta Frith has characterised children with

AS as having 'a dash of autism'. This leaves room for some confusion regarding diagnostic terms, and it is likely that quite similar children across the country have been diagnosed differently, depending upon where they were evaluated and by whom.

Since AS itself shows a wide range of symptom severity, many mildly impaired children receive no diagnosis at all and are viewed as 'unusual' or 'just different,'or are misdiagnosed with conditions such as attention deficit disorder. The inclusion of AS as a separate category in DSM-IV, with fairly clear criteria for diagnosis, should hopefully promote greater consistency of labelling in the future.

The Numbers of Children with AS

Many studies that have been conducted to date suggest that AS is considerably more common than 'classic' autism. Whereas autism is reported to occur in about 4 in every 10 000 children, estimates of Asperger syndrome have been as high as 20–25 in 10 000 children. This means that for each case of unequivocal autism, the community can expect to have several children with a picture of AS. The excellent study conducted by Gillberg's group in Sweden concluded that nearly 0.7% of the children studied had a clinical picture of AS to a greater or lesser degree. Some researchers state that if one includes those children who have many of the features of AS, but as generally less severe presentations along the spectrum as it shades into 'normal', then it does not appear to be a rare condition at all.

Asperger syndrome is much more common in boys than in girls, but why this should be is not known. It is also fairly commonly associated with other diagnoses, again for unknown reasons, including attentional deficits and mood problems such as depression and anxiety. In many cases there is a clear genetic component, with one parent (most often the father) showing either the full picture of AS or at least some of the traits associated with it. Genetic factors seem to be obvious in AS in comparison to classic autism. Traits such as intense and limited interests, compulsive and rigid style and social awkwardness are also more common, alone or in combination, in relatives of AS children. Sometimes there is a family history of autism among relatives, strengthening the impression that AS and autism are related conditions. To confuse the issue, however, less severe developmental disorders may also be found across the extended family. These include dyslexia and dyspraxia. Other studies have demonstrated a fairly high rate of depression, both bipolar and unipolar, among the relatives of children with AS. It is probable that for

AS, as for autism, the clinical presentation is characterised by many factors, including genetic ones, such that in most cases there is no single identifiable cause.

Diagnostic Definition and Criteria

The recent DSM-IV criteria for a diagnosis of AS, with much of the language carrying over from the diagnostic criteria for autism, include the presence of the following.

1. Qualitative impairment in social interaction involving some or all of the following.
   - impaired use of non-verbal behaviours to regulate social interaction;
   - failure to develop age-appropriate peer relationships;
   - lack of spontaneous interest in sharing experiences with others;
   - lack of social or emotional reciprocity.
2. Restricted, repetitive and stereotyped patterns of behaviour, interests and activities involving the following:
   - preoccupation with one or more stereotyped and restricted pattern of interest;
   - inflexible adherence to specific non-functional routines or rituals;
   - stereotyped or repetitive motor mannerisms, or preoccupation with parts of objects.

These behaviours must be sufficient to interfere significantly with social or other areas of functioning. Furthermore, there must be no significant associated delay in either general cognitive function, self-help/adaptive skills, interest in the environment or overall language development.

The Swedish researcher Gillberg has studied AS extensively, and proposed six criteria for the diagnosis, elaborating on the criteria set out in DSM-IV. His six criteria capture the unique style of these children and include the following.

1. Social impairment with extreme egocentricity, which may include:
   - inability to interact with peers;
   - lack of desire to interact with peers;
   - poor appreciation of social cues;
   - socially and emotionally inappropriate responses.
2. Limited interests and preoccupations, including:
   - more rote than meaning;
   - relatively exclusive of other interests;
   - repetitive adherence.

3. Repetitive routines or rituals, which may be:
   - imposed on self; or
   - imposed on others.
4. Speech and language peculiarities, such as the following:
   - delayed early development possible but not consistently seen;
   - superficially perfect expressive language;
   - odd prosody, peculiar voice characteristics;
   - impaired comprehension, including misinterpretation of literal and implied meanings.
5. Non-verbal communication problems, such as the following:
   - limited use of gesture;
   - clumsy body language;
   - limited or inappropriate facial expression;
   - peculiar 'stiff' gaze;
   - difficulty in adjusting physical proximity.
6. Motor clumsiness.

These need not all be found in all cases.

Presentation of Asperger Syndrome

The most obvious characteristic of Asperger syndrome, which makes these children so unique, is their particular, idiosyncratic areas of 'special interest'. In contrast to autism, where the interests are more likely to concern objects or parts of objects, in AS the interests most often concern specific intellectual areas. Often, when they enter school, or even before then, these children show an obsessive interest in an area such as mathematics, aspects of science, or reading. Indeed, some have a history of hyperlexia or rote reading. At a surprisingly young age many develop an interest in some aspect of history or geography, wanting to learn everything they can about the subject and dwelling on it in their conversations and representational play. The first author has seen a number of children with AS who dwell on train timetables, astronomy, various types of plastics or parts of cars and ships.

Interestingly, Asperger's original clinical description dating back to 1944 shows that aspects of transport seemed to be a particularly common area of fascination (he described children who memorised the tramlines in Vienna down to the last stop). Many preschool children with AS are unusually aware of the route taken on car trips. Sometimes the areas of fascination represent exaggerated interests that many children display, such as dinosaurs, or Star Wars, etc. For many children these areas of preoccupation may be replaced by others. However, in some children the interests may remain into adulthood, such that the childhood fascinations become the basis for an adult career.

Another major characteristic of AS is that of socialisation, which is also quite different to that seen in autism. Most children with AS are observed by teachers and parents to be in 'a world of their own' and preoccupied with their own interests, although they are seldom as 'detached' as children with autism. Many children with AS who are of school age want to have friends. They are often sad, frustrated and perplexed by their lack of social success. Their problem is not usually a lack of interaction opportunity so much as in effectiveness in interactions. They have difficulty knowing how to behave socially. Gillberg has described this as a 'disorder of empathy', i.e. an inability to understand other people's needs and perspectives and to respond appropriately. These children with AS misread social situations, and their interactions and responses are frequently viewed by others as eccentric and off-putting.

Although good language development is a feature that distinguishes AS from other forms of autism, there are invariably obvious differences in the use of language by children with AS. Rote skills are often very strong. Their prosody affects aspects of spoken language such as volume of speech, intonation, inflection, rate, etc., which are frequently abnormal. Sometimes the language seems pedantic, lacking idioms and slang, and comments are taken too literally. Comprehension tends to be excessively concrete, and increasing problems often occur as language use becomes more abstract in the secondary-school curriculum. Pragmatic or conversational language skills are often poor because of difficulties in turn-taking, a tendency to revert to boring areas of special interest, and difficulty in sustaining the 'give and take' of conversation. Most children with AS have difficulties with humour and tend not to understand jokes. They often laugh at the wrong time despite the fact that quite a few show an interest in humour and jokes, where they find fascination in puns or word games. The common belief that these children lack humour is often mistaken. Many children with AS tend to be hyperverbal and do not understand that this alienates them.

The early language development of children with AS shows no single pattern. Some children demonstrate normal or even rapid achievement of milestones, while others experience early delays in speech but rapidly catch up to more normal language usage by the time of school entry. The differential diagnosis between AS and mild autism can be difficult to make at that time. Sometimes, during the preschool years, language factors common to those in autism are present, including perseverative or repetitive aspects of language, or repetitive use of phrases or lines drawn from a variety of often-heard sources.

The preschool child with Asperger syndrome

There is no single presenting pattern of Asperger syndrome in the first 3 to 4 years. The early signs may be difficult to distinguish from more typical autism, strongly suggesting that when evaluating young children with autism and apparently normal intelligence, the possibility should be considered that they may eventually present a constellation of symptoms that is more compatible with Asperger syndrome. Other children may show early language delays but rapidly improve between 3 and 5 years. Some of these children, particularly the brightest ones, may show no evidence of early developmental delay except perhaps some motor dysfunction. Usually on close assessment of the child between the ages of 3 and 5 years some signs of the syndrome will be found, and in most cases a comprehensive assessment at that age can be a positive experience for both the parents and the child.

This is important because, although these children may appear to relate quite well within the family setting, problems often arise when they enter a nursery. These may include the following:

- a tendency to avoid spontaneous interactions or to have weak skills in interactions;
- problems in holding simple conversations or a tendency to be repetitive when conversing;
- odd verbal responses;
- a preference for fixed routines and difficulty with changes;
- difficulty in controlling social/emotional responses with anger, aggression or excessive anxiety;
- hyperactivity;
- appearing to be lost in their own interests, with a tendency to fixate on particular objects or subjects.

Although this set is similar to the early symptom list for autism, compared to those children the child with AS is more likely to have social interest in adults and other children, to have less abnormal conversational speech and not to appear so obviously 'different' to other children. Areas of particularly strong rote skills may be visible, including letter or number recognition, rote memorisation of various facts, etc.

Primary-school children with Asperger syndrome

The child with AS often enters nursery without having been assessed and diagnosed. In some cases there may have been behavioural concerns (e.g. hyperactivity, inattention, aggression or outbursts) in the preschool years and concern about 'immature' social skills and interactions. Many of these children are viewed as being 'strange'. Despite this, most children with AS enter a more mainstream setting. Often curriculum progress in the infant years is relatively good and encouraging. Rote reading is often good, and simple number operations may be very proficient. Motor skills for writing and crayoning are often much weaker. Teachers frequently comment on the child's 'obsessive' areas of interest, which they find inappropriate in group activities.

Most children with AS show interest in other children, although it may be muted, but they have great difficulties with friend-keeping skills, the depth of their interactions being relatively superficial. Conversely, they may appeal to adults because of their 'old-fashioned' ways.

The presentation throughout primary school varies considerably from one child to another, and their problems often range from mild and easily managed to severe and impossible. This variation is associated with variables such as intelligence level, consistency of management at school and home, temperament, and the severity of complicating factors such as hyperactivity/attentional problems, anxiety, learning problems, bullying and peer support or rejection.

Secondary-school children and Asperger syndrome

As the child with AS moves into secondary school, the most difficult areas continue to be those of socialisation and behavioural adjustment. Many children with AS are in mainstream schools at this age, and their specific developmental problems may be more easily overlooked if they are bright and do not appear to act too eccentrically. They are frequently misunderstood at this age by teachers and pupils. Secondary-school teachers have less opportunity to get to know most pupils really well, and problems with behaviour or study habits may be incorrectly attributed to emotional or motivational problems. In some settings, particularly relatively unstructured ones such as the canteen, games or playground, the pupil with AS may become involved in escalating conflicts with supervisors, teachers and pupils who are not familiar with their impaired interaction skills. This frequently leads to more serious behavioural problems. Stress builds up in the AS pupil until he or she reacts in a dramatically unacceptable manner.

During early adolescence, when the pressures to conform are at their highest and tolerance is at a minimum, pupils with AS may be excluded, bullied or teased and rejected. While experiencing such rejection but considering friendships, their behaviour may increasingly involve testing out in the form of outbursts and aggression. Depression is unfortunately common as a complicating and worrying feature, and in the experience of the first author there is often a degree of suicidal ideation that terrifies the child's helpless parents.

If there are no significant learning disabilities, academic performance can be good, particularly in areas of particular interest. However, this apparent strength disguises subtle misunderstandings of information, particularly in abstract or idiomatic language. Attentional and organisational difficulties are usually present, and there are often uncomfortable tensions between AS pupils who need to do things 'their way' and teachers who want it done 'according to the book'. Parents find the unending battle of trying to explain their complicated children to specialist subject teachers exhausting and fruitless.

Tolerance of individual differences usually increases again to some extent by the stage of late secondary education. If pupils perform well academically, they may experience a degree of respect from others. AS adolescents may form friendships with other pupils who share their interests in computers or fantasy. Given proper management, many AS pupils develop better social skills and a general ability to 'get on' more comfortably with others by this age, which makes both their own lives and those of their parents a little easier.

Adulthood and Asperger syndrome

There is limited high-quality research information about the eventual outcome for pupils with AS. It is only recently that AS has been differentiated from autism when examining outcomes, and generally only severe cases were recognised. The available data that exists suggests that, compared to other forms of autism, children with AS are much more likely to grow up to be independently functioning adults with regard to education, training, employment, marriage and parenting.

A useful source of data on outcomes is derived indirectly from the study of those parents and other relatives of AS children who may themselves have AS. This data indicates that AS does not entirely affect potential for a fairly normal adult life. These adults commonly gravitate towards a job or profession that relates to their own areas of special interest, and sometimes they become very proficient. Both authors have had intelligent students with AS who successfully completed first-degree and even postgraduate courses. None the less, even in these cases the students continue to demonstrate varying degrees of subtle differences in social interactions. They are challenged by the social and emotional demands of relationships, although many of them do marry and have children. Their rigidity of style and egocentric perspectives make interactions difficult, both within and outside the family, and failure of their relationships is depressingly common. There is also the risk of mood problems such as depression and anxiety, and the true nature of other problems may go unrecognised among a welter of standard treatments.

Gillberg has estimated that perhaps 30 to 50% of all adults with AS are never evaluated or correctly diagnosed. These people are viewed by others as 'different' or eccentric, and they may receive other psychiatric diagnoses. Both authors have met a number of individuals whom they believe fall within the category of AS, and many of them have been able to utilise their special skills, often with support from loved ones, to achieve what we consider to be a high level of adaptation both personally and professionally. Many of the highest-functioning and most intelligent of our students with AS become highly respected in academic society for their single-mindedness and consuming interest in advancing our knowledge in their various fields of study.

Semantic–Pragmatic Disorder

No description of muddled diagnosis would be complete without a brief description of children with semantic–pragmatic disorder. Many of the most colourful and acidic battles that the first author has witnessed between psychiatrists, speech and language therapists and psychologists have concerned the differentiated diagnosis of autism, AS and semantic–pragmatic disorder. What takes the enjoyment out of these tub-thumping sessions is that there are usually two parents and a child anxiously awaiting the outcome.

Semantic–pragmatic disorder was originally defined in the literature on language disorder in 1983 by Rapin and Allen, when it was classified as a syndrome. This referred to a group of children who presented with some mild autistic features and specific semantic–pragmatic language problems.

Parents often described them as model babies or, by contrast, babies who seemed to cry too much. Many of these children babbled little or very late, and continued to use jargonised speech much longer than other children of the same age. Their first words were late, and learning language was tedious. Many of them had other speech disorders as well, with phonological problems being fairly common. Problems were usually first noticed between the ages of 18 months and 2 years when the child had few if any real words.

As with many parents of children with autism, the parents of children with semantic–pragmatic disorder wondered whether their children were hearing impaired, because they did not appear to respond to speech. Assessment generally found that most of these children had good hearing, although inevitably some were found to have otitis media and had grommets fitted.

The problem is usually to do with accurate reception and processing the meaning of language. Early on in their lives, semantic–pragmatic disordered children are found to have comprehension problems, and find it difficult to follow instructions that are not part of their normal routines. Comprehension problems usually improve or respond well to speech and language therapy, so that by the age of 4 years many of these children appear superficially to function well.

Soon after these children reach school, teachers and parents both become aware that there is something 'different' about them, but they find the subtle difficulties hard to describe. Sometimes the children appear to follow very little conversation, while at other times they give detailed explanations of events. Later on, many of them become good at mathematics, science and computer studies, but have great difficulty in writing a coherent sentence or in social interaction with other children. They often show difficulty in sharing and taking turns. They sometimes appear aggressive, selfish, bossy and over-confident, or shy and withdrawn. Many of them therefore became recognised as children with behaviour problems and subject to management regimes which do not always work, the children being left confused about what they were doing. One can be forgiven for finding many parallels with the description of children with AS.

Present Perception of Semantic–Pragmatic Disorder

Semantic–pragmatic disordered children have many more problems than just difficulty in speaking and understanding words, and it is justifiably defined as a communication disorder rather than as a language disorder. It appears that the main difficulty for children may lie in the way in which they process information. They find it more difficult to extract the essential meaning, and tend to focus on detail. Consequently they fail to understand the possibly serious generalities of social situations, and become confused when people around them do not react as they predict.

Because children with semantic–pragmatic disorder find it difficult to focus their listening, they are easily distracted by noises outside the classroom or someone talking on the other side of the room. They may butt in on conversations which have nothing to do with them, and they are often described by staff as inattentive or impulsive. They may find loud noise in the classroom distressing, and may comment on this. Sometimes when children with semantic–pragmatic disorder are trying very hard to concentrate they may not hear speech at all, and they may ignore general instructions in the classroom while they are trying to work. Many class teachers say that they sometimes have to stand in front of their children with semantic–pragmatic disorder or touch them before they respond. A common complaint of mainstream schoolteachers is that they need physically to stop the children doing whatever it is they are engaged in before they can take in new instructions.

Many children with semantic–pragmatic disorder do well, sometimes above their age level on formal language assessments, and this can conceal their subtle comprehension difficulties. These difficulties in understanding language are often apparent by the time they are 5 years old. Children with semantic–pragmatic disorder can often respond to long instructions because the relevant objects are there to hand, but find comments and questions such as 'Where did you come from then?' or 'What are you doing later?' or 'That was very clever of you!' much more difficult. This language requires more than listening and understanding words, as there is also a need to understand what the speaker was intending, and many of the clues to that pass by the child with semantic–pragmatic disorder. These include body posture, tone of voice and eye contact.

As children with semantic–pragmatic disorder have difficulty in understanding what other people are thinking when they are talking, they cannot understand when people are lying to or deceiving them. Many parents of children with semantic–pragmatic disorder have reported to us that their children have been led astray or had money taken off them as a result of this.

Talking to others

As well as subtle comprehension problems, children with semantic–pragmatic disorder also experience difficulties with talking. These are not always picked up by parents or staff because so often such children chat fluently. It is the particular way in that they use language that identifies them as a group. Children with semantic–pragmatic disorder appear to learn more by memorising than by knowing what the individual words really mean, so they cannot use language with the same range and flexibility as other children. Children with semantic–pragmatic disorder remember large sections of adult phrases and, because they are not sure which sections are more important than others, they learn everything accurately, including the intonation pattern and accents of the people they listen to most. A fundamental characteristic is that they say a lot more than they really understand. Some children with semantic–pragmatic disorder use a flat voice when they are echoing other people's language, and are then accused of cheekiness or mimicry.

Children with semantic–pragmatic disorder often remember to use this echoed language appropriately so that they sound adult-like in contrast to their social immaturity. Also characteristic is their inability to give an account of an event or to discuss a picture story which they have not rehearsed; they then grope for words and their account is very disjointed.

A common characteristic of their conversation is a very high proportion of echoed social phrases and very little on how people feel or think. In addition, the delayed social development of children with semantic–pragmatic disorder means that they do not make distinctions between people readily. Adults, children, teachers and parents are often treated in the same way. Thus the inappropriate or immature use of language by these children can be very embarrassing, and they experience high levels of disapproval and censorship as a result. This causes great stress to their parents, who have to bear the brunt of the aftermath of these conflicts, and several parents have told us that this is in many ways the worst effect of the disorder.

5

THE EFFECTS OF AUTISM ON PARENTS: PART I

Only a very few parents will know before their child is born that he or she will be handicapped. Unless there has been an amniocentesis or there is an extremely high risk of carrying on a genetic potential for disability, the majority of parents are unprepared for their children to be born with a disabling condition. In the recent past there has been an increase in the volume of research on the impact of handicap on the parents of the child. There has been considerable research activity investigating the experiences of the parents of children who are mentally retarded, physically disabled or chronically ill. Most of these studies have examined the immediate effects on the psychological functioning of the parents, the emotional impact of the diagnosis and the subsequent reactions of the parents to it. The perceptions and attitudes of parents towards their child's handicap have also been examined and, not surprisingly, there are many variations in their responses. Anger, anxiety, depression, confusion, denial, grief, helplessness, guilt, self-pity, terror and sorrow are but a few of the many emotions that may be experienced (e.g. Sarason and Doris, 1979).

As we have seen, autism has numerous impacts, some of which are immediate and devastating, while others are subtle and experienced over the long term. This chapter and the next one will consider the impact of autism on the parents and other family members.

GENERAL DIFFICULTIES EXPERIENCED BY PARENTS

Howlin and Rutter (1987) acknowledge that the parents of children with autism face considerable difficulties. Such children often present difficulties related to their unresponsiveness, challenging behaviour and long-term special needs which confront their parents with daily problems that last for years (e.g. Konstantareas, 1991). Successful work with the child with autism therefore generally requires successful work with the parents (e.g. Powers, 1991), and that topic will be addressed in a later chapter.

This chapter starts by explaining some of the particular difficulties that autism causes parents, and describing these in relation to the experience of families referred to the Family Assessment and Support Unit.

'It just creeps up on you'; autism in the family

As we have seen, many parents become aware of their children's developmental difficulties during the pre-verbal stage (Newson *et al.*, 1982). These concerns may not be sufficiently great at first to trigger a referral to the health or other services. Instead, a gradually increasing sense of unease gives way to alarm and sometimes desperation. One 32-year-old experienced mother with two previous children described her experiences thus:

Jane seemed such a good baby—hardly ever cried unless she was wet or hungry. She slept and didn't demand all my attention. Not like the first two. But, by the time she was two, we knew there was something wrong—she seemed so inactive after our boys. Week after week we seemed to have more and more little worries about the way she wasn't developing. That's how autism is—it just seems to creep up on you.

If practitioners are to work successfully with the parents of children with autism, it is essential that they understand the way in which such children develop within the family, and the special problems that the disability brings. It is particularly important to be aware of the feelings aroused in the parents on discovering that their child is autistic, and also the problems—both emotional and practical—caused by living with such a child.

First-time parents are more at risk of not recognising the early developmental signs of autism, but more experienced parents are not immune either. It is rare for parents to avoid having any anxieties about their developing baby but, as we have stated, few parents expect to have a child with a disability and, even if they are aware of the possibility, even fewer are prepared for the experience. The family with a child who is clearly handicapped at birth faces a tragedy which will result in a wide range of feelings. This range may include shock, helplessness, inadequacy, anger and guilt (Frude, 1992). For the parents of a child with autism, these emotions are heightened by the fact that the baby is invariably born healthy and apparently normal. Not only do they eventually discover that their child is handicapped, but they also experience feelings very akin to those of parents whose child has died. The parents of a child with autism slowly and remorselessly 'lose' the child they had expected, their hopes for normality often lasting well into infancy, only to be replaced by chronic sadness and fears about the future (e.g. Handleman, 1990).

Research conducted at the Child Development Research Unit at the University of Nottingham by Newson *et al.* (1982) involved interviews with the parents of nearly 100 'able autistic' children. The study reported that two-thirds of the parents recalled difficulties in communicating with their child at the pre-verbal stage, of whom 14 parents stated that these difficulties resulted in great concern at the time. The baby's mother often feels that the infant is remote and self-contained, that she does not gaze or smile at her or that she does not snuggle against her when held.

These experiences are portrayed vividly by Jane's mother, who was quoted above:

> *Jane would allow herself to be cuddled, but only if I didn't look at her. She always resisted sitting on my lap unless she was facing away. And I could go to her with my arms out, just as I had a million times with my boys, but she would never reach out to me in return. I would stand grinning at her, like some big Cheshire cat, just praying she would smile back at me. She never did. One day I found my husband doing the same—he was smiling at her, the tears rolling down his face, begging her to smile back.*

Even at this stage, many parents rarely voice their fears, not even to each other. If expressed at all, such concerns are often discounted by relatives and family doctors, who believe that the parents are over-anxious and tell them that 'All babies are different'. It is our experience that the parents themselves are often relieved to be given this advice, particularly if the child is their first-born. Such parents often have limited experience of other babies and are unable to compare their child's development with that of others. For other parents who rapidly go on to have another child the situation becomes particularly tragic when the second child begins to outstrip the first in the race for development.

The behaviour about which parents start to become concerned varies significantly from one child to another, but in general it is from the age of about 6 months that the disturbing features become more apparent. Such children may not reach out to be held or comforted, and they may be very selective about the objects they want. The parents may find that they are not emotionally differentiated from these objects. Later, the child may show worrying obsessions with particular objects and spend long periods of time running to and fro or becoming engrossed by particular movements, e.g. spinning objects, twirling and examining their hands, sniffing objects and people, fanning their faces, etc. Many such children may be terrified by everyday events and will almost certainly appear detached and 'cut off' from their surroundings. In turn, the parents experience alarm and then fear that their child should be displaying such inexplicable behaviour.

It is the area of speech and language development about which most parents, regardless of their experience of parenting to date, become particularly concerned. Children with autism may attach such little importance to language that they do not even respond to their name when it is shouted at them, and they show other marked communication difficulties which are well documented elsewhere (e.g. Aarons and Gittens, 1992). Paradoxically, some of these children may be intensely interested in a variety of quiet sounds or whispers, which may confuse those parents who had begun to suspect that their child had a serious hearing impairment.

With some exceptions, most children with autism are late to talk and nearly half of them never learn to speak (Howlin and Rutter, 1987). For those who do acquire speech, problems often arise with regard to the intonations and pitch of their speech (Aarons and Gittens, 1992). Thus the lack of early speech development or its abnormality of tone, as well as concern about hearing impairment, are common reasons for parents seeking professional advice.[1]

In addition, parents witness and become increasingly concerned about the developing stereotypical and obsessively repetitive behaviours that are displayed by many children with autism (Howlin and Rutter, 1987), and realise that they do not just have a child who will not speak, but they also have one whose behaviour is completely beyond their comprehension.

> I think that's when Jane really seemed to move away from us. She no longer seemed to retain any vestige of the daughter we had longed for, no matter how hard we worked to keep her. We didn't stop loving her for one minute, but she seemed beyond our love. It just wasn't enough.

It is often at this point of hopelessness that parents are at their most desperate for a diagnosis.

'What do they mean by autistic tendencies?'; the impact of diagnostic confusion

Faced with their perplexing child, parents are keen to find professionals who can give them answers to their myriad questions. However, it is the experience of many parents of children with a wide range of handicaps

---

[1] As one mother put it, 'His voice sounded flat and robotic, just like his stare at me'.

that their initial contact with professionals is far from satisfactory (Frude, 1992).

The parents of children with autism are no exception, and of those that we have worked with, few found that their first contacts with professionals led promptly to an adequate diagnosis or onward referral to someone who was able to make a diagnosis. Many parents were given more to worry about with partial diagnoses. Worse still, many found that the individual pathology of their child's condition was ignored in favour of a concentration on parental or family dysfunction, a trend that is both aversive and counterproductive (Konstantareas, 1990). One parent described her own fraught experiences and questioned the value of the increasingly common tendency to tell parents that their child has 'autistic tendencies' (Hockey, 1991).

Her account describes how her son was given a variety of labels, including autistic tendencies, and was eventually diagnosed as dyslexic. Such a process is obviously both unhelpful and distressing. In taking up this debate, Aarons and Gittens (1991) discuss the value of 'autism' used as a *context* in which to understand better a child's special needs. In doing so they reiterate the benefits of autism viewed as a continuum disorder, which is made possible through the use of the well-known triad of social impairments described by Wing and Gould (1979).

As this diagnostic description of autism is now internationally accepted (World Health Organisation, 1993), there is little need for professionals to talk of 'autistic tendencies'. Parents are quite capable of understanding that their child has a more or less severe degree of impairment on the autistic continuum compared to other children who are also diagnosed as autistic. They are equally capable of recognising that the nature of the condition will vary with age and maturation, and that their child will move to take up different positions on the continuum as time passes (Randall and Gibb, 1992). An explanation of this type can be extremely reassuring, as the following quote indicates.

> We didn't like the news when we heard that Jane was autistic, but it put an end to the uncertainty. Up until then we had thought it was our fault, but it was explained to us that autism is an organic brain dysfunction. We weren't responsible for Jane's problems, and we could move on from there more positively.

The information available from parents is a vital ingredient of the diagnostic process, and it should be placed alongside other sources of information (Lord, 1991).

Unfortunately, not all 'diagnoses' are delivered by those trained to give them. Autism has become the property of a wide variety of professionals who are all willing to make a diagnosis, as the following quote from a teacher in charge of a nursery shows.

We had this little girl, Gail, in the nursery. Her behaviour was weird and she had little or no language—even at age four. She certainly couldn't handle more than single part instruction, although we knew she wasn't deaf. Anyway, I saw a TV programme about holding therapy and autistic children. Some of those little kids were just like Gail. I asked her mum the next day to take her to the doctor—I said I thought Gail was autistic.

Many parents have reported to us a kind of numbing shock after this type of approach, but many of them then go on to say 'Well, she is a professional. She must be right', or words to that effect. Gradually a sense of deep loss develops, which some have likened to bereavement—they mourn a child who can never be seen by them in the same way again. Aarons and Gittens (1992) write of the child becoming the personification of a label.

Challenging behaviour and the family

Apart from the need for diagnosis, the most likely cause of referral to the Family Assessment and Support Unit is the presence of severely challenging behaviour. It is not just the bizarre and ritualistic behaviour of the mobile infant with autism that starts to cause concern. It is the frequent frustration–aggression reactions (e.g. tantrums) which often accompany this that gives rise to great anxiety (Howlin and Rutter, 1987), and it is hardly surprising that the age range 2–5 years is described by many parents as their most fraught time, given the often incomprehensible behaviour of their children.

Jane got hooked on an old blanket. It was an extra large one and she kept tripping over it. It had to be carried everywhere otherwise she'd just scream and kick—people used to get exasperated in shops because we were so slow moving around with the damned blanket. We only got rid of it when the psychologist told us to snip small bits off it when she was asleep. Eventually she ended up with something the size of a large handkerchief—then she gave it up altogether. It worked without tears, but you feel so stupid and inadequate, snipping bits off a blanket in the middle of the night.

Sometimes the 'cure' for the problem seems so trite that, although it works, it demeans the parents. Some of them, like Jane's mother quoted above, feel silly, while others blame themselves ('why didn't I think of that? I could kick myself').

Jane got really frightened of car tyres crunching on our gravel drive. She would cry and cry—once started she was so difficult to control. Her poor dad had to leave the car out until she was asleep before he could put it away.

And finally:

> *People keep looking at us. They think we made her the way she is.*

At a time when most parents are proudly showing off their children's skills, the parents of children with autism pray that no one will notice how odd their little child is ('will they notice how he lines up his cars, how he can't talk, how he can't . . . ?', and so on). The fear often leads to a near-overwhelming temptation to shut their child up in the house so that his or her autistic foibles will go unnoticed.

The potential list of specific difficulties associated with autistic behaviours is long and complex. As professionals we want to help the parents to cope well and empower them with the skills which they need in order to cope (Gibb and Randall, 1989a), but we cannot always ignore the impact of our strategies on their constructs of themselves as parents.

Personality characteristics of parents of autistic individuals

Although the insidious idea that autistic individuals are created by the personality and child-rearing practice of their parents has been laid to rest (Cantwell *et al.*, 1976), there still exists a belief that certain personality characteristics occur relatively commonly among the family members of autistic people. The evidence for this belief is the subject of this section. It is an important issue because, if true, these personality characteristics may have a bearing on the way in which autistic individuals are responded to and the way in which support services are delivered.

Many studies have made use of self-report questionnaires to assess parental personality attributes. Most of these (e.g. McAdoo and DeMyer, 1978; Cantwell *et al.*, 1979) have not demonstrated differences between these parents and control groups. Although this may indicate support for the view that there is no effective difference, it is also true that such questionnaires are probably insufficiently sensitive to detect any subtle attributes that may exist. They are designed to measure broad facets of personality structure rather than subtle traits within those facets. Thus, for example, two people may have the same score as significantly intro-verted on the Eysenck Personality Questionnaire (EPQ); one of them may be quiet but perfectly approachable, whereas the other may be distant and withdrawn. Cantwell *et al.* (1979) found no differences between the parents of dysphasic and autistic children on the EPQ extraversion and neuroticism scales, but noted that there were oddities of personality to be found mostly among the parents of children with autism.

In one well-known early study, Cox *et al.* (1975) found no significant

differences among the parents of children with autism compared to those
of dysphasic children. Their study examined the variables of 'warmth',
'demonstrativeness' and 'responsiveness'. Of these, 'warmth' was rated
according to tone of voice, facial expression and gesture, words used and
the quality of (warm) interaction shown by the parents towards their children. Five standardised situations characterising emotional representation were given to parents, who were asked how they would respond.
Ratings of the two variables were recorded for these responses. There
were no significant differences between the two groups of parents on
these variables.

A different picture emerges when clinicians are asked to interview the
parents of autistic and non-autistic children (e.g. Wolff *et al.*, 1988). The
clinicians did not know which group the parents belonged to and
rated them 'blind'. The results suggested that the parents of children
with autism were more likely to show schizoid traits, including lack of
empathy, poor emotional responsiveness, impaired rapport with the interviewer, a degree of over-sensitivity to experiences, solitariness, anomalies
within social communication and idiosyncratic special interests.

A more detailed examination of social communication reveals interesting findings. In one recent study, parents of autistic children were found
to have significant abnormalities of social language use (e.g. Landa *et al.*,
1991). Landa and her colleagues argue that previous studies of the characteristics of the parents of children with autism have suffered from
methodological or conceptual weaknesses. They point out that some
studies may inadvertently make use of parents whose own difficulties
may have been genetically transmitted to their children. For example, the
parents of non-autistic but otherwise disturbed children have been
selected to compare with the stress of having an autistic child. If these disturbed non-autistic children have genetically based aetiologies, then it is
likely that they will share traits with their parents which will mask or
otherwise distort potential discrepancies with the parents of autistic children (Landa *et al.*, 1992). A second defect raised by these authors concerns
the point already made above, that some of the personality tests used may
not be sufficiently sensitive to illuminate those traits that are observed by
clinicians. The authors speak of the tests as encompassing many domains,
including non-verbal communication behaviour, affective behaviour and
social cognition.

They argue persuasively that these difficulties can be resolved by
simply focusing on a single aspect of social behaviour. Their choice was
an essential ingredient of effective social communication, namely pragmatic behaviour. There is considerable evidence at the level of clinical
assessment to support this choice. As early as 1958, Kanner and Lesser
reported that the parents of children with autism spoke pedantically and

were disdainful of small talk. The study by Wolff *et al.* (1988) described the most differentiating variable of all in respect of parents with autistic children as 'over-' or 'under-' communicativeness. Also included were 'excessive guardedness' and disinhibition. These are all ingredients of problematic social communication.

Turning to the literature, Landa *et al.* (1991) highlight particular variables that have been identified as appropriate for an assessment of pragmatics (e.g. Roth and Spekman, 1984). Essentially, these variables concern the use of verbal language that is inappropriate for the social context. Thus pragmatic defects observable in individuals with autism include problems of following the rules of politeness and social etiquette in conversation.

Included in this are difficulties concerning the amount and type of background information that should be provided to help people to understand what is being said to them (Baltaxe, 1977). In addition, a well-known problem experienced by autistic people with good language skills concerns reciprocity of conversational exchange (i.e. being able to maintain a conversation that is of interest to all participants), an essential skill in this being the ability to make a smooth transition from one topic to the next (Dewey and Everard, 1974). Landa and her colleagues felt that if the parents of autistic individuals exhibit abnormal pragmatic behaviour that is conceptually similar to these difficulties, but milder in degree, then people who are in conversation with them may regard them as socially odd. These researchers developed the Pragmatic Rating Scale (PRS) to help to test the hypothesis that pragmatic deficits are more likely to be found in the parents of autistic individuals than in the parents of non-autistic individuals.

In total, 43 parents of 28 children with autism took part in this study. Very strict criteria were used to ensure that these parents represented the full spectrum of autism, which included meeting the criteria for autism based on the Autism Diagnostic Interview (ADI) (LeCouteur *et al.*, 1989), which utilises information provided by the mothers. The children themselves were assessed directly using a structured observation schedule, namely the Autism Diagnostic Observation Schedule (ADOS) (Lord *et al.*, 1989). In addition, each child received a neurodevelopmental examination and was accepted only if their non-verbal IQ was above 30.

The control group represented the general population, and consisted of 21 adults whose children did not have autism. Of these, some had children with Down's syndrome, and all controls were selected for comparability with the parents of children with autism with regard to social class, high-school education and gender. All of the parents were educated in the USA and spoke standard English as their first language. Apart from one African-American in each group, all subjects were Caucasian.

The Pragmatic Rating Scale was based on 19 pragmatic behaviours selected to reflect abnormalities observed in the relatives of individuals with autism during clinical interviews. The PRS was completed by interviewers who had not met the parents before, and who were unaware of the group membership of the parents. Ratings were made of conversational behaviour observed during the session, which was based on 2 hours of cognitive and language testing. A 15-minute conversation was held midway through the session, and this was also rated. The examiner was required to initiate the conversation, attempt to stimulate new subjects, and make the kinds of enquiries that would normally occur in any social exchange. At times during the conversation, the interviewers would create circumstances in which the parents might demonstrate pragmatic deficits. For example, occasional misunderstandings of the parents' statements were introduced, and the parents were rated according to whether or not they were able to make adequate revisions of what they had said in order to facilitate understanding. In addition, the parents were asked to describe their occupations, hobbies and interests, in order to determine whether they could use terminology that the interviewer could understand in a properly detailed description. The fact that the parents were rated during formal structured test situations as well as the informal conversational situation made possible a comparison of pragmatic difficulties arising with or without the guidance of structure. Thus pragmatic behaviour was sampled over a range of behaviour, including initial and final salutations, responses to explicit instructions, 'small talk', conversation during unfamiliar tasks, when enquiries and requests for additional information were made, and ordinary social conversational behaviour. A variety of topics was offered to the parents, and this enabled the rating of their responses to reflect adequately their pragmatic behaviour.

The results demonstrated that the PRS could reliably distinguish parents of individuals with autism from the controls. These differences could not be the result of intellectual or cultural differences and, as a group, the parents of autistic individuals showed a larger number of defective pragmatic behaviours than did the control group.

The differences between the groups appeared on three specific scales of the PRS. The first of these was labelled the Disinhibited Social Communication Subscale, and the traits recorded on this include preoccupation with detailed topics about which the individual was overly talkative, confusion when recounting or describing (often going off the subject), making abrupt changes of topic, overly candid remarks, and poor synchronisation of communicative behaviour. Readers will no doubt see similarities between these traits and those characterising individuals with autism who are high functioning, or those with Asperger syndrome.

The second subscale, labelled the Awkward/Inadequate Expression Subscale, is composed of conversational traits that affect expression and understanding. Thus individuals tended to show inadequate clarification, gave rather vague descriptions, provided poor background information to aid comprehension, made terse remarks and showed a generally awkward expression of ideas. Landa *et al.* (1991, 1992) believe that these pragmatic deficits imply a rigid linguistic rule system which lacks sufficient flexibility to give adequate expression or understanding in social conversations. They remark that this 'linguistic inflexibility' is a milder version of the impairment of communication found among individuals with autism. The last and least common deficit was represented by the Odd Verbal Interaction Subscale. The traits subsumed in this subscale include the initiation of contextually inappropriate verbalisations, an odd sense of humour, restricted conversational flow, excessive formality in communication style, and atypical greeting behaviour. The authors remark that these traits demonstrate difficulties in the means whereby a conversational partner is put at ease and a pleasant conversational tone is established. This careful study reveals subtle but important deficits of pragmatic conversational behaviour among the parents of individuals with autism. With regard to the reasons for these deficits, one possibility is that the parents' conversational behaviour is in some way modelled or otherwise perturbed by the presence of their autistic offspring. Taking care of a person with autism is an extremely tiring and stressful responsibility, and fatigue and stress could possibly lead to impairment of the efficiency of many skills, including those concerned with conversational pragmatics. If it were the case that the parents of children with autism did simplify and restrict their conversational skills in order better to meet the needs of the child with autism, then this idea might have some merit. However, these parents should not demonstrate such significant abnormal traits in the absence of their children. In any case, Snow (1972) found that parents of children with autism do not simplify their language when in the company of their language-impaired child, despite being instructed to do so. It is unlikely, therefore, that being the parent of a child with autism is going to affect the conversational skills shown in relation to another, unimpaired adult in the absence of their autistic offspring. In any event, if this explanation was valid then one would expect to see nearly all parents of children with autism adopting such a strategy. In fact, over half of the parents of children with autism were rated as displaying normal pragmatic behaviour.

The alternative explanation is that there is a genetic basis for the pragmatic deficits. This is an appropriate hypothesis in view of the fact that the genetic mediation of autism is fairly well established (e.g. Folstein and Rutter, 1988). It should not be surprising, therefore, to find pragmatic impairment among the parents of children with autism. Indeed, other researchers (e.g. August *et al.*, 1981; Wolff *et al.*, 1988; Piven *et al.*, 1989) have reported a family communality of social and cognitive deficits where autism is present. These deficits are recorded as being milder but conceptually similar to those shown by individuals with autism.

The similarities of persistent traits, although at a level of less severity than in individuals with autism, is a much-repeated theme throughout the relevant literature. For example, Gillberg (1989) reported a study of the parents of 23 children with Asperger syndrome. Social deficits were found in 11 of 23 fathers, and were judged to be similar to but not as severe as those normally found in Asperger syndrome. Bolton *et al.* (1994) reported a higher rate of mild autistic-like social deficits among the siblings of 99 autistic people compared to the siblings of 36 Down's syndrome controls.

These and other studies led to a well-designed research study by Piven *et al.* (1994), who tested the hypothesis that the relatives of autistic people would show personality characteristics that could be regarded as milder but similar features to full-blown autism. They predicted difficulty in social interactions manifested as a lack of interest or as aloofness in interpersonal relationships, reduced emotional expression or undemonstrativeness, an inability to appreciate the social–emotional behaviour of others through unresponsiveness, and rigid or stereotyped behaviour reflecting the characteristic of rigidity. The researchers tested these hypotheses by comparing autistic individuals and controls with Down's syndrome. This study overcame many of the methodological difficulties of previous investigations through an extremely careful selection of parents and autistic individuals. The method of selection and confirmation of eligibility was very similar to that described for the study by Landa *et al.*, and similar checking was performed in order to ensure that the diagnosis of autism was correct. The parents of Down's syndrome children served as controls because of the need to control for the effect of caring for a handicapped child on the socio-emotional functioning of parents. The parents of Down's syndrome children are no more or less likely to have psychiatric disorders than members of the general population.

After the selection procedures were complete, the study included 87 parents of 48 autistic children and 38 parents of 20 Down's syndrome children. The design of the study allowed for both self-reporting and informant categorisation of personality types. In order to achieve this, the Modified-Personality Assessment Schedule (M-PAS) was used. This instrument was employed at the end of a 2- to 3-hour interview that started with a semi-structured social history including major life events, social life and educational and employment history. It was followed by another interview designed to assess the effects on family members of having a handicapped child, during which a modified version of the Schedule for Affective Disorders and Schizophrenia-Lifetime (SADS-L) was used. By the end of this process, all subjects and informants had become familiarised with the interviewer, and consequently their responses to the M-PAS were likely to be accurate.

The results showed that the parents of children with autism scored significantly higher on three characteristics of the M-PAS, namely Aloof, Untactful and Undemonstrative.

The study by Landa et al. on pragmatics of communication refers to one significant pragmatic deficit among people with autism as that indicative of poor understanding of the 'rules' of conversation. The conversation of many people with autism is off-putting because it is essentially directed at the interests of the autistic person alone. This might be regarded as a lack of tact, and therefore a finding of 'untactfulness' as a persistent trait in the parents of children with autism is not surprising. Piven and his colleagues examined the subject and informant responses relating to this characteristic, and were able to define the types of behaviour shown by the subjects that led to them being regarded as 'untactful'. Essentially, they seemed to react in a manner which put other people off by appearing callous and unfeeling. They seemed unable to respond appropriately to the distress of others, and their reduced capacity to relate led to difficulties in relationships. Piven et al. (1994) chose to interpret this characteristic as an impairment of social cognition, and related it to such impairments found in individuals with autism (e.g. Baron-Cohen, 1988). They relate to the theory-of-mind research in which a central cognitive deficit is revealed as an inability to understand the different perspectives of other people in the social environment. It is clear that the kind of pragmatic deficits that are inherent to the conversations of these parents may also be the product of the same central cognitive dysfunction. Piven et al. (1994) concluded that the characteristics (aloof, untactful, undemonstrative and unresponsive) are 'conceptually reminiscent of some features of autism, but milder and for the most part not impairing. The possibility exists that these characteristics may result from the stress of having an autistic individual in the home. Alternatively, these characteristics may be expressions of the underlying genetic abnormality in autism' (Piven et al., 1994, p. 792).

PARENT-CHILD INTERACTIONS

It may be that the tendency towards 'aloofness' is at the heart of findings about the ways in which parents relate to their children with autism. One study of parent–child interactions at preschool age revealed significant results with regard to child compliance (Lemanek *et al.* 1993). It is well known that a variety of different handicaps are associated with increasing non-compliance in children. However, it is also the case that the way in which parents interact with their handicapped children may either increase or diminish this non-compliance. Thus children with Down's syndrome tend to respond better to parental directives than to suggestions (e.g. Maurer and Sherrod, 1987), whereas children with autism benefit from higher levels of structure (e.g. more frequent task-related reminders and instructions; Clark and Rutter, 1981). Another relevant finding was reported by Cunningham *et al.* (1981), who showed that whereas the compliance rates of mentally retarded and non-handicapped children do not differ significantly, the mothers of mentally retarded children use more commands and respond less positively to compliant behaviour. A related finding emerged from a survey by Sigman *et al.* (1986), which reported that children with autism were generally less compliant with suggestions made by their parents (e.g. 'Would you like to . . . ?') than children with mental retardation or no handicaps at all.

The study by Lemanek *et al.* (1993) examined compliance in children with language impairments, autism and mental retardation. Children with language impairments constituted an important comparison group because of the overlapping characteristics of this group with the other two groups. Compliance was assessed within a demand situation which was established by giving parents a list of tasks for their children to complete. Two categories of child behaviour were coded, namely compliance and non-compliance, of which non-compliance consisted of three distinct behaviours—refusing instructions, ignoring parents and leaving the area. Three categories of parent behaviour were also noted, namely structure, instructions and cues, and reinforcement. The structure category was composed of the following four distinct behaviours:

- gaining the child's attention (verbally);
- gaining the child's attention (non-verbally);
- removing extraneous and distracting materials;
- ensuring physical proximity.

The category concerning instructions and cues consisted of the following behaviours:

- verbal instructions (positive and negative);
- provision of models or demonstrations;
- use of gestures;
- prompting (verbal and non-verbal);
- engaging in other types of speech (i.e. relevant or irrelevant speech).

The category of reinforcement included the use of verbal reinforcement (e.g. praise) and non-verbal reinforcement (e.g. physical or meteoric reinforcement).

The results of this study were very interesting. For both the mentally retarded and autistic groups, increased compliance was brought about by greater use of verbal parental prompts. However, increased compliance for the language-impaired and non-handicapped groups was associated with greater parental use of positive and negative instructions. Compliance was also associated with greater parental use of verbal/non-verbal reinforcement.

Non-compliance was associated with increased use of verbal and non-verbal 'attention-getting' behaviours by the parents in all four groups. It was also correlated with removal of extraneous items and, for the language-impaired group, with increased physical proximity.

Children with autism were the least compliant, and their parents made greatest use of structure and cue behaviours (i.e. verbal and non-verbal attention-securing, physical proximity and non-verbal prompting) when attempting to gain the child's compliance. The results appeared to indicate that the parents of children with autism used demands for compliance more than the parents of the other groups of children. Unfortunately, this increased use of structure was not augmented by an increased use of effective instructions and cues (except for non-verbal prompts). Although the parents of children with autism showed more prompting and an increased rate of success in gaining their child's attention, they failed to extend their behaviour in other ways. They had a greater need than the other groups of parents to acquire a wide range of instruction and cue-usage behaviours.

A further finding concerned the nature of tasks chosen by the parents for their children in each group. Whereas no significant group of differences was found, implying that the parents of children with autism selected the same types of tasks as the parents of other children, there seemed to be little indication that the parents of these children understood how to relate the nature of tasks to their children's needs. Too many verbally oriented tasks were chosen, which clashed directly with the main handicapping feature of the children with autism, who would have been better off with a higher proportion of non-verbal tasks. The authors of the study suggested that the parents of children with autism may expect their children to perform tasks beyond their capabilities.

It is clear, therefore, that there is a weight of evidence to suggest that the parents of children with autism show significant differences to other populations of parents with regard to persistent traits of behaviour. Although an argument can be advanced that these traits arise from the struggle of living with a child with autism, there is no satisfactory explanation for the fact that these traits are as likely to be found among the parents of very young children with autism as in those with older children. It is clear that professionals working with these parents must take into account these subtle differences, and need to be prepared to modify their service delivery accordingly.

6

THE EFFECTS OF AUTISM
ON PARENTS: PART II

Much of the research on the functioning of families with children who have developmental disorders has focused on the stresses encountered when bringing up an intellectually disabled young person at home, and describes the potential stressful and adverse consequences for the families (e.g. Byrne and Cunningham, 1985; Levy-Shiff, 1986). This research has mirrored the increasing facility for early identification of children with such disorders, and the politico-educational trends towards needs-based resource application. In addition, many more people with profound multiple handicaps are now surviving because of improved medical care, and their long-term requirements are demanding, full-time and stress-evoking for family members. These stressors are obviously considerably less for those families whose children are educated in residential establishments than for those whose children remain at home and attend day school (Kazak, 1989). Nevertheless, one cannot underestimate the impact of children's learning disabilities on all family members, including siblings. A common finding throughout the research literature is the relationship between the amount of support given to families in order to reduce stress levels, and age.

There are strong indications that lower levels of support are available to families of older individuals (Suelzele and Keenan, 1981). In some cases, the staff of residential facilities provided this support and so became indispensable parts of the families' resources (Kazak, 1989).

The first chapter described some of the research evidence indicating the particular stresses that are experienced by the families of children with autism, and Chapter 2 looked briefly at stress and social support in caring for a child with a disability. These stressors have been well documented (e.g. Bristol and Schopler, 1984; Schopler and Mesibov, 1984; Cutler and Kozloff, 1987). The severity of the disorder at any level can leave parents exhausted to a degree that is dependent on their stress tolerance. Many of them experience chronic pessimism, and risk breakdowns in their functioning (e.g. Marcus, 1984). The failure to make respite care arrangements can also add to these difficulties (Factor *et al.* 1990).

PARENTS AND MEDICATION

Given the stressors that impact on families, it is perhaps surprising that more parents do not seek to medicate their child with autism, particularly in the context of extremely challenging behaviour. Only 15% of the families we spoke to made use of drugs to help with behavioural problems. This may be due to the fact that there is little research evidence available on drug intervention strategies with autistic children, or information on its effectiveness. Despite an early claim by Campbell (1975) that medication can promote development and improve functioning in children with autism, the majority of practitioners working in the field view medication as a last-resort strategy, and use it only to suppress unwanted symptoms for short periods (Sloman, 1991). In addition, there is considerable wariness about side-effects, particularly in the case of neuroleptic medication, which is known to cause tardive and withdrawal dyskinesia (Gualtieri, 1991).

As a result, few children remain on medication for long, and the population that is being medicated fluctuates rapidly. This is not conducive to effective clinical studies on the effects of medication. However, from the clinical evidence it does seem clear that the acceptability of medication is positively correlated with such factors as severity of symptoms, information about the disorder, and the positive experiences of other parents. It is negatively correlated with family support and family resources. Thus families with poor resources and/or few supports are more likely to decide to use medication.

Some of the best studies on the decision of parents to use medication have been conducted in relation to attention deficit hyperactivity disorder (ADHD). For example, Rostain *et al.* (1993) found that a previous history of using medication was weakly positively correlated with a decision to use medication with an ADHD child. Knowledge of ADHD was negatively correlated with the willingness of mothers to accept medication, and it has to be acknowledged that a previous study by Liu *et al.* (1991) showed that behavioural treatments for ADHD were rated by parents as more socially acceptable than medication. It was also found that the mothers' knowledge of ADHD was negatively correlated with the acceptance of a psychostimulant drug regularly used to treat ADHD children. Thus the more the mothers of these children knew about the disorder, the less likely they were to make use of medication. It is particularly interesting to note that, in the context of the ADHD population, Rostain *et al.* (1993) found that family factors such as socio-economic status (SES), parenting stress and family coping style were not predictive of a willingness to use medication.

Konstantareas *et al.* (1995) found that the parents of children with autism frequently opposed the use of medication, even when the clinicians working with them suggested it. Many are quite likely to do this even when the overall family functioning is being disturbed by the child's severely challenging behaviour, for which the drugs were being recommended. This group of reluctant non-drug users is far larger than the few parents who clinicians know use medication even when there is no particularly good clinical reason for doing so.

CASE STUDY 6.1

Our doctor and the child psychiatrist both offered us medication to help control Sammy's terrible temper. She would throw herself around, hold her breath and punch at her ears. They suggested sedation and we agreed for while, but it didn't help; she was still bad-tempered and so sleepy that she lost a lot of her skills.

We know that now there is no medical cure for autism; it's all down to us and Sammy's teachers. Autism isn't a medical condition, and there's no point in taking medicine for it.

Konstantareas *et al.* (1995) consider that two factors are very important to parents when they are trying to decide whether or not to use medication. The first concerns child characteristics which, particularly at the lower end of the range of intellectual functioning where more severe behaviour problems are likely to be found, make the children a greater management challenge to the parents. The second concerns family systems that are unable to withstand additional stress from the child because they are already nearly overwhelmed by other impositions. Thus work by Bristol (1987) and Konstantareas and Homatadis (1991) demonstrates that parents are significantly affected by the many and changing demands that their autistic child imposes on the family, and that older children tend to be more stressful, such stress being augmented by lack of resources and family support. Not surprisingly, many such families find that the problems presented by the symptoms of the child with autism exceed their coping skills.

A recent and careful study by Konstantareas *et al.* (1995) evaluated a number of factors which may contribute to the decision to allow the medication of a child with autism. Five variables were isolated as being particularly influential, namely presence or absence of speech, irritability, intellectual level, family size and family stress. Thus higher levels of parental stress, and the child's ability to speak as opposed to being mute, were significantly correlated with the decision to medicate children. It would appear therefore that what the child with autism has to say to a highly stressed family may add to that stress rather than diminishing it. Surprisingly, low intellectual ability, mutism and odd facial appearances (generally associated with greater neurological impairment), as well as poor social acceptability, were not positively correlated with a decision to medicate. Given these findings, it is probably not entirely unexpected that the severity of symptomatology also did not correlate positively with the decision to medicate.

The perception and opinions of doctors and other practitioners with regard to medication of children with autism is also influential. Their opinion on the validity of medication for such children is unlikely to change until the relevant research literature demonstrates a significance and role for it over and above the simple suppression of unwanted behaviours. If it is found to be therapeutically valuable to children with autism in much the same way as stimulants have been found to help children with ADHD, then it is possible that prescribing practices will change. Some of this research evidence will be considered in a later chapter.

Parents and respite care

Many studies have demonstrated that respite care is one of the support services that families identify as particularly beneficial to them in their struggle to cope (e.g. Apolloni and Triest, 1983; Bristol and Schopler, 1983; Salisbury and Intagliata, 1986).[1] Provided that respite care is of a high quality, parents value it highly, and many of them comment that it has improved the quality not just of their lives but also of the child's siblings (e.g. Marc and MacDonald, 1988; Wigham and Tovey, 1994).

CASE STUDY 6.2

Stephen and Jenny have three children with a one-year gap between each of them. The youngest, Nicholas, is currently 12 years old and is severely autistic. His behaviour at home is exceptionally dangerous and includes trying to cut his brother and sister with pieces of glass, setting fire to their clothes and throwing large stones at them. He has some speech, and repeatedly shouts 'No, no, no!' when they come into the room.

His resentment of them is such that neither parent dare show them any affection when he is present. All spare time was becoming dominated by

---

[1] In total, 73% of the parents we talked to stated a firm wish to have access to high-quality respite care.

Nicholas in that he demanded and got his own choice of activities on every occasion. Fortunately, his brother and sister were able to get some support from a siblings group, but they longed to have some 'quality time' with their parents without the difficulties associated with Nicholas.

In the end we gave in—we accepted respite care, something we always swore we would never have. Nicholas went into a small Unit with three other children and excellent, very experienced staff. He really enjoyed it and, over several months, he has learned to share us with the others. We are delighted with the outcome.

Although respite care tends to be used most by families who have limited support networks (Cohen, 1982), it is not unusual for families with good support networks to use it as well, although on a less frequent basis (in the first author's experience). The greatest source of satisfaction that families report from the use of respite care is the reduction of immediate stress levels (Potasznik and Nelson, 1984). This is consistent with the findings of other researchers (e.g. Bristol and Schopler, 1983) who have demonstrated that parents in lower-stress groups tend to perceive greater adequacy of their support services than parents in higher-stress groups.

The issue of non-professional support networks is of interest in that, as has been mentioned above, the more frequent users of respite care services tend to be those families that have lower levels of support from families and friends. In general, however, it is the severity of the child's difficulties that appears to be the primary factor distinguishing between users and non-users. Thus Halpern (1985) demonstrated that users of respite care had children who were more severely retarded, more physically incapacitated and more adult dependent than those of non-users. Marc and MacDonald (1988) added serious behaviour problems to this list of severe disabilities.

With specific reference to the families of children with autism, the study by Factor *et al.* (1990) made use of 36 two-parent families, each with an autistic child aged between 7 and 17 years. In total, 19 of these families made use of respite care and 17 families did not. Factor *et al.* postulated that users would tend to have more seriously affected children, and also that they would report higher levels of stress. The variables that were measured included family stress, which was self-recorded on a questionnaire evaluating resource availability and stress levels. The functional skills of the children were assessed using a developmental profile questionnaire, also completed by the parents, which provides quantified data on five major areas of functioning, namely physical, self-help, social, communication and academic functioning. The results showed that the users of respite services reported that their children had more severe difficulties than the children of the non-users with regard to difficult child characteristics, and significantly more physical incapacitation. In addition, the developmental assessment data indicated that the children of the respite user group tended to be more significantly impaired than those of the non-respite-user group.

Factor *et al.* also postulated that non-users would have higher levels of perceived social support from their networks than users. A different group of 28 families was used, and data were collected on the Interpersonal Support Evaluation List (ISEL; Cohen *et al.*, 1985), which is designed to assess the perceived availability of various types of social support.

As before, children in the user group tended to have more significant difficulties, and their families showed higher stress levels. The ISEL data confirmed the hypothesis by demonstrating that the non-users did in fact have more social support than the user group. The results of an incomplete survey also support these findings. Unlike some of the previous results described above that relate to the choice of whether or not to accept medication, severity of autism in terms of different behaviours was the reason most frequently cited by parents for making use of respite care. This was closely linked to the impact of autism on the siblings, and the difficulties that the parents perceived in being able to give time and attention to their other children.

The absence of useful and emotionally supportive informal networks was also found to be an initial factor among the parents to whom we spoke. Those parents who were given practical as well as emotional support were less likely to use respite care and, even when they did, they used it less frequently than those parents who had little informal support. It would appear therefore that parents prefer to use extended family and friends rather than formal respite support services.

However, some of the parents in our survey reported that extended family support can be a two-edged sword. On the one hand it is supportive, available and accessible, but on the other it can be associated with polite criticism, bad advice and subtle pressures caused by tension between extended family members.[2] As one parent commented, 'We accept help when it's offered and then we are expected to be eternally grateful as it gets thrown back at us.'

THE SIBLINGS OF CHILDREN WITH AUTISM

Chapter 1 has already described some of the difficulties experienced by the siblings of children with autism. Although it is logical to expect that

---

[2] In total, 57% of the parents we interviewed had experienced tensions of this type.

having a severely handicapped brother or sister will be a significant stressor on siblings, the picture is far from simple, and other factors also have an influence. For example, the developmental characteristics of these siblings are also significant. Just as the parents of children with autism show marked personality variation from the norm, leaning towards the characteristics that define autism but being less severe, so the siblings of children with autism may also show developmental anomalies. An investigation by Narayan *et al.* (1990) does not support this view. Their study was designed to assess, among other variables, the presence of educational delay in the siblings of autistic children compared to those of matched controls. Although their study did not use formally standardised instruments to measure academic progress, careful interviewing of the parents was used to determine whether the children showed evidence of 'global' or 'specific' problems in accessing the curriculum.

However, their results did not support the hypothesis that there would be significant problems for the siblings of children with autism. The rates of 'global' and 'specific' difficulties did not differ between the siblings of autistic children and the controls. However, when the children of extended families were examined, a significant number were found with specific developmental delay. The first finding is supported by the work of Baird and August (1985), who used autistic children with IQs above 70. The study by Narayan *et al.* (1990) also involved high-functioning autistic children. By contrast, August *et al.* (1981) found that a significant proportion of the siblings of retarded and severely autistic children were cognitively impaired. There was a very high rate of both global and specific developmental delays.

Sibling adjustment

All teachers and parents are aware that sibling interactions are essential and powerful shapers in developing socialisation, because they help to develop important instrumental and affective relationship skills (Cicirelli, 1985). Important lessons learned from older siblings include cognitive, social affective and other skills, as well as the development of positive self-esteem. In addition, Dunn and Kendrick (1982) showed that positive and frequent interactions with siblings can provide an important source of emotional support, whereas poor-quality and infrequent sibling interactions can have a negative effect on adaptation.

Sibling interactions for children with autism are so valued that there have been several attempts to devise appropriate training measures to encourage positive interaction (e.g. Strain and Danko, 1995). Being aware of the significance of sibling interpersonal contacts in the process of child development, many researchers have studied the psychological response of siblings to their ill or disabled brothers and sisters (e.g. Hanson *et al.*, 1992). Other researchers (e.g. Howlin, 1988; Morgan, 1988) have been concerned with the psychological adaptation of siblings within the context of the disruptions and reorganisations of family life that are brought about by the presence of a child with a disability. Howlin's paper in particular has much to offer in terms of strategies for including and involving the siblings of children with autism, and her words on this subject provide invaluable guidance for professional support staff working with families.

The common assumption is that the siblings of children with disabilities are more likely to experience problems of psychological adjustment than are the siblings of healthy children. Researchers in this area are consistent in listing the types of stressors that the siblings of handicapped children may experience, including changes in family roles, restructuring of the family's functioning and activities, loss or absence of parental attention, feelings of guilt, a sensation of shame often brought on by the negative evaluations of their peer group, and perplexity at the bizarre behaviour that children with autism may display. Morgan (1988) described increases in parental stress that have residual effects on the non-handicapped children in the family, and it has been noted that small families may be more vulnerable than larger ones, since there are fewer siblings to help the parents in their task of coping.

Despite the prevailing and fairly logical view that siblings of children with handicaps will experience more stressors and so display more psychological difficulties than children without a handicapped sibling, the findings concerning the impact on siblings are in fact equivocal. Whereas some studies (e.g. Ferrari, 1987) report that there are detrimental influences on the siblings of handicapped children, others have reported that any such difficulties were not discernible (e.g. Dyson, 1989). In one interesting study (McHale and Pawletko, 1992), the siblings of children with disabilities were found to spend more time on domestic tasks than their handicapped brothers and sisters, and also than the siblings of children without handicaps. In addition, mothers spent more time helping and playing with the disabled child than they spent on their non-disabled siblings. This apparent lack of attention given by the mothers to their non-disabled children is more apparent than real, because the mothers of children with handicaps actually spent more time playing with their non-disabled children than did the mothers of children without handicaps. This suggests that the mothers of children with handicaps have made efforts to 'repay' their non-disabled siblings by giving them extra attention.

The same study also reported that the mothers of children with disabilities found themselves using more power-assertive discipline strategies and less positive love for their handicapped child than for his or her non-disabled siblings. Not surprisingly, this differential response to dis-cipline was associated with higher levels of anxiety and depression among the siblings of disabled children.

What is clear from this last study is that the logical view of siblings of children with handicaps is over-simplistic, and that there are complex interactions between differential maternal treatment and possible nega-tive emotional consequences which affect the disabled and non-disabled siblings quite differently. With specific reference to children with autism, Morgan (1988) suggested that the siblings without autism were at higher risk of poor psychological adjustment than the siblings of children with other disabilities. As yet, however, research which has investigated this possibility has produced no more unequivocal results than those across the range of disabilities and their effects on siblings (e.g. McHale *et al.*, 1986; Mates, 1990).

The study by Rodrigue *et al.* (1992b) sought to clarify some of this com-plexity by using a tightly controlled research study to examine the psy-chological adjustment of siblings of children with autism compared to those of children with Down's syndrome and those of non-handicapped children. Of particular concern to this survey was the siblings' perceived self-competence and their parents' perceptions of their social and behav-ioural functioning. It was postulated that the siblings of both the Down's syndrome children and those with autism would have lower perceived self-competence and generally poorer personal/social/behavioural adjustment than the siblings of non-handicapped children. These researchers also sought to examine the relationships between sibling adjustment and other variables such as age and gender while controlling for the degree of disability in both the autism and Down's syndrome groups. These other variables included marital satisfaction and child adjustment.

This study involved 39 biological siblings of children with either autism or Down's syndrome. Of these, 19 children (10 females and 9 males) were siblings of children with autism and 20 children (10 females and 10 males) were the siblings of children with Down's syndrome. In total, 20 children (12 females and 8 males) were selected as the biological siblings of devel-opmentally normal children. All of the families were intact with regard to marital status, predominantly white, middle to upper-middle class, and were matched on the basis of the targeted child's gender, race, and sibling's age, gender and birth order, as well as family size and socio-economic status.

In addition, the targeted children were matched on the basis of mental age, rather than chronological age, in order to prevent possible confound-ing of disability and adaptive behaviour. Thus although the siblings of the targeted children were of approximately the same ages, the average age of the targeted children was significantly different to allow for the effects of learning difficulties among the two disabled groups. Thus the average age of the children with autism was nearly 11 years, that of the children with Down's syndrome was nearly 12 years, and that of the non-handicapped target group was only 3.8 years. Use of the Vineland Adaptive Behaviour Scale enabled the average functioning of the three groups to be determined, and there was only approximately one developmental year of difference between the highest and lowest of these groups.

Measurements were made using standardised tests of perceived competence and social and behavioural adjustment with regard to the siblings. In addition, a scale of marital satisfaction was given to the parents in order to assess both parents' level of marital satisfaction.

The results were interesting. The siblings of children with autism did not differ significantly with regard to perceived competence and social/behavioural adjustment. Although the siblings of children with autism showed higher internalising and externalising problem behaviours when compared to the other siblings in the study, their average scores on both dimensions fell within the normal range. This suggests that they are not especially vulnerable to adjustment difficulties, a finding that is consistent with other studies (e.g. Dyson, 1989).

Whereas other researchers (e.g. Howlin, 1988; Morgan, 1988) stated that a multiplicity of child, sibling and parental characteristics represent potential negative influences on the adjustment of siblings of children with autism, the study by Rodrigue *et al.* (1992a) revealed only two variables that were significantly associated with sibling adjustment, namely siblings' age and marital satisfaction. This study demonstrated that older siblings of children with autism showed higher rates of internalising and externalising behaviour problems. This is a reasonable finding, and it suggests that the longer a child is exposed to a brother or sister with autism, particularly with severe difficulties, the more likely it is that he or she will experience psychological problems. In addition, McHale *et al.* (1984) suggested that older children are more likely to have had extensive experience of being responsible for domestic and care tasks in respect of the disabled child, and so become influenced by cumulative stress.

It is pleasing to note that this study also suggests that higher levels of marital satisfaction among the parents of children with autism are associated with higher levels of self-esteem in the siblings. Other research (e.g. Henggeler and Borduin, 1990) demonstrated that the effects of high levels of marital satisfaction were positive not only for the parents but also for their children, and this may be associated (e.g. Rodrigue *et al.*, 1992a) with better adjustment for both parents and siblings when there is a child with a developmental disorder in the family.

In summary, the results of this study suggest that the siblings of children with autism are not always susceptible to influences that create difficulties in psychological functioning. Nevertheless, there are variables which interact with the factors associated with having a brother or sister with autism that may lead to such difficulties. Marital satisfaction is one of these, and increasing age is another. It would seem, therefore, that the siblings of children with autism who are most at risk are those who are older and whose parents experience less marital satisfaction than is the norm. Clearly these are important findings, and all clinicians and other professionals working with families where there are children with autism, must be aware of them and take them into account when designing family support and intervention services.

PARENTS AND CHALLENGING BEHAVIOUR

All parents, no matter how satisfactory their children's development may be, will worry about behaviour management many times throughout their parenting career. Even when children are not testing limits or causing any particular concerns over challenging behaviour, their parents may still be placed in situations in which they compare their children's behaviour with that of the child next door or the other children arriving at school and wonder if they are doing enough to ensure that their children are developing the right kind of social behaviour to advance their future in today's world. Parents of children with autism tell us that they are preoccupied with both types of concern. First, they are often beset by a spectrum of challenging behaviours which defy their best efforts to understand them, and secondly, as their child with autism and his or her peers grow older, the differences in social behaviour and all that that means for their child's future become increasingly apparent.

The parents we have spoken to show great sensitivity in their understanding of the difficulties that their children face. They are capable of going well beyond simple labels of challenging behaviour (aggressive, disobedient, destructive, dirty, etc.) to state more precisely how the unique deficits of autism lie at the heart of these problems. Parents speak of challenging behaviour which they attribute to their child's dysfunctional social skills, narrow or obsessive interests and severe communication difficulties. As Schopler (1995) points out, all too often they find that their previous experiences of parenting their children without autism are of little help because the core deficits of autism prevent their affected child from learning in the same way.

Most of the parents (74%) in our survey have received little effective help from professional workers. As will be seen later, the majority feel that the professionals with whom they have had contact simply did not have

enough time to provide them with the information, support and monitoring that they needed, and others had been told 'Your child is autistic;
you can expect this sort of behaviour'. Where parents have been helped
effectively it is because the professionals concerned have assisted them
not just in looking at the behaviour which is causing major problems and
finding a means of repressing it; instead, they have been helped by examining in more depth the antecedents to this behaviour and understanding
the triggers that set it off. Parent management training in appropriate
techniques will be discussed later in this chapter, but it is clear that it presents parents not only with the possibility of immediate or partial solutions to challenging behaviour, but also with the strategy or strategies that
could enable them to cope better as new and equally difficult situations
arise. In essence, we found that the parents who had been more successfully assisted in tackling challenging behaviour knew either how to use a
constructional approach to provide their child with new and compensat-
ing behaviour, or how to alter the environmental antecedents such that
the challenging behaviour was less likely to occur. Both approaches have
their roots in behavioural psychology, and despite the bad press that this
discipline has received in the context of autism because of the over-narrow
way in which some practitioners have advocated it, it is a source of great
pride to many of the parents with whom we have worked that they have
acquired such techniques and now use them efficiently to benefit the lives
of their children with autism.

Challenging Behaviour:
Operational Definitions and Criteria

If we are to discuss strategies for coping with challenging behaviour, we
must first be sure that we know what is meant by that term. We need to
understand that challenging behaviour is not simply behaviour which
challenges the authority of parents, teachers and others who are important to the child but that it is also behaviour which may interfere
significantly with opportunities for the child to develop. For example, a
child with autism who desperately needs the input of a speech and language therapist is unlikely to be able to benefit from that input if he or
she spends the sessions constantly spinning and swirling.

At both clinical and service levels there are good reasons why challenging behaviour should be given as clear-cut an operational definition
as possible. At the clinical level, the needs of children and young people
whose behaviour is challenging must be clearly understood if intervention programmes are to be designed for them successfully. At the service
level, the needs of people with challenging behaviour must be taken fully
into account if they are to receive the services that they require, particu-

larly when they are living with their families within the community. In the context of challenging behaviour the challenge is to find the means whereby the environment can be adjusted such that the antecedents for this behaviour are no longer present. It is at this service level that Emerson *et al.* (1987) proposed the following definition:

Behaviour of such intensity, frequency or duration that the physical safety of the person or others is likely to be placed in serious jeopardy, or behaviour that is likely to seriously limit orderly access to the use of ordinary community facilities.

This is a very useful definition because it introduces the notion that children with challenging behaviour may well be their own worst enemies in that they prevent themselves from obtaining the maximum benefit from family and community resources and furthering their own development. The following examples show just how challenging some behaviours may be to the opportunities for the young people who display them.

Jenny has to have her hands in mittens, otherwise she pounds her ears until they bleed.

Tommy cannot be taken out by his mother because he screams every time he sees a dog.

Gillian cannot be given weekend leave because of her history of absconding.

Libby has no friends; other youngsters won't associate with her because she has refused to wash or change her clothes for three months.

Unfortunately, this aspect of challenging behaviour is often forgotten, and indeed there is a danger that it may simply be viewed as a rather more refined way of talking about violent or aggressive behaviour. Although violent and aggressive behaviour is indeed challenging, it is completely incorrect to conceive of challenging behaviour in such a narrow and restricted way.

The judgment as to whether or not a particular behaviour is sufficiently challenging to warrant intervention is a crucial one, and particular criteria are desirable to help make this assessment. The criteria proposed by Zarkowska and Clements (1989) are of considerable value because they can be adapted to a wide range of clients whose behaviour is challenging. Their criteria are as follows.

- The behaviour is inappropriate in nature or severity, given the individual's age or level of development.
- It is dangerous to the individual (e.g. self-injury, running into the road).
- It is dangerous to others.
- It causes significant stress to those who live and work with the client.
- It disrupts or impairs the quality of other people's lives to an unreasonable degree.
- It constitutes a significant additional impairment for the client because

it blocks opportunities for learning new skills, and may exclude a person from new learning experiences.
- It is contrary to generally accepted social norms.

Bearing the definition of Emerson *et al.* (1987) and these criteria in mind, it can be seen that both the challenging behaviours presented by people with autism and related difficulties make the work of families, teachers, community support personnel and others very difficult indeed. The parents with whom we have worked describe violent behaviour that includes aggression directed at others as well as self-injury, destructive behaviour towards property and stereotyped behaviour which is stigmatising and associated with rejection by the community as the most significant causes of worry that they experience. They are not alone in this, as many research studies (e.g. Horner *et al.*, 1990) have reported similar fears and observations from the parents of people with severe disabilities around the world.

The fears that parents report are numerous, but the commonest and most significant of these is a recognition that the challenging behaviour displayed by the child or young person with autism in the family represents a significant obstacle to the creation and stability of family life and interaction, such that the quality of life, both for the individual with autism and his or her close family members, is greatly reduced. Despite the commonality of their fears, it is clear that each family is unique and that the problems presented by the child or young person with autism impact on them in different ways. It is therefore important that information about the types of problem that each family experiences is obtained and matched to the types of resources that are required to improve family stability, adaptation and routine functioning (Bailey *et al.*, 1986). The next section will consider some of the evidence that is influential in determining the nature of these resources.

Parents' Reports of Challenging Behaviour in the Context of Autism

Published research in this area dates back over nearly three decades and has examined the challenging behaviour of people with autism and related disabilities in the context of its impact on families. Much of the research has focused on the simplistic use of contingency management strategies (i.e. the manipulation of rewards and punishments) to modify specific challenging behaviours, and the ways in which such strategies can be taught to parents and, occasionally, to siblings (e.g. Dangel and Polster, 1984). Some of these techniques have sometimes relied on ethically dubious aversive techniques (see Sheldon, 1995; Wing, 1996). Such techniques are fairly powerful, and it is not surprising that the outcomes have been generally favourable. This continues to be the case, even though some of the earlier work was limited in that the families taking part had usually been few in number and narrowly defined in relation to socio-economic and cultural characteristics (Bernal, 1984). When such difficulties are negated by extended sample size and widening the source of families selected, then the results are still positive, but some families do not show the same ability to benefit (e.g. Robbins *et al.*, 1991), and some researchers (e.g. LeLaurin, 1992) argue the need for individualised programmes to aid the provision of assistance for a wider range of families.

Despite this obvious conclusion and the recognition by most professionals that support for families must be tailored to the individual strengths, circumstances, predilections and needs of those families (e.g. Turnbull *et al.*, 1986; Dunlap and Robbins, 1991), there has been surprisingly little research on identifying which services are particularly in need and which varieties of support are most valued by the families of children and young people with autism. The straightforward requests and clinical narratives of surveys such as the one conducted by ourselves teach us that a wide diversity of services are valued and needed. This has been established by other authors as well, as required services include support groups, personal counselling, respite care, behaviour management training, functional skills training and parent groups (e.g. Bristol, 1984). In fact, there is no lack of evidence of the services that the parents of children and young people with autism believe they require, but what is lacking is any evidence of the efficacy of these services in relation to the amelioration or prevention of challenging behaviour.

Furthermore, there is the issue of who judges resources given to parents in relation to challenging behaviour to be more or less useful. Professionals will clearly take a different perspective to family members. Thus an educational psychologist who is concerned about challenging behaviour in the school as well as the home context may greatly value a purely behavioural approach that is consistent between the two locations in an attempt to replace the challenging behaviour with a more acceptable and adaptive behaviour. However, the family, already 'worn down' by a long history of such behaviour, may find respite care a much more valuable option, even when that causes further confusion to their child with autism because it considerably extends the range of caretakers and sources of inconsistent behaviour management. It is a saddening fact that in making judgements of the efficacy of various resources, there are few studies which have actually sought the opinions of parents. Much useful information is derived when this does occur.

Before considering the outcomes of our own survey on parents' judge-ments, it is useful to review one previous survey that has been conducted recently. Dunlap *et al.* (1994) conducted a survey in order to obtain pre-liminary information from parents about their children's challenging behaviour and the resources that the parents find or anticipate to be most helpful. The researchers asked parents of individuals with autism to give information about the frequency and nature of their children's challeng-ing behaviours, the specific strategies that they had found to be useful in tackling these behaviours, the resources that they had found most helpful, and the resources that were felt to be most urgently needed in order to address challenging behaviour effectively.

This study made use of a questionnaire, entitled 'Surveys of Families and Their Response to Behaviour Problems', containing 22 items, which was sent by post to 133 families on the mailing list of the Autism Society of Florida. A total of 79 questionnaires were returned, of which 78 ques-tionnaires could be subjected to full analysis.

Of the 22 items in this questionnaire, 10 items request descriptive infor-mation about the family member with autism (e.g. age, medication, com-municative abilities) and the family context (e.g. number of siblings). A further 10 items require information about the challenging behaviour dis-played by the individual with autism, and about the resources which the family have found helpful or might anticipate to be helpful in the future with regard to challenging behaviour. Two other items require informa-tion about services currently being received by the families, and whether the families were willing to be contacted for additional information. The items included a mixture of open-ended, multiple-choice and fill-in formats.

The results were instructive and mirror our own similar findings. The first finding of note was a wide diversity of challenging behaviours, including many cases where destructive activities were reported to occur more than once a day. The diversity of descriptions included aggression towards others, self-injury, pica, destruction of property, temper tantrums, stereotypical or self-stimulating behaviours, withdrawal and messiness. Destructive behaviour was reported to occur at least once per day by 40% of the parents. Self-stimulation was reported to be the most frequent type of worrying and challenging behaviour (61% of cases), followed by with-drawal and temper tantrums, which were noted by 38% and 23% of parents, respectively. It must be remembered that individuals with autism engage in a variety of challenging behaviours, and therefore some parents were faced with very severe problems caused by a combination of such behaviours.

The parents' responses concerning the strategies that they found most useful in addressing behaviour problems showed an overwhelming pref-

erence for behaviour contingency management procedures. These procedures specifically referred to manipulations of reinforcers and/or
punishers which included such techniques as time-out, working for
privileges, ignoring bad behaviour and response cost (a system of fining
a child for inappropriate behaviour in relation to preferred activities,
pocket money, etc.). This finding, which closely mirrors our own, is in
direct contrast to the view of many professionals who have decried the
use of such simplistic behavioural strategies, and this contrast warrants
consideration. The preference for contingency management strategies
was overwhelming, as other categories of successful strategies were
reported by only 10% or fewer of the parents. These included the provision of predictable daily structure and routine, having other activities
available, making use of activities that involve communication (e.g.
'talking to the person', medication and making sure that younger people
with autism had sufficient food or sleep). It is of particular interest that
there were few differences in these findings across the different age
groups of the survey.

With regard to resources which parents had found most helpful, there
was strong agreement that teachers, other family members and informative published materials were regarded highly, whereas doctors, psychologists, social workers and the church were found to be least helpful. It
would seem, therefore, that professional personnel do not perform well
in the estimation of parents when it comes to helping them to deal with
the challenging behaviour of their children and young people with
autism. There are also age group differences to be taken into account. For
example, the highly valued helpfulness of teachers is less commonly
reported among parents of adolescent autistic adolescents, with less then
40% describing their child's teacher as being very helpful. In addition, the
perceived helpfulness of support groups was found to be highest during
the preschool years, when parents experienced the greatest uncertainty,
and this also diminishes as age increases. Unfortunately for those of us in
the caring professions, the usefulness of doctors, psychologists and social
workers is perceived to be low during the preschool years, and gets
steadily lower as age increases. It would appear that these groups of
professionals are valued no more highly by parents in the context of
challenging behaviour than they are in the context of assessment and
diagnosis. The responses of parents to questions relating to resources
which they felt were most needed were also diverse, with no single category of response being selected by more than 30% of the parents. The
range of resources included 'skills-building', which involved either the
child or the parents learning new skills, and related to this parents
identified the need for better trained professional staff among doctors,
psychologists, teachers and others, who could then be more helpful to

them in tackling challenging behaviour. Again, therefore, there is a strong feeling among parents that many of the professionals with whom they come into contact are not appropriately trained to meet the needs of their children and families. This pattern of responding was common across all age groups of autistic individuals surveyed.

Our own survey yielded similar findings. Parents found teachers marginally more helpful than other professionals, and were particularly disappointed with doctors (general practitioners, psychiatrists and paediatricians) and psychologists. Many of them made disparaging remarks, of which the following is typical.

> Our psychologist was much more concerned with the difficulties teachers experienced with Jimmy. She more or less said that if we were devoted to him and gave him lots of stimulation then we would be alright. She completely ignored the kicks, punches and bites his little sister gets every day, and the screaming tantrums we just don't know how to control.

One family that was surveyed had been referred to a child protection team because a social worker felt that their methods of restraining their 10-year-old autistic son were 'too power-assaultive and on the verge of abuse'. They were accused of not listening to professional advice. However, at the child protection team conference it was agreed that they had never received any advice.

As may be clearly seen, there is a considerable impact on the families of children with autism where severely challenging behaviours are to be found. Research evidence suggests that where these behaviours are of the externalising variety (e.g. hyperactivity, non-compliance, poor rule-governed activity, aggression), families experience greater stress with them. Parents report a greater negative impact on social life and feelings about parenting, less positive feelings towards parenting, and higher child-related stress than do the parents of normally developing children. Moreover, research (e.g. Donenberg and Baker, 1993) suggests that it is the externalising behaviour rather than the condition itself which causes the difficulties. Thus families with other young children who display externalising behaviours (e.g. attention deficit hyperactivity disorder) experience the same levels of stress, even though ostensibly the condition has less severe consequences for children.

Parents from our survey group were clear that the major problem they experienced with the externalising behaviours of autism concerned non-compliance. Whether deliberately or because of poor communication skills, their children simply could not or would not comply with important instructions. The stress of this seems to be particularly acute during the preschool period, and in one study (Arbelle et al., 1994) young autistic children aged 3–5 years were compared with a mental-age-matched group of mentally retarded and normal children in an observational study of compliance. These children were forbidden to eat a sweet offered to them by the experimenter. Behavioural response, affect and gaze patterns were used as measures across the three groups. It was found that the children with autism exhibited significantly less compliant behaviour with regard to the parental prohibition than did the children in the two control groups. The main correlation for this non-compliant behaviour was with chronological age and not with mental age, language development or parental behaviour. Affect and gaze patterns of the autistic children were different to those of the controls, but these patterns were not correlated with compliance behaviour. This research indicates that children with autism are significantly less compliant with parental prohibition because of the autism, and not because of other factors linked with their intellectual abilities or certain characteristics of their parents. This suggests, as is indeed revealed by our own survey, that no matter how effective parents may be in coping with their children with autism, there are likely to be stress-evoking challenging behaviours associated with non-compliance. As one parent to whom we spoke said, 'Even the best parents need help with autism.'

7

FAMILIES AND CHALLENGING BEHAVIOUR

A BEHAVIOURAL AND SYSTEMIC PERSPECTIVE

As has been stated previously, those strategies which families value most highly with regard to the resolution or amelioration of challenging behaviour displayed by their children with autism are the ones which may be loosely defined under the heading of contingency management. These strategies are essentially behavioural and make use of operant and social learning theory. However, many authors have argued against the use of such strategies, and indeed there have been many difficulties surrounding the rapid fall-off in their use by families. Wing (1996) has provided a useful résumé for parents on the limitations of the behavioural approach when it was applied in an inflexible manner over a decade ago. She relates this approach to three major criticisms that have been made. First, whether autistic or not, the children cannot learn higher levels of skills than their 'in-built potential allows' (Wing, 1996, p.104). Secondly, she refers to the quite alarming use of harsh methods to discourage inappropriate behaviour (although her characteristic of description is an approach that was used with children with autism and individuals with learning disabilities many years ago). Thirdly, she points out that many psychologists who practised behavioural methodologies 'thought that the reasons for any behaviour were irrelevant to its management and all one had to do was to apply the methods strictly according to the rules' (Wing, 1996, p.105).

Many parents reading this information would be alarmed at the prospect of using behavioural methods to deal with the challenging behaviour shown by their children. Yet, as in most complex issues, there is a middle ground, in this case where effective behavioural principles can be combined with other approaches to provide effective and family-sensitive solutions. This section is based on the work carried out by the authors in various locations, but mainly in the Family Assessment and Support Unit where they are currently based. Before this, however, it is perhaps desirable to alleviate some of the anxieties that the critics of behaviourism have raised among the parents of children and young people with autism.

Turning to the first point made by Wing (1996), that children cannot learn more than their in-built potential allows, one has to accept the truth of this and acknowledge the fact that no one can learn successfully at levels beyond those imposed by the capacity of their thinking and reasoning abilities. Thus a child with severe intellectual impairment at a school for children with severe learning difficulties is unlikely to be expected to master trigonometry. Similarly, those of us with only average motor skills will never acquire the grace and fluency of a world-class gymnast. However, there are many examples in everyday life where people routinely make use of skills which are based on principles well beyond their knowledge and potential understanding. For example, the majority of drivers who are safe, competent and capable of consistent good standards of behaviour on the road drive their vehicles with no understanding whatsoever of what is happening inside the internal combustion or diesel engine that is propelling them. Similarly, most people reading this book will be able to use a wide range of electrical appliances without having any knowledge or understanding of the nature of electrons. Most of us can tell the time competently, and yet we have no real understanding of why there are 24 hours in a day and 60 minutes in an hour.

The same is true of our social behaviour. The complex array of dealings with other people that we engage in daily on a routine basis, and which enables us to maintain satisfactory relationships with most of these people, is based on principles which do not concern us as we apply those skills. We are aware that such principles exist, and we refer to moral development as we watch young children acquire increasingly complex social behaviour. Yet the vast majority of children acquire social skills ahead of understanding. Simple greeting behaviour and 'waving bye-bye' are largely the products of imitation and parental encouragement. No lessons in moral philosophy are applied alongside such encouragements to assist the child in understanding why it is good to 'wave bye-bye', or to say 'Hello, Nanna' when their grandmother enters the room. In other words, both children and adults acquire and use skills whose theoretical basis is often unknown to them.

It is at this level that parents part company with professionals who, being aware of the limitations of the behavioural approach, are willing to use it when children are clearly without 'the in-built potential' to understand the theoretical or philosophical underpinnings.

Parents want solutions. They tell us that they want their children to be able to understand why they should behave in certain ways and not others. They also tell us that this understanding is peripheral, and that family life proceeds more smoothly if children behave in certain ways and not others. There is less stress, family members like each other more, and happier times can be enjoyed by all. At a logical level, it is obvious that a behavioural approach which reduces the amount of wrist-chewing, face-fanning and twirling in which a young child with autism engages, such that he or she is then more able to access learning opportunities, should be applied even though the young child in question has no idea of the processes involved or the reasons for applying them. It is perfectly possible, using behavioural methodologies of the type known as contingency management, to provide children and young people with autism with a wide range of basic skills of which they may not understand the purpose, but which nevertheless lead to an improvement in the quality of both their lives and those of their family members.

In a later section we shall examine a range of behavioural approaches to problems that have been identified by families as particularly challenging.

Turning to the second criticism, namely that behavioural psychologists have in the past used excessively harsh punishers to suppress unwanted behaviour, one must again acknowledge that this was the case. There are horror stories of children being subjected to electric cattle prods in order to suppress self-mutilation, the use of deprivation of food and water in order to heighten the motivation to 'win' pieces of food or small drinks by performing in particular ways, and various unpleasant forms of restraint given grandiose titles such as 'positive practice over-correction' which merely demonstrate to the young people that they are absolutely helpless in the hands of a stronger adult.

Such practices are unacceptable and, indeed, if used in this country without appropriate licence would result in prosecution and subsequent action being taken under the Children Act 1989. Critics will argue, quite correctly, that there are more insidious forms of equally harsh disciplinary procedures, and that even the simple withdrawal of privileges, as in response-cost or time-out strategies, may be aversive to some children and young people with autism. For these reasons, the majority of contingency management procedures make use only of positive reinforcement, and do so in a way that, following functional analysis of the behavioural profile of the individual, seeks to replace the maladaptive and challenging behaviour with behaviour that is acceptable and developmentally appropriate.

Turning to the fact that many psychologists and social workers practising behavioural methodologies feel that the reasons for certain behaviours are irrelevant to their treatment, it must be pointed out that this is hardly the case in modern times. It is a vital component of the behavioural approach that the antecedents of behaviours are studied carefully in the hope that they can be modified such that there is no reason for the individual to present that particular behaviour in the first place. One simple example is that of a 10-year-old girl who displayed extreme forms of school refusal behaviour such that she was frequently unable to settle at any time during the school day, and had to be brought home early. Her behaviours included temper tantrums, eye gouging, physical assaults on teachers and other staff, and less severe behaviour such as spitting and swearing. After a fruitless period of family therapy based on a quaint notion that the child was showing some separation anxiety that had been induced by dysfunctional family dynamics, a behaviourally orientated educational psychologist performed a functional analysis to examine the antecedents of this child's disturbing behaviour, and discovered that the primary antecedent concerned the frequent changes of taxi driver on the transport that took her to school. In common with many children with autism, she was unable to tolerate such rapid fluctuations in a sequence of events that she needed to have highly structured and routinised. The problems resolved when the taxi company ensured that the girl would have the same driver each day. This is a simple example of how behavioural psychologists do take into account the immediate underpinning reasons for particular challenging behaviours.

Critics may well point out that this antecedent was not necessarily the cause of the child's distress, and would suggest that more work should be done to understand why she responded in this way to variations in an everyday event. The answer to this is simply to point out that, as yet, our understanding of the effects of autism are not up to such an investigation, and they are certainly not up to ameliorating those effects at the core level of impairment.

The role of parents

For many years now parents have been trained to implement a variety of behavioural programmes in order to ameliorate such diverse problems as aggression towards others, self-stimulation, self-injury and the development of new adaptive behaviours, including independence skills (e.g. eating, dressing) and rudimentary communication (e.g. Harris *et al.*, 1981). Those responsible for such training have never made any claims that these procedures are a 'cure' for autism, but have simply stated that both the children and their parents are better able to cope with the severe effects of autism. What has become clear, however, is that it is not possible simply to stop at the point where, using didactic procedures, parents acquire behavioural management skills (e.g. Harris, 1984a). Even when such training has been successful, there remain clinical difficulties that exceed the daily direct management of challenging behaviour. To ignore these is to risk a process whereby parents become disenchanted with what they have learned and cease to apply it.

During the early 1980s there were many reports of successful parent training initiatives whereby parents acquired the ability to use contingency management strategies to teach their children with autism a variety of new and adaptive skills. These included rudimentary self-care skills such as learning to eat with a spoon, as well as much more complex skills such as acquisition of the rudiments of communicative speech (e.g. Harris et al., 1982).

In reviewing the success of these initiatives, Harris (1984b) reported that new problems were raised by the apparent success of these parent-training interventions. Thus while many parents were able to achieve a high level of skill as behaviour modifiers, they were found to reduce their application of these skills over a period of 1 year after acquiring them. A variety of reasons were given for this, and parents acknowledged that they were not doing what they felt they 'ought' to be doing. Some of these reasons will now be considered.

As early as 1976, Mealiea highlighted many limitations of early behavioural approaches to clinical problems, and commented that the narrow scope of treatment represented a lack of awareness of the wide impact such an intervention can have on a family, and which could actually cause deterioration of relationships and functioning. Later, Patterson et al. (1975) reviewed their work on sophisticated behavioural approaches to problems of aggression, and reported that their behavioural intervention strategy was insufficient to help the majority of the children referred to them. They discovered that many of the families required help in areas that ostensibly had little to do with the antecedents of the child's aggression. These included marital conflict or the need for extensive parental support within the home which, if successful, brought about changes in functioning which might then beneficially influence the behaviour of the children. Pursuing this theme, Patterson and Fleischman (1979) reported that there is a need to examine more carefully how changes in the family as a whole can lead to beneficial changes in the child who displays challenging behaviour. There is no reason to believe that such comments do not also relate to families where a child with autism is present. Harris (1982) began to examine the possibility of using behavioural training approaches alongside those which examined and influenced family systems.

In her later paper, Harris (1984b) sets out in detail her reasons for bringing together the powerful behavioural methodologies with systemic family work, and she argues strongly that the use of behavioural methodologies may have unfortunate and undesirable effects on families if there is no attempt to examine family issues beyond the narrow focus of the behavioural training. For example, she warns:

> If the therapist attempts to teach the mother of a pre-school, autistic child to help her child to feed and dress herself, but ignores the mother's depression about the child's diagnosis and the father's lack of involvement in the family as his response to stress, a situation is created which is likely to generate failure. It is difficult for a person who is depressed to find sufficient motivation to get up in the morning and faithfully carry out a behavioural program even if, intellectually, that person (knows) it ought to be done. A father who feels himself to be an ineffective parent and spouse may increasingly avoid coming home. Indeed, the risk of heightening the parents' guilt may be run since they will find themselves failing to do things which have been defined as important for the child. This may increase the tension between them and lead to a further deterioration of family life. Similarly, if the parents of an adolescent autistic child come to a therapist concerned about how to deal with their child behaviour problems and the therapist fails to at least consider the question of how that family can help the youngster in the process of separation from the family, but instead focuses exclusively upon behavioural programs to address the presenting problem, the therapist may, in the long run, be contributing to the maladaptive functioning of the entire family. (Harris, 1984a, p.132)

She then goes on to point out that behaviourists who practise only from the systemic viewpoint risk causing further problems for the family by not attending to the immediate presenting problem. She states that behavioural training is critically important in the intervention process for families where autism is present.

> Living with a child that bangs its head, wets the bed, wanders around the house at night, and does not speak, is an exhausting, discouraging, defeating and sometimes enraging experience. Learning the skills to bring these behaviour problems under control and return a sense of peace to the house provides parents and siblings with a feeling of efficacy and makes the autistic child easier to integrate into family activities. For many families the primary focus of treatment should be didactic training in behaviour modification, but the therapist must be ever aware that the intervention must be flexible enough to go beyond these bounds to focus upon the context of the family which will be implementing the procedures. (Harris, 1984a, p.132)

THE EFFECTIVENESS OF FAMILY THERAPIES IN RELATION TO AUTISM

As has been mentioned previously, the predominant view in the early 1960s was that autism was a product of dysfunctional parenting. This view reflected a general trend in that period whereby most attempts to treat childhood disorders were of an out-patient or in-patient variety, and whatever successes were achieved often did not last once the child had returned to the natural setting of the family. Since that time, behavioural methodologies, in particular the impact of social learning theory and family therapy, have brought a strong psychosocial dimension to intervention in childhood emotional and behavioural disorders. Unlike child psychotherapeutic procedures and straightforward behavioural techniques of childhood behaviour modification, more recent approaches based on family therapy and behavioural psychology are much more focused on the family context of children with such disorders. This welcome movement has seen a gradual integration of therapeutic approaches which, although they may have quite disparate theoretical foundations, are nevertheless able to provide a comprehensive package to assist the children, family members and other relevant contexts such as school, respite-care facilities, and so on.

Estrada and Pinsof (1995) reviewed the scientific evidence for the effectiveness of family-based approaches to the treatment of several childhood disorders. They made use of the broad definition of family therapy given by Gurman *et al.* (1986) as 'any psychotherapeutic endeavour that explicitly focuses on altering the interaction between or among family members and seeks to improve the functioning of the family as a unit, or its subsystems and/or the functioning of individual members of the family' (p.565). They point out that although this generous operational definition of family therapy can include the traditional forms (e.g. structural, strategic) there have been few, if any, rigorous evaluations of such models with regard to the childhood disorders under investigation, including autism. In the absence of such evaluations they restricted their work to a review of the outcomes of parent management training (PMT) as a model of intervention. The underlying assumption is that challenging behaviour may be sustained by maladaptive parent–child interactions.

Kazdin (1993) lists several common characteristics of PMT strategies. First, the activity specifically targeted at the amelioration of the child's challenging behaviour is conducted primarily by the parents themselves. There is little or no direct intervention by a professional worker with the child. Secondly, the parents are taught to identify, define and observe the problem behaviour, making careful note of antecedents and consequences as they do so. Thirdly, the direct training of the parents covers social learning principles and behavioural procedures, including the manipulation of positive reinforcement, and sanctions (e.g. time-out or response-cost, contingency contracting, and negotiation). Fourthly, these strategies are usually taught through a specific range of activities which may include interactive discussion, imitation training, role play, audio visual work, home-based practice and feedback.

Thus far, much of the description of PMT makes use of behavioural technology and principles. Increasingly, however, a systemic approach is adopted either directly or indirectly (Estrada and Pinsof, 1995). This approach complements such behaviourally oriented practice by including concepts concerning the following:

- a perception of child and family disorders as a constellation of inter-related systems and subsystems;
- the necessity for considering the whole family context when making an assessment of the importance of any single variable;
- recognition that similar behaviours may result from different sets of initiating factors within the systems and subsystems;
- acknowledgement that even successful interventions will cause multiple outcomes which include effects on the relationships within the family system; and
- awareness of the fact that family systems and subsystems are dynamic and that they change over time (Mash, 1989).

As Estrada and Pinsof point out, many of those families who fail to respond successfully to parent management training do so because of factors operating within the family system and subsystems. Thus families where there are multiple risk factors associated with, for example, parental psychopathology, social–cognitive deficits, socio-economic disadvantage or marital disagreements, are less likely to pursue the PMT approach consistently, show less evidence of success even when they do complete the course, and fail to maintain gains over time (e.g. Dumas and Wahler, 1983; Kazdin, 1993). In cases where these factors are present, the support workers and therapists must take them into account at the systemic level or risk causing harm by doing only part of the necessary work.

The increasing trend towards adopting behavioural approaches in combination with family-oriented approaches has led to significant improvements in the modification of challenging behaviour and recognition of the value of parents as teachers and advocates for their children with autism (Estrada and Pinsof, 1995). There are now many examples of such programmes in successful operation, and Estrada and Pinsof (1995) have reviewed 12 programmes which make use of social learning theory and operant conditioning principles, take into account family-based factors, and resulted in excellent outcomes in terms of parenting skills and management of children's challenging behaviours. A recent study which illustrates the combined approach is that of Zappella (1990), who describes an ethnologically oriented family therapy whereby close relationships were fostered between autistic children and their parents, who then became agents of behavioural change.

PARENT-IDENTIFIED STRATEGIES FOR CHALLENGING BEHAVIOUR

Given that there is a movement towards involving family members much more closely in the assessment, resolution and monitoring of challenging behaviour, it is appropriate to survey parental opinion about the most worrying forms of challenging behaviour that they face from their children with autism, and strategies which they have found to be effective in resolving or ameliorating these problems. The survey of parents conducted by this Unit has led to a clear hierarchy of difficulties experienced, and also to many intelligent and sensitive strategies for resolution. A caveat, of course, is that not all parents would share this hierarchy of difficulties, and not all of them will have experienced success in following the strategies described below. It is also the case that on many occasions the strategies have been suggested by professionals but 'made to fit' particular family circumstances. The inventiveness that families show in adapting behavioural strategies and the response they make to systemic family work that may accompany this indicates to the authors that, given confidence and empowerment with appropriate information, the families of children with autism are able to provide assistance to those children that often exceeds anything available through the statutory services.

Before describing the hierarchy and its attendant strategies, it is worth making some general points about the underpinning of efficient responses to the challenging behaviour of individuals with autism.

TACKLING CHALLENGING BEHAVIOUR: GENERAL PRINCIPLES

Many excellent books and papers have been written that provide appropriate information about the general underpinnings of successful strategies in tackling challenging behaviour. For example, Wing (1996) provides a full and easy-to-read set of general principles (pp.104–108) and Eric Schopler (1995), in Chapter 8 of his invaluable *Parent Survival Manual*, gives an excellent account of behavioural management strategies. Parents and professionals are well advised to read these.

Our work with parents indicates that they are able to develop considerable insight into the factors associated with challenging behaviour among children with autism. During the course of the many interviews we have conducted with them, they have been able to identify from their own experiences the antecedents of inappropriate behaviour. Wing (1996) provides a list of some of the most frequent autistic antecedents of such behaviour, and these are reproduced here in terms of the parents' observations.

1. Over 80% of the parents we interviewed were well aware that interference with the daily routines of their children and/or with their children's preferred activities is the most likely antecedent of a wide variety of difficult and inappropriate behaviours, including destruction of objects, temper tantrums, interpersonal aggression and severe noncompliance.
2. Significant intolerance of unfamiliar situations, events and people are circumstances from which parents try to shield their autistic children in order to avoid anxiety and outright fear. This was true for over 55% of the families to whom we spoke.
3. Parents also seek to protect their children from embarrassing themselves because of their poor understanding of the rules of social behaviour.
4. A significant majority of parents (71%) accept the fact that their children with autism do not cope well with instructions and cannot understand the explanations from which their children without autism have benefited.
5. Most parents express sadness that their autistic children are unable to make known their feelings, needs and emotional state using conventional communication. Instead, the parents have learned to recognise the sometimes very faint cues of distress and try to prevent the emotional outburst to come.
6. Parents are aware that many of the children are hypersensitive to a wide variety of perfectly normal everyday stimuli such as bright lights, particular noises, crowds, particular people, and other commonplace regularly encountered events. Over 35% of the parents surveyed could list their child's idiosyncratic hypersensitivities.
7. Many parents acknowledge that their children show fears of specific objects, or of specific objects in particular locations, and know how to avoid these.
8. Parents learn to recognise the signs by which pain, discomfort, hunger, thirst, needing the toilet, etc., are made clear by their children with autism, and they react accordingly.
9. Parents try hard to shield their children with autism from tasks that are too complex and stressful. Many of them try to ensure that teachers and other school staff are aware of how their children respond to apparently excessive pressures. Unfortunately, they often find that the response at school is inconsistent.

Wing goes on to describe some general rules for coping with inappropriate behaviour which can be applied when the reasons for the behaviour are understood. She suggests several rules that are particularly
appropriate for the individual with autism, and it is noteworthy that
many of the parents interviewed by us have been able, largely without
professional help, to develop similar rules for themselves. They include
the following.

1. Trying to preserve 'sameness' in the child's daily routine and domestic environment. They appreciate that one of the main problems which
   autism imposes on individuals in an inability to make sense of the
   everyday world that most people inhabit more or less competently and
   without fear. They understand that in order for their children with
   autism to 'cope', they as parents must try to reduce significant fluctuations in daily life. Whereas over 35% knew this should be done, only
   25% of those realised that this was a double-edged sword. They recognised that such endeavours now merely made it more difficult for their
   children to cope with unpreventable changes later. As one mother
   stated, 'I fought hard to get one-to-one support at school for my daughter from the same aide. I didn't realise just how dependent this made
   her—the problem is far worse now.'
2. Parents are aware that it is not possible to keep routines and environment exactly the same day after day, and they understand that the
   needs of their other children without autism must sometimes take
   precedence. Accordingly, they understand that necessary changes in
   routines need to be ushered in gently. In cases where their children
   have good understanding or verbal communication most parents have
   developed strategies for quietly and precisely stating what changes
   will occur and when, and for how long they will last. They do this gradually and repetitively whenever circumstances allow. Many parents
   also understand that they cannot rely on one form of communication
   alone. They try to make adaptations in order to convey a particular
   message to their child with autism. For example, one mother told us
   how she now not only gave precise descriptions about what would
   happen when the family went on holiday, but she also drew with her
   autistic son a whole series of pictures which depicted the likely events.
3. At times parents can go to inordinate lengths to ensure that their child
   with autism will not be subjected to stress by stimuli to which he or
   she is over-sensitive. For example, one father told us how he would
   drive his autistic son at least 50 miles away from their house, which
   was adjacent to an airfield, whenever there was an air display, because
   his son could not tolerate the noise of different types of aircraft to those
   he was used to.

4. Wing describes how regular physical exercise is alleged to diminish aggressive behaviour and stereotypes in people with autism. Many of the parents we spoke to were aware of this at their own level, and described how they frequently used physical exercise at particular times when their child seemed 'edgy' and they predicted the onset of a period of aggression or tantrums.
5. Finally, the parents of children with autism maintained greater vigilance with regard to minor health matters for their child with autism than they did for their other children because they were aware that even minor ailments frequently led to a heightened incidence of challenging behaviour.

Although parents have managed intuitively to develop these procedures for negating the antecedents of many aspects of challenging behaviour, they are frequently unaware of the basic rules that govern appropriate strategies for behaviour change. Wing (1996) has listed a further six rules that are based on theories of learning. These are inconsistently understood by parents unless they receive adequate parent management training.

1. Wing describes the basic rules of reinforcement and the use of rewards to strengthen desirable behaviour. She comments that it is often difficult for children with autism to know what is rewarding for them. The parents of children with autism are acutely aware of this difficulty, and many try for too long to use the kinds of reinforcers that benefit their children without autism. They respond well to brief instruction about the assessment of potential reinforcers.
2. Parents appear to be aware of the manipulation of antecedents by preventing the occurrence of events or circumstances which they know are likely to spark off inappropriate behaviour. Unfortunately, they experience difficulty in convincing other people, particularly members of the extended family, that it is better to avoid such behaviour rather than punish it or deal with it in some other way when it occurs. This seems to have a specific intergenerational characteristic in that several parents reported that their own parents had difficulty in accepting this avoidance strategy. One father told us 'my mother refused to accept the need to avoid confrontation. She made our lives miserable by demanding that we allowed Kirsty to "try to do it right so that she could learn what happens when she does it wrong".'
3. The problem of extended family mentioned above also leads to difficulties with regard to Wing's third rule that inappropriate behaviour should not be rewarded. Although parents often sense that they can inadvertently strengthen unwanted behaviour by simply attend-

ing to it in a particular way, they frequently experience grave difficulties in, for example, dissuading grandparents from doing just that. They often find themselves unable to prevent others or indeed themselves from reinforcing unwanted behaviour. As one mother told us, 'How can I not attend to him, when for the tenth time that day he tries to run out of the house and on to the road? What am I supposed to do—let him get run down? He couldn't manipulate one anymore then, could he?' This parent was understandably annoyed at times when told by a community nurse to ignore behaviour which was clearly designed to gain her attention.

4. Most parents do not develop for themselves the concept of response competition, and they tend to do so only after appropriate training. Consequently, most of them remain unaware that it is often better to try to replace a challenging behaviour with an adaptive one, rather than continually confront the challenging behaviour in the hope that it will eventually go away. This leads to daily confrontations and loss of tempers, and equally importantly it creates the impression of failing, which further damages the parents' self-esteem.

5. Wing talks of timing being crucial in order for the response to challenging behaviour to make clear that the behaviour is unwanted. Generally speaking, immediate reinforcement or sanctions are necessary to help the child with autism to understand that the response is being made to the particular behaviour that is being targeted. Many parents find this extremely difficult to achieve, and indeed sometimes it is not practicable. Nevertheless, many of the parents whom we interviewed continued to practise deferment of rewards or sanctions much as they were able to do with their children without autism. They believed that the poor response to this reflected an inability to learn, rather than a failure of an inappropriate strategy.

6. Related to the issue of timing is that of inconsistency. Often because parents hope for results too quickly in relation to challenging behaviour they switch from one strategy to another, allowing insufficient time for any of them to work. This inconsistency then combines with inconsistent behaviour from relevant others, such as extended family members, to create an inappropriate learning situation for the child with autism.

PARENTS' STRATEGIES FOR TACKLING COMMON PROBLEMS OF CHALLENGING BEHAVIOUR

The following strategies and case studies relate to specific problems of challenging behaviour which were frequently identified by the parents in our survey. The order in which these problems are presented reflects the frequency with which they have been identified by parents. In a sense this represents an order of priority, although it is quite clear that any one of these types of challenging behaviour can be exceptionally serious.

Sleep Problems

The most common cause of anxiety that parents reported, and at the highest level of severity, concerned the poor sleep patterns of many of their children with autism. Although these children did not appear to suffer greatly as a consequence of having too little sleep, the psychological and physical health of their parents was threatened by their poor sleep patterns. Many parents reported that many of the stresses they experienced, including marital conflict, were associated with lack of sleep caused by the waking habits of their child with autism. Most of the parents who had experienced this difficulty reported that the frustration and stress caused by being woken night after night had led them to punish their children, in some cases quite severely. Two of the parents we spoke to reported that, when in desperation they had spoken to their health visitors about their response to this sleep disorder, they had been reported to their Local Authority Social Services Departments and investigated by the local child protection teams.

Medication was frequently used by some parents when they could persuade their general practitioners to give them an appropriate prescription. Many more would have liked medication but were refused it. One parent shamefacedly confessed to giving her autistic son her own sleeping pills on three occasions so that she and her partner could get some sleep.

Those parents who claimed positive effects from using medication felt that it was useful for helping their child to fall asleep more quickly and in enabling them to stay asleep for longer periods. Other parents felt that the medication they were given was of little value, either because the dosage recommended was too low or because it simply seemed to make their children more alert and active.

Our survey revealed that many parents, with or without guidance from professionals, were able to utilise a wide range of ingenious strategies to help to resolve the problem.

Where the main problem had been that their child was unable to go to sleep at an appropriate time, a common strategy had been to create an environment that naturally relaxed the child and made him or her want to pay attention to pleasant stimulation until such time as sleep arrived.

We found that simply playing the Aladdin video with the sound right down kept Sam in bed watching contentedly until he nodded off. Sometimes we were able to read to him as well, and that felt wonderfully normal.

Some children are unable to go to sleep at approximately the right time simply because they will not remain in their own bed. Several parents have told us that they have actually tried to practise restraint by using sheets or dressing-gown cords to 'strap down' their children in the bed. These methods were always unsuccessful and led to a great deal of insecurity on the part of the child, as well as feelings of guilt on the part of the parents. One reasonably successful strategy depended on the use of an activity reward for remaining in bed:

Janey would spend all her days playing with a snowman globe, tipping it up and down and watching the snow fall. She could peer intently at it until all the snow had fallen and then tip it up again. We had stopped her having this during the day because it was too distracting, but it worked well at night to reward her for staying in bed. Most nights, unless she is poorly, she just quietly drops off to sleep watching the snow. It relaxes all of us.

Many parents whose children wandered around the house at night rather than remaining in bed found that increasing their pattern of exercise did much to reduce this difficulty. 'Buying Simon an exercise bike was the best thing we ever did. Five miles at top speed is all he needs to help him relax enough to go to bed properly.'

Some parents told us that they had felt that their children's inability to remain in bed was due to insecurity about being left on their own. Sadly, too many of these parents had received either no advice at all or bad advice, and had ended up taking the child into their own beds, creating a habit that was far more difficult to break, with more serious consequences to the parents' own relationship than had been caused by the original wandering habit. Some parents found that they could help their child to master this insecurity by simply remaining in the vicinity while they went off to sleep.

CASE STUDY 7.1

For two years Sam would sleep only if he was in our bed, we dreaded every night from the age of three onwards. It wasn't that he wouldn't go to bed, it was just that he would not stay in it

The psychologist helped us design a simple strategy for getting over this problem. First of all one of us would lie down on his bed with him; we played with him until he fell asleep. Next we sat on the bed and played with him, and then one sat on a chair beside his bed. As he got used to each little change, so we introduced another one. Eventually the chair was moved pro-

gressively further from the bed until it was just in his bedroom doorway. Finally we were able to stand just inside the room until he had gone to sleep.

A smaller number of parents felt that their primary problem was that their child woke periodically during the night and left the bed to disturb the household and possibly even leave the house. These parents claimed that their child might not be fully awake during these venturesome occasions, and they had experienced terror that their children would experience some calamity as a result. The response of many parents was to create partial barriers, and we note that Schopler (1995) in his *Parent Survival Manual* provides anecdotes of a similar nature (pp. 150–151). The parents he describes showed awareness of the need for a child to be able to leave his or her bedroom if it was really necessary, but the partial barricade might be sufficient simply to make the child return to bed rather than breach it when he or she was only half awake. The following case study describes a similar plan.

We found that Mike (aged 4) would not move far from his bed if we laid an old quilt on the floor by it. He didn't like the squashy sensation of walking on it when he was half asleep. That meant he stayed close to his bed until the baby alarm alerted us and we got to him. We found that provided he didn't move around too much he didn't really wake up and we could put him back to sleep fairly quickly.

In general terms, the majority of sleep disorders that we have encountered in children with autism are very similar to those presented by other children of up to about 8 years of age. These are often the product of inappropriate bedtime routines on the part of parents. For whatever reason, the fact of their child's autism and the constellation of behavioural symptoms that this presents to parents causes them to adopt inappropriate routines and 'so create a rod for their own backs'.

Self-Injury

Many parents reported their distress at having to watch their child deliberately injure him- or herself. Even when they suspected that this was a manipulative form of attention-seeking they still found themselves unable to quell their anxiety. Hand-biting, eye-poking, head-banging and ear-slapping are among the most common of the self-injurious behaviours reported, and they are normally shown by children with the most severe form of the disorder.

Many explanations exist for this type of behaviour, the most common one being that the self-injuring children are simply attention-seeking.

They have learned that this behaviour, painful as it may be, brings large rewards in terms of adult attention. Another explanation is that the children have learned that causing themselves pain leads to a sense of well-being. This situation may arise because the behaviour produces a response at the biochemical level whereby naturally occurring opiates rather like morphine are released into the bloodstream, and this leads to an increased sense of well-being.

A third hypothesis is that self-injuring children are showing that they are bored and need stimulation. It is certainly the clinical experience of the first author that distracting a self-injuring child with an interesting activity can reduce the frequency and severity of self-injury. It is also noticeable that the most severe and frequent self-injurious behaviour is found in those children who have little or no means of communication. This implies that it is a form of communication, and that parents and psychologists must be careful to try to interpret the message that the child is attempting to communicate. Once this has been done, it is often possible to alter the antecedents that give rise to the self-injurious behaviour, such that the child no longer needs to communicate in this way. Typically the antecedents concern some break in or disruption of a ritual that the child with autism enjoys or depends upon for his or her security.

CASE STUDY 7.2

We took a long time to discover that Matt began to bite his forearm about 5 minutes after we turned off the TV or radio. Even though other things were happening and we weren't exactly ignoring him he still liked the background noise.

His biting got really bad and on one occasion he needed four quick stitches at the Health Centre. We were both distraught about it because we had been told by the school that children with autism only hurt themselves when they were bored. That made us bad parents! We didn't stop to think that he did it at school as well.

It was a trainee psychologist who came up with the idea about the radio. She made us look hard at what happened just before he started biting. We wrote down everything we did before and after; there were a couple of consistent things more or less every time. One of them was turning off the radio or TV.

Now Matt has got his own radio and he turns it on and off whenever he likes. We find that control has been very good for him. He doesn't bite himself hardly at all and he seems far more relaxed.

Another approach that frequently works when the manipulation of antecedents has not done so is to provide the child with a more adaptive behaviour instead of the self-injury. For children with little or no communication, the use of behavioural techniques such as shaping to provide a simple signing system for indicating their needs provides them with a more adaptive and acceptable response.

Jimmy started Makaton signing when he was five. We were very dubious at first because we were still hoping for normal talking. We soon noticed that the signs meant he could get through to us quicker. In no time he learned 'drink', 'eat' and some others. The more signs we all learned the less he punched his head.

In the past, this distressing behaviour has given rise to some very dubious treatments which merely suppressed the behaviour instead of resolving it. Even now it may be necessary to use arm splints to prevent a child from biting his or her wrists so badly that blood vessels are severed, and many children have to wear plastic helmets to prevent them from damaging their heads or ears as a result of chronic head-banging. Such measures are reasonably acceptable in the short term, but they are completely unacceptable if they are all that the self-injuring child receives by way of intervention. Such protective devices do not resolve the problem, and at one level they may simply remove from the child a form of communication which was at least reliable for gaining people's attention. These protective devices should only be used as part of a functional analysis of the meaning of the self-injurious behaviour and a satisfactory therapeutic response to it.

Self-biting

This is the form of self-injurious behaviour that parents report causes them greatest distress. Analysis of most of the situations in which they report this behaviour indicates that the child or young person feels under some pressure because he or she is no longer in a routine, or because there has been a change in the child's handling characteristics.

Sally bit herself everywhere she could, even her shoulders. The behaviour was really bad when she went to the speech therapist at the health centre. There was a new one who didn't know Sally and who clearly didn't understand autism. She put a lot of pressure on Sally by trying to treat her like a child who 'wouldn't' rather than 'couldn't'.

Sometimes the only solution to self-biting is to use a protective device that stops the young person from injuring him- or herself. This also has the added benefit of preventing parents from being anxious that there will be serious injury. Schopler (1995) gives an excellent example in his *Parent*

Survival Manual (p. 96), which is very similar to a case with which the first author was involved. In both instances the mothers of the respective children became more relaxed following the use of a protective device, and the children in question realised that there was little point in pursuing this behaviour in order to obtain the distressed response from their mothers. However, as stated before, it is necessary to use some form of additional training to help the child to show adaptive behaviour when the device is removed.

Although the majority of children who self-injure by biting themselves are severely or profoundly affected by autism and/or learning difficulties, some higher functioning children may also exhibit self-biting when they are unable to communicate their needs.

CASE STUDY 7.3

Callum was diagnosed with Asperger syndrome when he was 8; before that he was treated as a child with minimal autism.

He had many behaviours for getting our attention, including biting the backs of his hands. He went through about 10 months of having badly marked hands because of this. We found out that it was simple frustration. If he couldn't talk to us about what he wanted to talk about, then he would do it to wind us up.

CASE STUDY 7.4

Donald was a 10-year-old boy with autism and little communication, but good cognitive skills, who was educated in a mainstream school only 100 yards from his house. He seemed to be happy with his educational and domestic arrangements, and his parents were both very distressed when he began a pattern of wrist chewing that took him to the casualty department of the local hospital on two occasions for stitches. The more the parents became distressed with this behaviour the more it was perpetuated, and at first an assumption was made that it was a behaviour reinforced or initiated by parental distress. It was only when a neighbour's child told the parents that Donald was being bullied by three boys waiting for him just inside the school entrance that it became obvious that his wrist chewing was a response to being bullied. An arrangement was made with other children in his class to escort him beyond the school gates and the bullies were dealt with by a 'bully court' (Sharp and Smith, 1994). As soon as the bullying behaviour ceased the wrist chewing also ceased, and the next phase was to provide Donald with a simple phrase which he could use to communicate with his parents when future bullying occurred.

Head-banging

Many children with severe and profound learning difficulties bang their heads against both hard and soft objects. Often this is no more than a gentle tap, insufficient to raise as much as a small bruise, but quite enough to terrify parents. Under these circumstances it is generally an attention-seeking device and it is reinforced by the parents who, not unnaturally, pay attention to it. However, in cases where children are banging their heads against hard objects such as radiators, doors, table tops, windows and walls, there is a much more serious problem to be resolved. The antecedents and consequences of this behaviour must be carefully established and modified in the best way possible. A frequent antecedent is the presence of painful ear infection leading to the child head-banging or delivering punches to his or her ears. The most effective solution that the authors have discovered is to attempt to find a distracting behaviour such that the child is then encouraged to do something adaptive.

Jane punched her ear because she was in pain a lot of the time. She would come up to us and start ear punching until we gave her Calpol to ease the pain. We soon learned how to get her to bring us her special medicine spoon instead. We did this by physical prompting and fading, using gentle rubbing of her hands as a reward. We noticed that after she had her medicine she started to rub her own hands as well. This showed us that she was starting to feel better.

Sometimes attention-seeking children can get into a habit of severe head-banging in order to provoke a response from one or both parents. One family reported that their 8-year-old son, Paul, was of this type. Their solution to the problem was unusual but very effective.

Once Paul started to bang his head we would fetch his favourite Postman Pat video and prompt him to watch us putting it on top of a cupboard out of his reach. He stopped immediately.

On other occasions parents found that head-banging behaviour is a kind of barometer of their children's inner state. As has been mentioned previously, head-banging as a self-injurious behaviour can occur at times of stress, and when routines have been changed or new teachers have been assigned there is a greater likelihood that this type of behaviour will be manifested.

Claire took ages to adapt to anyone new. Supply teachers or new non-teaching assistants caused her to bang her head hard for up to 2 weeks. We found that we could reduce this by repeating favourite activities associated with the absent teacher or aide.

Eye-poking

Eye-poking does not appear to be a behaviour that is used for attention-seeking purposes or indeed to communicate some unmet need. Instead, it appears to be related to a need for stimulation caused by pain. Parents report that when their children engage in this behaviour it is generally with their eyes closed, and they poke or bang against the eyelid. Those children who poke or push at their open eyes cause much greater distress. Favell *et al.* (1982) reported on a 22-year-old profoundly handicapped man with limited vision. Apparently he would frequently press a finger against his open eye. Staff had tried to intervene by physically removing his finger from his eye, and by giving the man many activities to engage in. Despite these responses the eye-poking continued. However, the researchers reported that when bright, colourful and visually dramatic toys such as prisms, mirrors and shiny toys were given to him, his eye-poking decreased. He was also given special instructions to help him to play appropriately with these toys.

This case is reminiscent of one known to the authors which involved a 15-year-old blind, autistic boy named Sam.

CASE STUDY 7.5

Sam had been blind from birth and was diagnosed as autistic. He was wonderfully active in the surroundings of his residential school and its grounds. Visitors to the school were amazed at his ability to find his way round the huge rambling building with complete confidence and virtually no collisions. His sureness was attributed to echolocation; he could be heard making clicking noises whenever he moved around.

His social contacts were extremely affected by autistic behaviours, and staff were only able to get his attention through the use of physical prompts. These had to be very gentle and well signalled by verbal warning and stroking, which he enjoyed.

However, his foster carer during the school holidays was less enthusiastic about him. She reported that he spent several hours each day poking both eyes and making wailing noises. She found the eye-poking very worrying because he did it vigorously and hurt himself. When she tried to restrain him he became even more distressed and started biting his wrists as well.

On investigation it was discovered that the foster carer had suppressed his 'weird clicking noise' because it irritated her. No one had explained that this was vital for his mobility and that she was effectively robbing him of a further sensory information channel. He poked his eyes as a means of distracting himself from the cause of his distress. This stopped as soon as she allowed him to echolocate.

These two case-work examples revealed successful strategies arising from the manipulation of antecedents. In the first example given by Favell *et al.* (1982), practitioners made use of heightened sensory stimulation to distract the client from serious self-harm. Another novel approach also heightened sensory stimulation by applying a vibrator to an eye-poking child's hand (Wells and Smith, 1983). The vibrating sensation was sufficient to distract the child and provide a competing response.

The second example shows how a child's distress was eased by simply restoring his capacity to gain stimulation and so reducing his distress from non-stimulation.

Temper Tantrums/Aggression

Most of the parents in our survey felt that the aggression directed towards others by their children with autism during temper tantrums was a product of their frustrated attempts at communication. However, prolonged bouts of screaming, punctuated by kicking, hitting, biting, spitting and pushing other people, create severe family pressures. These behaviours are common among children with autism, and frequently follow a pattern from some kind of frustration, perhaps in communication or denial of a want, progressing through a series of escalating difficult behaviours to full-blown aggression.

Many parents had tried a variety of punishers, mostly without success. Smacking and shouting at children remain the two most common forms of punishment in the UK, but most parents had either never used such methods or very quickly found that they were ineffective. It is likely that the main reason for these standard but undesirable punishments being ineffective is that they do not teach the child with autism anything new. There is simply no point, as most of the parents rapidly found out, in subjecting a child to such unpleasant events unless they are capable of substituting the undesirable behaviour with adaptive behaviour.

Included among inappropriate or unsuccessful punishers is the use of the phrase 'No, don't do that' spoken in a loud and irate voice. Many parents claim that this does little to stop the behaviour, and that it may frequently send the child off into fresh paroxysms of rage.

Parents have found a number of strategies that can be effective. Of these, the most commonly employed is that of distraction, i.e. simply pointing out something to the child that they have not seen, or even making some kind of unusual response such as clapping the hands, singing loudly or simply pointing out of the window and saying 'Look at that' enthusiastically. In cases where it is impossible to adopt such strategies because of the location of the behaviour (e.g. the supermarket) parents find that the only successful action is simply to withdraw their child.

Once the immediate angry tantrum is over it is then desirable to think carefully about what happened before the child developed it. Very often this reflective analysis pinpoints particular antecedents in the form of poor communication skills specifically related to some activity, event or circumstance. Then it is often effective to teach the child some form of communication which they may use to signify their future need should those circumstances arise again. Whatever the form of communication that is decided upon, it should then become a competing response for the tantrum behaviour under the same circumstances.

Brendon used temper tantrums to tell us that he wanted to watch his favourite videos. For some reason, he came to believe that we would stop him and this made him angry. Perhaps because we gave into him he kept on communicating in this way. The speech therapist taught him and us the sign for TV and we rewarded him for using this by letting him have Postman Pat. His tantrums disappeared and we noticed that he became much more receptive to learning other signs.

Stereotypic Behaviour

These behaviours appear to be self-stimulatory because they seem to have little function other than to bring about heightened states of arousal. Parents report that they find them distressing because they are so obviously bizarre and mark out their child in public places as demonstrably different. There are many different forms of these behaviours, but the most common ones reported by parents in our survey include spinning objects (e.g. the wheels on toy vehicles), observing spinning or twirling objects (e.g. cloths tumbling in a front-loading washing machine) and sensory-motor activities such as face-fanning, finger-flicking and hand-flapping. Some parents report that their children incessantly lick their hands or particular objects, many of them then smearing the saliva onto their face or nose.

Some researchers argue that this type of behaviour occurs when children do not know how to use objects appropriately and therefore gain little if any stimulation from them. Under such circumstances licking one's hands may provide a reinforcing level of stimulation which the child might not otherwise experience.

A wide range of methods have been employed to stop such behaviour, including a severely punishing behaviour called over-correction (Foxx and Azrin, 1973). The first author has had much experience of this and has argued with colleagues against its use because it is demeaning to the child involved. For example, one child who constantly fanned his face was physically guided into fanning his own face and the faces of five other people in the classroom as soon as his spontaneous face-fanning began. It is clearly a severe punisher in which children are physically overwhelmed by an adult and forced to do something which makes their handicapping behaviour all the more obvious. Nevertheless, there is considerable research evidence that this form of over-correction is effective in suppressing stereotypic self-stimulatory behaviour.

Another technique that is used, which is similar to that employed for self-injurious behaviour, is known as sensory extinction, and simply deprives the child of the reinforcing sensation that the stereotypic behaviour provided (Aiken and Salzberg, 1984). Schopler's *Parent Survival Manual* gives an example (Schopler, 1995, p. 32) in which a young girl who constantly licked her hands was made to wear plastic gloves. She did not lick her hands when the plastic gloves were on and, furthermore, the plastic left a residue on her skin after the gloves had been removed. She found this unpleasant and the taste prevented her from licking her hands for considerably longer afterwards. The same process of sensory extinction is evident in the following case study.

CASE STUDY 7.6

When she was about 10 years old Sarah went through a phase of fanning her face with her left hand. This happened when she wasn't doing anything. If we tried to restrain her gently she brought up her right hand and punched her ear with it.

The psychologist encouraged us to try various tactics, but the one that was most successful involved simply placing a cot blanket over her left arm; that seemed to act as a restraint even though it was very light.

We were worried that she would return to face-fanning as soon as we phased out the use of the blanket, but the psychologist persuaded us to try anyway. Sarah did develop an attachment to her blanket, but eventually she only used it when she was watching the TV or listening to music. Finally, she seemed to forget all about fanning her face and only punched her ear when she was upset or 'in pain'.

Some stereotypic behaviours can be rapidly converted into a functional benefit for the child. For example, a 7-year-old girl with autism who repeatedly and obsessively poured water from one jug to another was allowed to pour water in this way only if she co-operated with her schoolwork on communication.

The last case study shows how stereotypic behaviour that is reinforcing to a child with autism can be used as a major activity reward to secure adaptive skills. Other colleagues have made use of children's predilection to twirl and spin bright objects, watch front-loading washing machines in operation, and engage in heel-and-toe rocking in order to reward a wide variety of desirable behaviours.

Overactivity

This behaviour is commonly found among children with developmental disorders, and the parents who responded to our survey felt that it was of moderate significance. Very few of them had failed to find satisfactory responses to their children's overactivity, and some of the solutions were ingenious. In general, however, the best solution seemed to be to provide times during which the children could be extremely energetic. Many parents had established daily exercise routines which took place before and after school. Most of the children had grown out of their excessively overactive stage by the age of 8 or 9 years, but many of them continued with their daily exercise routine. The parents observed that not only is their undesirable overactivity reduced after exercise but also their distractibility is diminished such that they seem to be more capable of attending to family life, their schoolwork and their social environment in general. One mother explained that a 2-mile run on the jogging machine before breakfast each morning made more difference to her son than the medication he had been taking for overactivity prior to starting this exercise.

CASE STUDY 7.7

Rachael was horribly overactive; we couldn't take her anywhere if it meant going into a building. She caused damage in shops and once made a dash for the altar in our local church. The damage she kept doing to our home has cost us thousands.

Then we discovered by accident that swimming calmed her down. It happened when she had some sessions in the school's hydrotherapy pool which is used sometimes as a starter pool for beginning swimmers. The warmth and the flotation effect definitely calmed her down. Her teacher suggested that we try getting her to go for a swim after school every day. This was no problem for us, as her dad goes nearly every day anyway with Sarah's brother, Paul. Her sister or I go as well to make sure she is alright in the changing room. It works well and she looks forward to it. Her activity level has dropped a lot and we can certainly take her out more now. Some days she doesn't want to go, but fortunately her activity level doesn't really change much.

Some parents explained that they had gone so far as to get a dual diagnosis. Their children were described as being autistic with attention deficit hyperactivity disorder. Although it is not generally satisfactory to apply such a plethora of labels to a child, it did enable these parents to access methylphenidate, a stimulant drug that is frequently used for the control of overactivity. Of the parents of the four children who were on this medication, the parents of three children believed that the drug had been a success, while the parent in the fourth case took her child off the drug because of unwanted side-effects and because she was unhappy about using medication in this way.

It was noticeable that the problem of overactivity seems to be present up to middle adolescence but not thereafter. Even so, a daily exercise routine can be most beneficial. Some studies have demonstrated that adequate physical exercise decreases self-stimulatory behaviour, increases attention control and is associated with more appropriate play and academic responsiveness (Watters and Watters, 1980). In addition, other studies have shown that exercise can act to reduce stereotypic and other repetitive behaviours such as hand-flapping, but only when the exercise is vigorous and continuous (over a period of 15 minutes) (Kern et al., 1984).

Destruction of Property

This particular form of challenging behaviour is the sixth most frequently alluded to by parents in our survey. Functional analysis of antecedents and consequences revealed that in almost every case the destruction taking place was not a form of vandalism which was reinforcing in its own right. Instead, the behaviour was either a form of aggression, in which case the strategies described for aggression are appropriate, or else it was a simple response to objects of attraction. Unfortunately for parents, the objects of attraction may be their precious mementoes, which are played with and destroyed, or objects such as a piece of loose carpet which can be pulled at until the threads break away. This type of behaviour accounts for the repeated tearing of wallpaper and shredding of clothes shown by many learning disabled children with autism. The first author remembers clearly one 15-year-old boy with severe learning difficulties and autism who was seen to have a small piece of thread dangling from the side of his mouth. A member of staff went to remove this, and gradually pulled on it. Eventually 16 metres of thread from the hostel curtains had to be removed from the boy.

Since the objects which get destroyed are often objects of amusement, and their use and destruction provide positive reinforcement, the logical way to deal with such behaviour is to keep these object away from the child. Many parents report that this leaves their house looking less than homely because only those objects which cannot be destroyed are left within arm's reach of the child. One parent described their home as 'Alcatraz' and showed the first author ingenious locks that he had made to prevent his child from getting into cupboards, the refrigerator, the airing cupboard and the bathroom.

Those conducting the survey have had interesting dialogues with many parents of children with autism on the Internet. None of them appears to have found effective ways to stop this aimless and non-malevolent destruction other than removal of objects. However, many have found that once the behaviour has stopped because there is no longer anything left for the child to destroy, then it has become possible for them to teach more adaptive behaviours, including the use of toys. Some parents report that once this phase has been reached they are gradually able to bring out objects that would previously have been destroyed. One parent told the first author that 'As long as I brought out one item at a time and let him (the child with autism) get used to it for 2 weeks or so, it was then as if he regarded it as immovable and untouchable. I could then bring out another object. In that way I managed to get my sitting-room looking like it was part of a real home after about 4 months.'

Some destruction is related to specific types of objects. Many parents told us that the only objects that their children destroyed were those that the children made use of in some other type of play. For example, one 6-year-old boy with autism and severe learning difficulties loved to jump from a height of about 3 to 4 feet on to the floor. His mother's dining-room table provided an ideal take-off point and despite her most serious threats and rather inconsistent punishment, he managed to reduce the table to matchsticks over a 3-month period. A 7-year-old girl with autism who learned how to throw was so delighted with this new skill that she chose the family's pictures as targets and aimed apples, marbles, snooker balls and other hard objects at these pictures. Not only did she smash them in an orgy of destruction that lasted for 2 days, but also her missed shots left large dents in the plasterwork. It was only when the authors suggested that the parents should set up a bright and attractive target in the back garden for her to use that she stopped this type of destruction.

The parents in our survey identified that this destructiveness, as a form of challenging behaviour, is invariably also associated with temper tantrum-like behaviour. In addition, much of the destructiveness that parents report is associated with low levels of development and severe intellectual impairment. The parents feel that their children do not know how to entertain themselves and that the destructiveness they display is little more than an attempt to find satisfying outcomes for simple behaviours. As previously described, many parents have responded to these behaviours by keeping rooms as free from ornaments and bric-à-brac as possible, and also by having wall coverings that are easily emulsioned over, and sticking down pieces of peeling wallpaper as soon as they are noticed. Such measures reduce the opportunity for destruction and so represent a valid manipulation of antecedents. Careful preventative work of this type is considered by many parents to help their children to engage in less destructive behaviour as they gradually learn more adaptive play skills.

Some parents discovered that a successful strategy for preventing destruction of treasured objects and the general fabric of the house is to provide their children with material that can be shredded or otherwise destroyed. One mother reported that she kept old magazines (not newspaper, which left print stains) and paper bags available for her 5-year-old boy to shred as a reward for adaptive behaviour. She had been criticised by her neighbours for doing this, because they felt that this was merely rewarding his tearing behaviour rather than replacing it. However, she did report that over a period of time the child became bored with simple shredding and began to lose interest not only in that but also in the destructive shredding that he had engaged in previously. Where the behaviour of destructiveness is associated with annoyance and frustration, then the comments made above in relation to aggression are apposite. Many children are destructive because they become frustrated by their inability to communicate, and parents, with or without professional guidance, have developed strategies for improving want-related communication skills.

Fears

Learning to be afraid of things that can be harmful is an essential part of child development. First of all the child must learn to be afraid, and then must learn to confine his or her fears to those objects or events that are truly dangerous. This is a complex process, and many children with autism fail to work through it successfully. Consequently, many of these children are terrified of harmless objects and routine events. One small boy with autism became terrified by the sight of his potty, and this had a marked effect on his toilet-training for over a year.

Clearly part of the problem is the inability of children with autism to communicate adequately what it is that they are feeling. As a result it is difficult for adults to know how or why a particular fear may be worsening.

In addition, many children with autism are hypersensitive to various stimuli, including loud noises, bright lights and particular smells. They apparently find these stimuli completely noxious and require professional help involving a psychological process of desensitisation in order to overcome their anxiety.

8

EDUCATIONAL AND OTHER STRATEGIES

Over 90% of the parents surveyed by us claimed that the worst problems and anxieties they faced during the early years after diagnosis concerned educational provision. Many felt that they were not listened to, and that the education authorities simply wanted to provide the cheapest option. Even when the parents were generally satisfied with the provision given, they still worried whether it met the exact needs of their child. In addition, another group of parents who had received a diagnosis from relevant centres were told that only a special school for children with autism would satisfy the needs of their children. This placed many parents in immediate conflict with education authorities who either could not or would not make such provision.

In this chapter we shall examine the problems that confront parents in choosing educational provision and process. Included in this examination is a review of mainstreaming children with autism, which is a necessary consideration given the number of such children who are placed in mainstream schools. Although there are good reasons for this movement, there are also difficulties of which many parents and educational personnel are unaware when such placements are made.

In the next part of the chapter, we shall examine those educational and other strategies that parents indicate as being optimal in helping their children to develop as successfully as possible. Finally, we shall consider the questions that parents need to ask before they commit their child and themselves to particular programmes that are claimed to be successful. It is vital that parents are aware of these, given that there is more variation among the methods alleged to suit children with autism than among those designed to develop the potential of non-disabled children, and that many of them have received little or no independent validation.

Educational Provision

The conventional wisdom of special educational philosophy is to experience the benefits of early education in an appropriate setting. Often this
means that children with special needs will enter the educational systems
earlier and for longer each week than their non-disabled peers. It is not
surprising that several parents have told us wistfully that they felt their
children were taken from them and shared with professionals too soon,
'almost before I had got to know him'.

Given that the emotional wrench may occur at any early age, parents
need to feel certain that they are acting in their child's best interests. Sometimes the choices they have to make are complicated and, as we have seen,
the information provided is of minimal value. Other family members may
put pressure on parents to deny the existence of the disability or to follow
some path that is viewed favourably by others who are powerful in the
family but who do not have parental responsibility.

Preschool opportunities

The number of playgroups and nursery schools that are prepared to take
children with autism is now high. This allows parents to consider placing
their child alongside those who are developing normally. This can be
beneficial in cases where children with autism are capable of learning
some skills through imitation. Even if they do not mix or show the parallel and social play of their non-disabled peers, they may still acquire
some appropriate social behaviour and the acceptance of their peers. This
can have far-reaching effects, particularly on dysfunctional behaviour at
home. As one mother told us, 'he changed completely after about a month
in the nursery unit; he became willing to let us play with him and make
a fuss of him instead of pushing us away and looking through us'.

Parents are often not warned that their child with autism may show
greater than normal distress at the start of nursery or playgroup placement. The social deficits at the core of autism make it difficult for the children to come to terms with the new environment, and their confusion is
often expressed in withdrawal and/or aggression. Many of the parents
who spoke to us had found that much of the distress that this causes to
the children themselves, their parents and the staff could be avoided
simply by phasing in gradually the number of people with whom the children have to cope. The children learn to work with one member of staff
first, and are then gradually familiarised with more staff before being
expected to become accustomed to other children. Often this means that
the first sessions are of reduced length, and that a parent is present to aid
this settling-in process.

Parents have had pressure put on them to have their children 'conform' to the typical school day, on the grounds that most children miss their parents initially but settle rapidly. This view reflects a complete ignorance of autism and should be resisted.

Some parents are offered places in multidisciplinary hospital units, often referred to as Children's Centres or Child Development Centres. Others may be offered places in specialist nursery units attached to special or mainstream schools. The attractions of the specialist staff are considerable, and parents may feel that such a placement is preferable even though a normally developing peer group is not available. The decision on which type of placement to accept is often difficult to make, and helpful education officials will try to ease this quandary by securing a dual placement so that the child experiences the best of both worlds. This is most feasible when the specialist unit is attached to a mainstream school.

Primary and secondary education

The range of provision available to the children of the families we surveyed was very wide. The majority of these children (31%) were in special schools catering primarily for children with severe learning difficulties, and most of the parents were aware that the officers of the LEAs believed that the primary handicap of their children consisted of severe general learning difficulties.

The next most frequent provision (25%) was for attendance at a wide range of free-standing (i.e. unattached to another school) special schools and units for children with moderate learning difficulties, including special schools for pupils with emotional and behavioural difficulties. Parents with children in the latter types of school were very dissatisfied with the provision, not because of the quality of teaching or support, but because of the total incompatibility of the majority of the pupils with their autistic children.

Following closely behind (20% of the children of surveyed families) was provision with non-teaching support in mainstream schools. Not surprisingly, the children who were placed in these schools tended to be high functioning and with some degree of speech and language skill. Most of the parents of these children were full of praise for the efforts made by the staff, and felt that their children were better served than they might be even in specialist schools for children with autism. However, most had reservations about the lack of training that teaching and non-teaching staff had received with respect to autism, and were condemnatory of the LEAs' failure to provide such training. As one mother put it, 'We are sure it is the right thing to help him (her autistic son) at school, but we often feel guilty that he isn't getting the specialist help we were told he needs.' This child had received the diagnosis of autism from a well-known and much respected centre for the assessment of children with social and communication disorders, and the parents understood that their child would be disadvantaged if he did not receive help that was available from certain specialist schools. This presented a huge problem for these rural parents who did not want their child to have a residential place that was necessary in order to obtain a place in one of these schools. 'I am afraid we were quite relieved to have the decision made for us when the LEA turned down our request to send him to the specialist school; we weren't ready to lose him into a hostel. I just hope he doesn't pay for our choice later.'

Not all parents were pleased with the mainstream school provision. A small number felt that it was their preferred choice and that the LEA had supported it. However, the teaching staff concerned had made clear that they did not want the autistic children, and they maintained an attitude of 'professional negativity' throughout. One child was suspended from the village primary school because his autistic behaviour was deemed to be 'unacceptable'. His mother told us:

> It was obvious that the class teacher did not want James in his class. He kept saying that he believed in integration, but only when children with special needs could 'fit in' with the rest of the class. His complete lack of flexibility rubbed James up the wrong way and we had months of tempers, letters from the head and short exclusions. James has been fine since we started educating him at home.

Finally, a small proportion of children (12%) attended specialist schools catering exclusively for pupils with autism. In general the parents were satisfied with the provision and allowed their children to put up with long daily journeys to and from the school, or residential arrangements that effectively parted the child from his or her family.

Ironically, however, some of these parents expressed a variety of guilty concerns about these placements, which is the reverse of the situation experienced by those whose children were in mainstream school. They expressed fears that their children might not prosper because, despite the specialist teaching, they 'seldom have the opportunity to mingle with kids who are developing normally. Paul (the son of these parents) picks up lots of undesirable habits from the other autistic kids, so he could probably pick up better habits if he saw normal children more.' Even those parents who fully supported the placement at the specialist school were relieved whenever there were opportunities for interactions with mainstream lessons, or when children from mainstream schools had lessons at the specialist schools.

Some parents who were in communication with each other cast doubt on the specialist nature of these schools. They had become aware that there was no particular specialist response that was a constant in them.

'It all depends on which school your child goes to as to whether he gets this approach or that. Surely they can't all work equally as well, and why do schools change their approaches as if they feel something better has come along?' This perceptive parent made some very negative assessments about a school that practised a TEACCH approach: 'just some of the time during the day and something else at other times. If it (TEACCH) is any good, why not all the time?'

Other parents felt excluded from the school and unable to visit the classrooms on the grounds that their presence would distract the teaching process. This explanation was not altogether convincing to some parents, who knew of other children in similar schools where there was no such prohibition.

Some parents felt that the specialist schools failed to live up to their claims of specialist skills, and there were sources of great dissatisfaction that led to removal of children. The reasons for this included the imitation of severely autistic behaviours which impacted on the home environment and which the staff allegedly did little about, inappropriate power-assertive methods of behaviour control and the encouragement of adult dependency.

The Integration of Children with Autism

There are various gradations of 'mainstream' education for children with special educational needs, ranging from attendance at a special unit attached to a mainstream school, but with no particular contact with the normal peer group, to full inclusion within mainstream classes and the mainstream curriculum. The majority of children with autism who are in mainstream schools fall somewhere between the two extremes. The children of the families that we surveyed who were in mainstream schools tended to be part of a normal year group and to be withdrawn on a more or less regular basis for specific activities. The underpinning philosophy of mainstream education for children with special educational needs concerns inclusion, and the view taken is simply that children with such needs should have their schooling in the least restrictive environment possible, i.e. the one that is closest to whatever is regarded as normality. According to its advocates, the benefits of such a process are as follows: the opportunity to learn alongside children who have normal cognitive, social and personal functioning and so offer good models for imitation; the availability of teachers who have higher expectations of children than those who teach highly specialised populations of children in settings detached from the normal educational process; higher self-esteem arising from the lack of stigmatisation that is so often linked with education in a free-standing special school; and the securing of a place in the normal community in which the child lives.

As laudable and logical as these ideals appear to be, it has to be said that for the most part they represent an act of faith on the part of educationalists, and there have been few attempts to subject either the processes or the outcomes of inclusion to systematic investigation. It is hardly surprising, therefore, that one finds few attempts to identify systematically the benefits and outcomes of inclusion for children with autism. This section will review what evidence there is for justifying a mainstream approach with regard to special educational needs generally, and will then look more closely at a few studies which concern children with autism or related difficulties.

A number of studies have evaluated the impact of inclusion on pupils with a variety of special educational needs. This includes a study by Carlberg and Kavale (1980), who conducted a review of all of the studies then available that met their particular criteria. They examined a total of 50 studies spanning the period from 1932 to 1977 which involved pupils with general learning difficulties, learning disabilities and those with emotional and behaviour disorders. They examined effects in relation to academic achievement and social/personal factors. The outcome of this complex review was general support for mainstreaming by an extremely small margin. There were differences between the groups of students such that those who benefited most from mainstream schooling were those with what would now be described as moderate learning difficulties and those with specific learning difficulties. Pupils with behavioural and emotional problems performed poorly by comparison.

The next major study (Strain and Kerr, 1981) examined academic and personal/social effects in relation to children with moderate learning difficulties (educable mentally retarded children as defined in American Educational Guidance having IQs of between 50 and 75). Their meta-analysis revealed support for mainstream placements in favour of special schools, particularly where individualised programmes could also be taught. Their study of personal/social effects showed an interesting change in trend, in that between the 1950s and 1960s pupils who attended special classes received better social ratings from their peers and teachers than did those in mainstream classes. During the course of the 1970s this trend was reversed, with higher ratings being given to those children with moderate learning difficulties in mainstream classes who also reported feeling better about themselves than did their contemporaries in special classes. This is indicative of improved self-esteem associated with education in mainstream classes.

Differentiation between level of disability and type of educational process offered between mainstream and special classes came under increasing scrutiny in the 1980s. Thus Madden and Slavin (1983) demonstrated that there were differences in relation to academic and social development according to whether pupils were in special classes, mainstream classes with additional support or other forms of support. They concluded that mainstream classes with additional individualised teaching produced better results than any other process and location. These effects were noted for both educational and personal/social development, but were only true for pupils who had mild special educational needs. Pupils with more severe special educational needs showed markedly better results for both educational attainment and personal/social development when educated in special classes.

The authors of studies reported during the early to mid-1980s appeared to be preoccupied with the educational and personal/social development of pupils with mild cognitive impairments. This is hardly surprising, given that such children represent the greatest proportion with special educational needs that schools and local education authorities must address. Ottensbacher and Cooper (1984) examined over 100 studies that investigated social adjustment of pupils with moderate learning difficulties, and they identified 40 studies which actually made comparisons between different types of educational placement, used satisfactory measures of social adjustment and made statistical reports. On this occasion the overall effect was very slightly in favour of special classes. However, when a comparison was made between special classes and mainstream classes with individualised support, the effect was reversed and children in the latter educational context did very slightly better than their contemporaries in special classes. Of great interest to those concerned about the needs of parents and families in the context of complex special educational needs, the studies that were meta-analysed by Ottensbacher and Cooper (1984) showed that there was a difference of opinion between teachers and other adults. It appears that teachers favoured special classes for children with moderate learning difficulties, whereas parents and other non-teaching adults favoured the provision of individualised teaching within mainstream classes. This finding strikes a chord with a plethora of studies relating to moderate learning difficulties around the world, indicating that whereas teachers espouse the concept of integration of the population of children with moderate learning difficulties, they are less happy about integration when it is related to specific children appearing in mainstream schools and attempting to cope with undifferentiated curricula (Randall and Gibb, 1988).

An important meta-analysis published in the mid-1980s examined the effects of inclusion on a variety of different handicapping conditions (Wang and Baker, 1985/1986). The populations included were those with moderate learning difficulties, specific learning difficulties, hearing impairment and a group referred to as having 'mixed handicaps'. There was also a group that accounted for about 17% of the population study, who were described as having an unknown handicapping condition. The meta-analysis of these authors suggested that inclusion was beneficial with regard to educational attitude and peer group interaction. However, the effect size was not large, and there was considerable variation, some of which actually suggested completely opposite outcomes.

In general, therefore, the outcome of research into mainstream versus special classes leaves one with much to ponder over. The overall effect in terms of educational attainment, personal/social development and self-concept favours education in mainstream schools with individualised programmes. Parents and other adults who are not involved in the teaching process seem to favour these arrangements, but teachers are less certain. Not all children with special educational needs benefit from inclusion. In particular, those with severe learning difficulties or emotional/behavioural problems seem to do better in special classes.

None of the studies mentioned above appears to have included investigations of children with autism in mainstream schools. There are only a few such studies, and methodological weaknesses rule out many of them. Mesibov and Shea (1996) report on some reviews that have examined the effectiveness of integrated settings in relation to children with autism or 'autistic-like' conditions. One group (Hoyson et al., 1984; Strain et al., 1985) examined integration in relation to preschool and young primary children with 'autistic-like' presenting problems. In these studies the degree of generalisation occurring with regard to social behaviours was observed in segregated and integrated settings. Unfortunately, the data were not analysed statistically, but the conclusion was drawn that learned social interaction skills generalised more efficiently in integrated rather than in segregated settings. One of the studies (Hoyson et al., 1984) also reported that the integrated settings brought benefits in terms of pre-academic skills. Mesibov and Shea (1996) reported these conclusions, but commented adversely on the methodological weaknesses of the studies, the lack of proper definitions of terms used, and a failure to describe exactly which social behaviours were improved. In addition, Mesibov and Shea pointed out that the post-intervention assessments were not rated by assessors who were blind to the purposes of the study.

A rather more well-designed study (Harris et al., 1990) made use of pupils described as 'high-functioning' in terms of recorded intellectual ability to examine the effectiveness of integrated and segregated classes. The children were of preschool age, and the measure used to determine the effect, if any, of the educational intervention was a ratio of language

age to chronological age as recorded on the Preschool Language Scale. Whereas the studies reported a significant improvement for both autistic and non-disabled children over time, there was no significant difference between the segregated and integrated settings.

Mesibov and Shea (1996) also describe a study by Myles *et al.* (1993), who examined social interaction among preschool children with autism during the presence or absence of non-disabled, age-matched peers. This is an important study which enables direct examination of the frequently cited arguments by integrationalists that the presence of non-disabled peers, particularly with regard to language and communication skills, has an uplifting effect on children with special educational needs. What is being examined, therefore, is the effect of non-disabled children, and not the more global influence of mainstream classes.

In this study the children with autism attended a school for 4 days per week, while the non-disabled peers attended only twice a week. This enabled behavioural observations of a variety of social behaviours within the classrooms with regard to both teachers and pupils during each condition. The reported results indicated that there was less interaction between teachers and pupils with autism when their non-disabled peers were present. The teachers gave less praise, gave less instruction and made fewer neutral or 'conversational' comments, but they did provide marginally more assistance.

The children with autism were found to initiate a minimal number of interactions with either teachers or pupils during both conditions. It was concluded that children with autism need more than the simple physical presence of non-disabled peers around them. Such a presence does not represent an alternative to structured programmes, specialised teaching methods and other specialist strategies. The authors also suggested that social behaviour and the development of functional skills are independent aspects of education that may require different settings.

Limited as these studies are, they certainly provide no support for any strongly worded arguments concerning the necessity for integration of children with autism into mainstream classes. The little evidence that does exist suggests that pupils with autism are even less likely to benefit from inclusion than children with other forms of special educational needs.

Autism and Learning in Schools

As is the case for all children with special educational needs, the development of functional independence, or something as close to this as the pupil can achieve, is a high priority. A particular problem for such pupils is not the learning of individual skills, but the sequencing of them. They frequently need direct instruction in order to be able to 'bolt together' individual skills into a sequence of behaviour with a functional goal. For the most part, they begin to use sequences of skills independently when they learn to manage without the guidance of their teachers and learn to recognise appropriate environmental cues. These cues should 'tell them what to do' without their having to be organised by other people.

Not surprisingly, the design and organisation of learning environments which facilitate access for pupils with autism is a complex task and one that demands great structure. As may be seen, therefore, it is an act of faith merely to assume that a pupil with autism who is able to learn would necessarily be able to learn by imitation from the behaviour of other better adapted pupils what to do and when. Thus the integration of many children with autism into mainstream classrooms may actually lead to de-skilling, because these children are unable to do more than imitate specific, unintegrated skills.

Assumptions are often made when proposing this type of integration that the mainstream classroom is a well-ordered, structured and pre-dictable environment. Very few classrooms have these characteristics, nor for the most part do they need them. Provided that certain gross activities are completed (e.g. attainment targets), then it matters little whether children move between groups, do craft work in the morning instead of the afternoon, or have 5 minutes of break time. Children with autism find such inconsistencies in a routine incomprehensible and distressing. In order to help them to cope, teachers' aides are frequently appointed to reduce insecurity and ensure that the child with autism is kept content and available for learning. Unfortunately, by doing this the very goal of integration may become overwhelmed by an involuntary increase in dependence. It is not sufficient to say of these children that they are not presenting challenging behaviour and that they are learning alongside their mainstream peers. Unless it can be demonstrated that they continue to acquire functional skills, which they can properly sequence so that they can move forward as independently as possible, then the integrated place-ment has failed.

Mesibov and Shea (1996) argue against a familiar statement in support of mainstream schooling, namely that if the child with autism is to learn skills to help him or her independently in the community, then he or she should learn those skills in the community in which he or she should live. They state that many skills are learned at an entry stage below that which is typified by the environment in which those skills are ultimately to be used. They cite as an example the fact that a concert pianist does not prac-tise only by giving concerts in front of large audiences. Many skills are practised, drill fashion, in 'safe' environments before they are practised in the environment for which they are intended. Once individual skills have been mastered, then it is possible to contemplate teaching their use in combination and gradually moving the pupil towards the intended environment.

A further difficulty arises in the way in which mainstream schools with children who are autistic rapidly acquire an aura of expertise which is conferred on them by onlookers. The first author, who in previous employment directed a large psychological service, was always amazed to be told that a particular primary school had previous experience of autism, and therefore education officers felt that the staff should be able to cope with other pupils with autism. This naïve view exists because of the assumption that one child with autism is very much like another. As the parents in the survey have made clear, their children are highly individualistic, and what may work for one child in a mainstream school may be an anathema to another. In view of the diversity that exists among pupils with autism, it is impossible to conceptualise any single educational institution being able to cope with all needs, regardless of whether that institution is a special school or a mainstream school.

It is also the case that when educationalists posit a universal specific to meet the needs of all special children, then there is less motivation to develop specialist strategies. With particular reference to autism, such a move would be disastrous, as it is only through the development of such strategies that progress can be made. This is not to say that general approaches do not work for all pupils with autism, but it is the case that not all children will respond equally or even positively to general approaches. There is a danger, therefore, that the clarion call for mainstream education for children with autism will lead not only to the inappropriate inclusion of pupils for whom it is unsuitable, but also to a reduction in those specialist resources that are starved of pupils.

As may be seen, therefore, not only is there a lack of research evidence to support the integration of children with autism, but also an examination of what such children need in order to be able to acquire functional independence skills suggests that it is most unlikely that generic mainstream approaches will suffice.

'High-Functioning' Pupils

Many will refute these pessimistic conclusions by referring to the suitability for integrated settings of those children who are increasingly referred to as 'high-functioning', a group which is often considered to include those diagnosed with Asperger syndrome. There is some merit in considering this group separately, as it is now generally accepted that they have other needs and a different range of skills to children with more typical autism (Trillingsgaard and Sorensen, 1994). Although it is difficult to find a satisfactory operational definition of what criteria the term 'high-functioning autism' actually refers to, it would appear that intellectual status is at the heart of them. Thus Ramsey *et al.* (1985) suggest a Weschler Full Scale IQ of 80 or higher as a criterion, while others are content to accept much lower Full Scale IQs, e.g. 65 to 70 (Gillberg *et al.*, 1991), or Weschler Performance Scale IQs above 70 (Lord and Venter, 1992). For many researchers, IQ is not a sole criterion, and some studies refer to better communication skills and potential for mastery with regard to basic social routines in everyday life (e.g. Tsai, 1992).

The study by Trillingsgaard and Sorensen (1994) presented a qualitative description of the experiences of a number of parents and teachers with regard to the integration of high-functioning children with autism into mainstream settings. Although this is only a small study (involving eight sets of parents, teachers and children whose experiences were investigated by means of a semi-structured questionnaire), the outcomes are important and can be compared with the experiences of the parents whom we surveyed. The paper gives a detailed description of the styles, processes and curriculum supports of the integrated settings that were investigated, and provides many insights into the impact of integration upon the children, their parents and their teachers. Essentially, the respondents were convinced that integration was 'the right thing' for each child, with the exception of one who was later moved into a specialised setting.

However, there were many indicators that this integration was being achieved at a considerable price. The authors of the study asked whether the teachers were fully aware of the children's difficulties, and pointed out that many of them had to struggle with the children's needs without expert support. The report also revealed that the parents themselves were used by the teachers as 'experts', not only with regard to their own children but also with respect to autism itself. The authors of the report asked the rhetorical question of whether this was an acceptable burden to place on parents who already had difficulties and exceptional stressors arising from running a family where autism was present. Certainly in the case of the child whose integration was discontinued there was significant evidence that the integration placed too great a strain on both the child and his or her family.

The children themselves were thought to benefit, with the exception of the child whose integration was discontinued. Yet one can question this conclusion, given that the majority of the children were isolated and without support in the day-to-day social context of the school. Unsupervised and unstructured times, such as morning and afternoon breaks, found the children by themselves with practical problems of adjustment that required expert intervention beyond the skills of the mainstream teachers. Furthermore, it is likely that the amount of time that needed to be invested in providing the children with the support they required was well beyond that which could reasonably be expected of mainstream class teachers. The authors concluded their study with a recommendation concerning the importance of designing a plan for guidance and supervision to support the children, school staff and families from the very start of the integration process. It was also recommended that each such integration should bring with it monitoring, training and direct intervention by psychological and psychiatric professionals with specific expertise in autism.

Given the resource constraints which currently afflict almost every education authority in the UK and abroad, the chances of such support being readily available are virtually zero. That is certainly the experience of the parents who were surveyed by ourselves, in that the comments they made about the integration process revealed difficulties every bit as acute as those identified by Trillingsgaard and Sorenson.

CASE STUDY 8.1

Emma went from a Child Development Centre to a mainstream infant school as a 'rising' 5-year-old. She had some previous sessions in the mainstream nursery, but only with her mother present. Her parents were delighted that she was to be integrated, but their hopes were soon shattered.

'We were told that there would be additional support for her from a teacher's aide, and that a speech and language therapist would supervise the special communication teaching she was supposed to receive every day. We were also told that a specially trained teacher would work with the class teacher to make sure that her learning was properly co-ordinated with the rest of the curriculum.

The first week we found that the teacher's aide was shared with other children in the school, not just those in the same class as Emma. The second week we discovered that the speech therapist was about to go on maternity leave and there was no replacement, and the third week we found that the specialist teacher was trained for dyslexia, not autism.

We complained to Mr . . . [Principal Education Officer (Special Needs)] who tried to be humorously reassuring. He went through Emma's Statement line by line and showed us how we had read too much into it. He pointed out that the bit about the teacher's aide did not specify that it would be one to one, and where it said full-time it just meant she would be avail-

able in the school all the time if needed. He joked that dyslexia was sup-posed to be a specific difficulty of language, and so is autism, so the spe-cialist teacher should be able to cope.

We tackled him on the missing speech therapist and he smugly pointed out that her work was in the non-educational provision bit of the Statement and was the responsibility of Health, not him. He then said Emma could have a place in an SLD (severe learning difficulties) school if we weren't satisfied. John (her husband) and I knew then that Emma would only get whatever scraps Education could afford for her.'

The next study also reveals a total lack of understanding of autism, with very serious consequences.

CASE STUDY 8.2

Mike started off in mainstream, but by the time he was 8 years old the school had permanently excluded him. The head said she didn't mind the autism; it was the antisocial behaviour she could not tolerate! We tried explaining that the behaviour problems were part of the autism, and so did the educational psychologist. The head said not all autistic children had such problems and she thought our parenting was an issue.

We tried to appeal, but as it was a Catholic School we were told by the Education Officer not to bother. He said that they could do as they liked and Catholic schools didn't like special needs kids anyway. He cracked a joke about the milk of human kindness and said Mike could go to an MLD school for the time being.

Mike only went for 5 days before he was beaten up by the Seniors, so we pulled him out. The Education Officer said that it was our choice and not the Department's, but he would do what he could. We asked for a reassess-ment and after 13 months with Mike off school we finally got a new Statement.

We were pleased that the Needs section stressed autism and spoke about the triad of impairments. It didn't name a school, but eventually, because we were desperate by then, we accepted an all-boys residential school. It only had 63 children and Mike could get home most weekends.

I know we were gullible, but it was only after a term that we found out that it was a school for emotionally disturbed boys with social and behav-iour problems. Mike was very unhappy there and we found out later that he spent a lot of time up a tree holding a stick. This was to avoid going into all the team games the school used to encourage the boys to work together. The education officer said that was fine; autism was a social disorder and Mike needed to learn to follow social rules.

We got an independent psychologist's opinion. He took one look at the

Statement and said 'Yes; it's got autism in the Needs section but all the rest is standard for EBD (emotional and behavioural difficulties) pupils.' He couldn't recognise anything in the Provision sections that actually referred to autism.

The tribunal accepted the independent opinion and finally Mike got a proper placement, but the Education people keep grumbling about the cost.

As may be seen from these case studies, the parents involved experienced significant problems when dealing with officials in their Local Education Authorities. Their attributional explanations for these difficulties imply a callow resistance on the part of education officers to spend money, disguised by apparent concern. Such experiences are depressingly common and have been admirably described by Bowers (1995). A more detailed commentary on of some of these problems is provided in Chapter 1.

The negative views that the parents in our survey held about the education officials with whom they had had to deal result in a deeply suspicious relationship which may interfere with other essential aspects of educational provision and process. Many parents reported that they felt so alienated by the struggle to gain a satisfactory Statement of Educational Needs that dialogue about what and how their children should be taught was strained and unpleasant. As a result, essential discussions about their children's Individual Education Programme were fraught and inconclusive. Many parents complained that they never felt comfortable again and believed that the discussions they had been invited to were merely conducted in order to comply with policy and legal dictates. Several parents complained that the language used about their children by the professionals was too technical and was intended, they thought, to exclude them from the discussions. Others complained of the large number of professionals who were present at the meetings, many of whom had little to say but were certainly intimidating by their very presence.

This is a serious situation, since it is only through the Individual Education Programme that the Statement of Special Educational Needs can be brought to life for the child to whom it refers. The involvement of parents should be an integral part of this process, and meetings about Individual Education Programmes 'serve as a communication vehicle between parents and school personnel and enable them, as equal participants, to jointly decide what the child's needs are, what services will be provided to meet those needs, and what outcomes are anticipated' (Simpson, 1995). Without this equal partnership there can be little possibility of newly acquired skills, whether they are taught at home or at school, generalising from one context to the other. Ultimately this leads to greater dependence on adults for children with autism, who are then robbed of opportunities for self-development.

Strategies Adopted by Parents

A glance at the various Web pages on autism from around the world reveals a bewildering variety of recommended strategies to assist the development of children with autism. Many of these are completely untested, and their only strength is derived from anecdotal evidence and recommendations. A sample of well-tried approaches which many parents have taken up or else support enthusiastically is given below.

Gentle teaching

The material that follows is taken from the home page of a non-violent approach for helping children and adults with special needs. The Web page is maintained by the Foundation for Gentle Teaching in The Netherlands.

Gentle Teaching is a non-violent approach for helping people with special needs and sometimes challenging behaviours that focuses on four primary goals of care-giving:

- teaching the person to feel safe with us;
- teaching the person to feel engaged with us;
- teaching the person to feel unconditionally valued by us;
- teaching the person to return unconditional valuing to us.

Gentle Teaching is a strategy based on a Psychology of Interdependence that sees all change as being mutual and bringing about a feeling of companionship and community—symbols of justice and non-violence.

How often do we hear ourselves and others say, 'You know . . . it is not difficult to teach a person to behave like we want him or her to. We just modify their behaviour—reward what we want and punish what we don't want.'

'If it doesn't work in the beginning, we'll just use some more punishment and we will succeed . . . or more structure, or more restraint, or more . . .'

Is it really so easy? It may be so if we are not interested in the emotional well-being of the other, when it doesn't matter if the other is afraid of us and when we are only focused on obedience. In reality we see that this approach doesn't work at all. As soon as we let go of punishment, restraint, or external structure, the challenging behaviour appears again in some form. Also, in many cases the behaviour we want to disappear is just replaced by another difficult one. Some people get the same punishment for many years without any 'success'.

A sad example of this is a woman who was treated with electro-aversive therapy for over 22 years . . . and still had self-injurious behaviour.

But the central question is not to do away with punishment; rather, it is to define what we want the person to become. The challenge is to mend shattered hearts, not broken bodies or brains. It is the emotional well-being that is central—feelings of being safe, engaged, loved and loving. And these do not come from reward or punishment, but from the teaching of feelings of companionship.

With Gentle Teaching we don't focus on compliance and obedience, but we focus on teaching the other to feel safe with us. We do this by looking at ourselves, at our beliefs and at the way we use our hands, eyes and words. We change our own posture, in order to help the other to feel safe. We do this because we know that most of the challenging behaviour comes out of fear and out of a broken heart, and not out of broken brains.

A Psychology of Interdependence

Gentle Teaching is not just another technique to deal with difficult behaviours of people with mental retardation. It is the expression of the Psychology of Interdependence, so it has to do with more than just challenging behaviours. It has to do with how we exist as human beings, how we see our self, how we see our relationships with important others, etc.

The Psychology of Interdependence is based on the following basic assumptions.

- Each human being is made up of mind—body—spirit.
- Each human being hungers for a feeling of being with others and having a feeling of companionship.
- Bonded relations are the fundamental basis for developing human basic values into a moral life and into personal life-goals.

In our work with people with mental retardation, the Psychology of Interdependence helps us to create a culture of life for those who need our help. Not just the people with challenging behaviours, but everyone.

Companionship

The central purpose of giving care to anyone is to establish a feeling of companionship. This is literally taught. It is more than being 'nice' to someone. It is an emotional prerequisite in all human beings, having a warm circle of significant others in our life who help us to feel safe, wanted and valued. Companionship expresses the feeling of belonging together and sharing the important events of life. The word 'companionship' comes from the Latin words 'com' (= together) and 'pan' (= bread).

Everyone needs to have companions in life. Without companions you feel lost and isolated. People with mental retardation, and especially those with challenging behaviour, have learned not to trust others or have even learned to be afraid of others. They don't have companions they can trust and they have to learn the feeling of companionship from the beginning.

People with mental retardation often don't know what a feeling of companionship is. They are submitted to others who are—at least in their own experience—domineering towards them, and an emotional gap grows between them instead of a bonded relationship. These people have to be taught a feeling of companionship. The first step in this process is that caregivers and important others have to find out what the Psychology of Interdependence means for themselves and for their stance towards the other. They can start creating a culture of interdependence, a culture of life, by changing their own behaviour and looking at the other not as a person with behaviour problems, but as a person who has not yet learned the feeling of companionship.

Basic Values

Everyone has personal objectives in life which are important. Not all objectives are equally important. One may be more important than the other. These objectives are the expressions of Basic Values, and together they form a profile of the personal quality of life expectations.

These are the eight basic values.

- Bodily Integrity—being healthy, being decently clothed, being clean, being well fed, etc.
- Feeling Safe—wanting to be with others, not being afraid to go outside, feeling relaxed in interactions with others, etc.
- Feeling Self-Worth—seeing oneself as good, being recognised as a person, feeling pride, expressing personal gifts and talents.
- Having A Life—sensing a life-plan, having daily structure and routine, having your own rituals and beliefs.
- A Sense of Belongingness—having a close circle of friends, loving others and being loved by others, having a home, feeling companionship.
- Social Participation—being able to have contact with the community, living with others, taking part in community life.
- Having Meaningful Daily Activities—enjoying one's daily activities, having daily activities which fit in with your life-plan.
- Inner Contentment—feeling inner harmony, feeling free from traumatic experiences.

Within these basic values there is no fixed hierarchy. Everyone has their own priorities, based on their own life experiences and the culture they live in.

At the start of our life, these basic values are not expressed in more or less concrete goals and behaviour to achieve our objectives. We develop our lifestyle and our objectives while we grow up, learning from our parents and other important people. The basis for this learning is a feeling of trust and safety with others, and an emotional stability within ourself. If we don't feel safe with others, we will not learn from them and we will not develop our personal lifestyle. As a result, we will be forced to live the lifestyle of people we are depending on, and we will be disciplined in many details of our life.

Often people with mental retardation didn't develop their own expressions of the basic values, or they didn't develop 'proper' expressions. For example, in order to feel safe you may be aggressive to someone else (attack is the best defence), or in order to create your own structure, you may act aggressively in order to provoke a predictable reaction from your caregivers.

When helping people in need, we have to determine how important the basic values are to them, and which expressions they have developed to achieve the important basic values. Then we can teach them other and perhaps more appropriate expressions, related to their priorities in life.

(Foundation for Gentle Teaching in The Netherlands)

Treatment and education of autistic and communication handicapped children (TEACCH)

Most of the parents we interviewed were aware of TEACCH, and many were actively campaigning to get this model adopted within the schools or Units that their children attended. It is a vindication of the model that not one parent had any reason to reject it from their own experiences. Most of the parents we spoke to who had children involved with TEACCH programmes wanted more rather than less use made of the model. The following material was provided by a French parent, Paul Trehin, of *Autisme France*.

Some Basic Information about TEACCH

TEACCH is starting to be well known all over the world for the excellent services provided to autistic people, and is often used as a model as a result. However, several misconceptions have been spread, and it seems to be helpful to give some basic information that will hopefully give a faithful description of the TEACCH Programme.

First of all, TEACCH is not a single approach, and still less a method. It is a state programme that tries to respond to the needs of autistic people using the best available approaches and methods known so far for educating them, and to provide the maximum level of autonomy that they can achieve.

Although some people have exported successfully from North Carolina and even from the USA some elements of this programme, the only complete implementation of TEACCH as a State Programme remains that in North Carolina. For the sake of my European friends, I should add that we were very lucky to be able to import some of the TEACCH programme into Europe, thanks to Theo Peters, a Belgian professional who received training in North Carolina and helped many European professionals and parents get up to date with modern views on autism. The programme in Antwerp is pretty close to most of the achievements of those in North Carolina, and constitutes a closer reference for visits in Europe.

Why do we think that TEACCH is a good model to follow?

Before I go any further in describing how the TEACCH Programme functions, I shall list a few of the considerations that led us to choose this programme as a model.

As parents who are quite involved in the Autistic Society activities, we have explored hundreds of methods, ranging from 'recipes' to full-blown country-wide systems.

TEACCH is one of the two programmes for autistic people that met our quality criteria, the other one being the UK National Autistic Society (NAS)-based School system for autistic children, which is good although not as comprehensive as TEACCH.

The following considerations were decisive in our choice of TEACCH over other approaches to autism:

- respect for autistic people, whatever the degree of severity of autism present;
- respect for parents and the association of parents in the programme as 'co-therapists';
- the inclusion of parents' opinions in decisions concerning younger children and more severely handicapped autistic adults;
- the inclusion of autistic people's advice to the maximum extent of their ability to communicate;
- warmth of professionals, mainly due to the next point;
- in-depth knowledge of autism from all points of view (medical, psychological, educational, social mainstreaming, affective), but with these professionals remaining open and approachable;
- lengthy experience with testable long-term results (30 years), and education constituting the backbone of the approach;
- continuous development of the teaching techniques based on university research programmes, integrating the most recent findings with long experience;
- a comprehensive programme from early childhood to adulthood, from the diagnosis of very young children to adult development assessment, and from low functioning to high functioning;
- adaptability of the approach—it could be adapted without problem to the French environment (or any other country), and the approach is flexible enough to be adaptable;
- last but not least, our overall impression that autistic people of all ages seemed to be happy and developing quite well towards maximum autonomy for their individual capacity. This was concluded both from our own observations and from what parents told us.

What is TEACCH? To answer this question, I hope that everyone will by now realise what an endeavour this represents.

TEACCH cannot be reduced to a technique, a set of techniques, or even a method. It is a complete programme of services for autistic people which makes use of a number of techniques in various combinations depending on the individual person's needs and emerging capabilities.

TEACCH stands for Treatment and Education of Autistic and Communication Handicapped Children, and is a Public Health Programme available in North Carolina. It was founded by Prof. Eric Schopler who was Director of the Programme until 1994. The new director is Dr Gary Mesibov. The head office is located in Chapel Hill, North Carolina, and TEACCH has a research section at the University of North Carolina Hospital.

There are several other offices and facilities in North Carolina, with a good geographical coverage. The services that are provided range from diagnostic and early counselling for parents and professionals, to adult community-based centres, with all of the intermediate stages such as psychological assessment, classes, teachers programmes, etc.

The TEACCH Programme supervises about 130 classes for autistic children. Several centres for adolescents and adults with varying degrees of mainstreaming according to the capabilities of each person are installed in either rural or urban areas. Depending on preferences expressed by the autistic people and their families, a rural or urban setting will be proposed.

What is done at TEACCH?

There are few programmes in the world that can claim 30 years of experience with autistic people. TEACCH keeps on evolving, and is continuously refining its approach, challenging old beliefs and incorporating new research results. It is also careful not to introduce techniques that are not yet proven on a large scale.

Unlike AIT, VT, holding and other approaches, the TEACCH programme does not use a single technique or method. No one at TEACCH will tell you that they are going to 'cure' autism.

The main goal of TEACCH for autistic children is to help them to grow up to have maximum autonomy in adulthood. This includes helping them to understand the world around them, acquiring communication skills that will enable them to relate to other people, and giving them the maximum opportunity to develop the necessary competence to make choices concerning their own lives.

The major thrust is towards improving communication skills and autonomy to the maximum of the child's potential, using education as a means to achieve that goal. Educational programmes are frequently revised as the child matures and progresses, since there are no good predictors of a child's evolution, and early assessment could be misleading.

Educational strategies are established individually on the basis of a detailed assessment of the autistic person's learning abilities, attempting to identify potential for further improvement rather than deficits.

The assessment known as the Psycho-Educational Profile (PEP) attempts to identify areas where the person 'passes', areas where the skill is not yet present, and areas where the skill is developing. These domains are then incorporated in an education programme for that person. This assessment has to be multi-dimensional because of the great variability in skills, even in the same autistic person, from one domain of competency to another.

In contrast to behaviour modification, these strategies do not work on the behaviour directly, but on underlying conditions that will foster learning experiences. They also make use of recent cognitive psychology research data on differences in particular areas of brain processing in autistic people compared to non-antistic individuals.

When behaviour problems occur, they are not treated directly either. The approach calls for efforts to understand the underlying reasons for these behaviour problems, e.g. anxiety, physical pain, difficulty with the task, unpredictable changes, boredom, etc. The effect is twofold.

1. By giving the person the means to understand his or her environment better, that environment becomes more predictable and less anxiety-provoking. This may necessitate proposing a simpler environment in the early phases of development, and then gradually reintroducing complexity as the child progresses towards increasing autonomy.
2. By giving a means of communication to the person, their comprehension and articulation abilities will enable them to understand better what they

are being told/asked and to express their needs and feelings in other ways than behaviour problems.

Direct behavior modification is not completely ruled out. It is reserved for those behaviours that endanger the person and for which the above strategy has not worked, at least so far. However, this situation is very rare.

(Paul Trehin, *Autisme France*)

The behavioural intensive approach of Lovaas

Many parents are very interested in this approach, which represents a marked contrast to the sentiments expressed in the previous paragraph. This approach is completely dependent on behavioural techniques, and its success relies on a high frequency and consistency of usage of behavioural techniques. The description which follows is taken from a paper prepared by the first author (Randall, 1995b).

The work of Lovaas
It is interesting to follow the development of behavioural techniques employed by Lovaas, who has been working in this area for several decades. He has an unfortunate reputation for using aversive behavioural techniques in institutions which were designed to 'punish' the behavioural manifestations of clients with autism. It has long been his contention that the more the client is exposed to behavioural interventions, the deeper and more rapid will be the adaptive learning. Consequently, Lovaas has an interest in working with families, because this facilitates the consistency, duration and frequency of this exposure to the behavioural programme. His strategies for work with parents and others were brought together in his Young Autism Project, which he described as 'a particularly intense and broad-based approach to the treatment of young autistic children' (Lovaas *et al.*, 1989, p.283).

Although Lovaas accepts that autism is the product of an abnormal central nervous system, which prevents or reduces the individual's learning opportunities in the context of a normal environment, like most other behaviourists he is primarily interested in quantifiable units of behaviour that can be recorded and used to demonstrate the changes brought about by intervention. The characteristic behaviours of autism, which include obsessive behaviour, rocking, twirling and ritual behaviours, are described by him as 'deficient behaviours' and 'excessive behaviours'. The deficient behaviours of autism include poor eye contact, poorly developed social behaviour, weak attention control and concentration, a restricted range of emotional behaviours (which include empathy), deficient speech and language, poor imagination and weak play skills. The excessive behaviours of autism are restricted to acts of aggression directed either at the client or at others, and common stereotypic or obsessive activities. It is his belief that the only way in which these behaviours can be modified and replaced by adaptive behaviours is through the use of intense behavioural methodology applied in all the environmental contexts of the client for as long as possible during the course of each day.

This approach, which eventually came to be known as the Behavioural Intensive Approach, has a number of key features:

- the need to approximate the learning opportunities that are available to the normal population. Children within this population learn all the time, from all the environments in which they find themselves and which are acquired incidentally, by direct teaching and by imitation;
- clients with autism, because of their organic deficits, do not learn in the same way or to the same extent when given these opportunities;
- therefore, to offset this difficulty, several adults have to be trained to provide the right kind of structured teaching to the child for as long as possible. Lovaas actually writes that the client needs this approach 'for virtually all of his or her waking hours' (Lovaas *et al.*, 1989, p.293);
- several adults should be trained to provide the instructions needed. They should work in a team which initially consists of people learning the strategies, one or more experienced people to facilitate the learning, the child's parents and possibly siblings;
- the inclusion of other family members is regarded by Lovaas as being vital in order to generalise the effects of the teaching.

Like all other behaviourists, Lovaas insists that his behavioural programmes must involve regular monitoring of the client from baseline onwards in order to determine the measurable effect of the intervention. The intervention generally hinges around shaping and imitation processes leading to the successful development of skills, together with the generalisation and discrimination associated with those skills.

Methodology
The majority of the intervention programmes designed by Lovaas and his followers commence with tasks that can be taught initially by prompting and then by imitation. Parents can be trained in these techniques and, with a small army of volunteers, can deliver the 'message' throughout the waking hours of the client. Lovaas outlines the stages thus.

- The teaching of simple *non-verbal imitation* leading to reinforcement, where imitation is defined as the establishment of a discrimination where the response resembles its stimulus and it is built by introducing contrasting stimuli in a distinguishing training paradigm.
- Gradually as the child grows more proficient in this type of imitation, so he or she can be moved towards *verbal imitation* training.
- Verbal imitation training invariably begins with single sounds, followed by combinations of sounds, and then words, leading eventually to short sentences.
- This carefully structured and intensive teaching at home should gradually be augmented by introducing the child to the behaviour of other children.
- Once the child has begun to imitate these other children in his or her own home, then it is possible to begin to generalise the learning environment into a school or nursery situation.
- Lovaas makes the point that moving the child into a school context will facilitate the generalisation of learning and broaden it from parents and adult carers to the peer group.

Generalisation
Lovaas regards the key to generalisation as the capacity to learn by imitating other children. He recognises that generalisation is one of the most difficult skills for children and young people with autism to acquire, because the core deficit of the disorder prevents such clients from readily extrapolating from one situation to another, no matter how similar those situations may be. Yet it is vital that all learning-disabled clients should be encouraged to acquire the skills of generalisation, since it is this that uplifts the development of simple single skills into the flexible framework that is necessary for the clients to experience real decision-making and choice as they go through daily life'

(Randall, 1995b)

Music therapy

Over the years of our work with the parents of young children with autism we have become aware of the enthusiasm many parents have expressed about the uses of music therapy. None of these parents were under any illusion that this therapy offered a 'cure', but all of them felt that it helped to bring their children into closer contact with the environment, including their social environment. Many of these parents have been keen to pass on their enthusiasm to other parents because they have been delighted with the outcomes. One Web site on the Internet makes use of Boxill's (1985) description to inform other parents about the nature of music therapy:

What does music therapy do?
- Facilitates creative expression in people who are either non-verbal or have deficits in communication skills.
- Provides the opportunity for experiences that open the way for and motivate learning in all domains of functioning.
- Creates the opportunity for positive, successful and pleasurable social experiences not otherwise available to them.
- Develops awareness of self, others and the environment that improves functioning on all levels, enhances well-being and fosters independent living.

One definition of music therapy
Music therapy is the use of music as a therapeutic tool for the restoration, maintenance and improvement of psychological, mental and physiological health. It is used for the habilitation, rehabilitation and maintenance of behavioural, developmental, physical and social skills—all within the context of a client–therapist relationship.

The overall aim of music therapy is to engage individuals actively in their own growth, development and behavioural change, and for them to transfer musical and non-musical skills to other aspects of their life, bringing them from isolation into active participation in the world.

Long-term goals of music therapy

- To improve self-image and body awareness.
- To increase communication skills.
- To increase the ability to use energy purposefully.
- To reduce maladaptive (stereotypic, compulsive, self-abusive, assaultive, disruptive, perseverative, impulsive) behaviours.
- To increase interaction with peers and others.
- To increase independence and self-direction.
- To stimulate creativity and imagination.
- To enhance emotional expression and adjustment.
- To increase attending behaviour.
- To improve fine and gross motor skills.
- To improve auditory perception.

This information is reproduced from Boxill, E. H. (1985) *Music Therapy for the Developmentally Disabled*. Austin, TX: Pro-Ed, Inc.

These methods, particularly TEACCH, have been reasonably well validated. Many other methods 'on the market' have not been, but their marketing often makes them sound attractive to desperate parents. A large number of these methods are old and tried strategies in new packages, while others are simply statements of faith which lack the support of research or theoretical foundations.

Helping Parents to Understand and Evaluate New Methods

It has been our experience that parents can become vulnerable to new programme ideas that come along—particularly from America and without the benefit of effective scientific scrutiny.

Tens of thousands of pounds are raised for very dubious 'treatments', and the public (and therefore other parents) seldom hear the outcomes. We have seen many disasters, including the breakup of families, because of the money and effort that have been invested in some inappropriate interventions.

Parents need help, support and guidance. Listed below are some of the issues that they need to explore, or of which they should at least be aware.

GUIDELINES TO PARENTS

Programme Description

- What is the intervention programme? Who does what, and how?
- Is there written information, a programme description, detailed brochure, etc.?

- Exactly what is involved for the child and their family?
- What is the length of the intervention?
- What is the frequency of sessions?
- How much parent time is required?
- What are the financial costs?
- Does the intervention programme focus on one particular skill, or is it a general, comprehensive approach?
- Do parents, care providers, teachers and others need to be trained in the intervention technique?
- Is there co-ordination between the intervention programme and other individuals/services working with the family (e.g. teachers, therapists, doctors)?
- Are the intervention programme goals individualised for each person and their families?
- Is there follow-up and/or support after the termination of intervention?

Rationale and Purpose of the Intervention

- What is the rationale, philosophy or purpose underlying the intervention programme?
- How is the philosophy tied to the specific intervention techniques?
- How were the philosophy and intervention methods developed (e.g. scientific research, clinical experience, application or extension from a related field such as learning disabilities or mental retardation)?
- Are you comfortable, or do you agree, with the philosophy of the programme?

Credentials of the Intervention Programme Director and Staff

- What is the background of the programme staff?
- What are their training and professional credentials?
- What is the staff's training and experience in autism?
- What is their understanding of the nature of the disorder?
- How much experience have they had in providing this type of intervention?
- Are the programme staff open to questions and input from the family or other professionals involved with the child?

Effectiveness of the Intervention

- What is the supporting evidence for the effectiveness of the programme? Are there publications about it in appropriate journals?
- Is there any independent confirmation of the effectiveness of the intervention programme?
- What are the possible negative effects or side-effects of the intervention?
- What impact might the programme have on the family's lifestyle?

9

AUTISM AND GROWING UP

As many parents have pointed out to us, the range of helpful literature on autism is very disproportionate in that virtually nothing has been written about autism in adulthood, in comparison with the mass of material examining childhood autism.[1] Consequently, parents have told us that even though they have expected little guidance from the professional services,[2] they were very disappointed to find how little literature there was to assist their own researches. Furthermore, of 23 families we spoke to who had adult children (older than 18 years) with autism, only two were actually aware of there being any autism-specific goals that guided the provisions made for their sons. Others complained or otherwise commented that the available provision was generic and merely 'contained' their adult children, whatever fine words might be printed in the 'prospectus' about the provision.

The most satisfied parents were those very few (less than 15%) whose adult children with autism were in specialised facilities, or those whose children were high-functioning and either in further/higher education or employment/training. As one parent said, 'At least we can see where he's going'.

The converse of this positive statement is that most parents cannot see where their adult children with autism are going. A lack of direction, obvious drift and impoverished sense of purpose distressed and bewildered many of the parents to whom we spoke. Several contrasted the educational provision in childhood and adolescence with the desultory services that their adult children now received:

---

[1] Patricia Howlin's (1997) excellent book *Autism in Adulthood* (London: Routledge) goes a long way towards redressing the balance, but was not available at the time when this chapter was finalised.

[2] An expectation based on experience with unhelpful services during the childhood and adolescence of their sons and daughters with autism.

> We had to struggle to get everything he needed from the LEA; little did we
> realise that there would be nothing to struggle for when he was grown up.

In addition, not only was there a strong belief that the available provision did not meet the needs of adults with autism, but in many cases there was great concern about issues that professionals would refer to as the 'values' base of the institution involved. Thus some parents spoke of a lack of privacy in both day and residential provision, and others described how hard-won skills were being eroded because care staff ran routines that simply did not allow clients to use their independence skills:

> For years her teachers, classroom assistants, brothers and us (parents)
> worked desperately hard to give her some independence. It may not have
> been much, but she knew we were proud—now she is too slow to suit the
> routines the staff prefer; they say they have to move things along quickly
> because there are so many clients to look after.

This particular young woman spent her days in a Local Authority Centre for Learning Disabilities. She was severely autistic but had greater intellectual abilities than the mostly severely or profoundly handicapped clients. The staff were not well trained, and devoted most of their energies to providing dedicated routine care for the clients. Their priorities were simply to make sure that the clients were well looked after physically and entertained. There were few concessions made to the further development of these clients, and individual educational programmes lay forgotten in files. Not surprisingly, on entry many clients gradually lost their previous independence skills.

This predicament was the most frequent concern of the parents we interviewed who had adult autistic children—a fear that what had been done at school (and further education college) was eroded by the lack of skill in day or residential adult provision. This chapter will largely deal with this area of great concern.

NORMALISATION

Whereas most Local Authorities provision policies speak of normalisation for their disabled clients, it is often the case that the practices of normalisation are not understood or conducted properly. This section will examine this philosophy in the context of autism.

Ideally, the services that an adult with autism should receive will be guided by the principles of normalisation, and it is usually the final years of schooling that serve as a preparation for the settings, objectives and values of the adult provision. In an ideal world there should be little difference in the objectives or the values, and even the principles of instruction should be fairly similar, so that the transition is as stress-free as possible. Unfortunately, this is seldom realised unless there is a very close liaison between school, college and adult services. All too often, as one parent old us, 'They use the same words but don't sing the same hymn'. What he meant by this is that he had heard similar sentiments expressed by education and social services staff, but that they had completely different ideas about the theory and practice underpinning those sentiments.

The principle of normalisation is attributed to Nirje (1976), and it is the central conceptual blank that underpins services now available to adults with disabilities. Wolfensberger (1972) developed this concept to include the utilisation of means which are as culturally normal as possible and linked to a subsumed concept of *social role valorisation*. He determined that the most explicit and highest goal for normalisation should be the establishment and maintenance of valued social roles for people who are otherwise at risk of social devaluation (Wolfensberger, 1972, p.235).

The issue of the values-base of practice is fundamental to normalisation, and may be summarised as the need of all individuals, regardless of disability, to be accepted and valued, and to have the same rights as all others to live as respected and contributing members of society. Logically, they should be able to do this in the normal community environment.

In its most optimistic form, normalisation requires that the services should be as non-specific as possible and open to all who need them. Some clients may need additional support to make use of these services, but the facilities themselves should be as ordinary as possible in the sense that they should not be seen to be only for the exclusive use of disabled people. The premise operating here is that segregated services are bound to be perceived as *special* services by non-service users, and that this will often lead to the service-users being viewed as special and possibly undesirable themselves. As a result, the service-users may be devalued and viewed as a permanent drain on society's resources. Clearly this concept of normalisation is attacked by those who provide specialist services and who claim that only specialist staff are able to provide for the needs of a population with a specific disability. Wolfensberger (1972) highlights two predominant arguments for specialisation, the first of these being the need for specialist staff and the second argument being that people with highly specific and severe disabilities cannot be regarded as 'normal' individuals, and should therefore be dealt with on a segregated basis.

The first of these arguments is completely circular. If all clients with highly specific disabilities were only ever cared for by individuals with specialist training to manage those disabilities, then it would be difficult to advance evidence that there were alternative strategies of value. Secondly, the possession of specialist skills does not automatically require a specialist environment in which to deliver them. At one time the casual observer could have been forgiven for thinking that the best environment in which to provide for the needs of the learning-disabled population was in several hundred acres of rural countryside, but the gradual closure of subnormality hospitals has allowed us to see that these clients are better served in normal communities. In short, this first argument against normalisation of specialist services is an empirical technical one which is as much rooted in tradition as it is in research.

The second argument is one of the conventional value-base held by powerful members of society. Wolfensberger (1972) includes professionals within this group of powerful people, and challenges the power and authority that they have over service users. Once the principle of normalisation is accepted, then those who must practise it should find their attitudes influenced such that they behave differently towards the service-users and communicate with them in ways which show a positive regard.

Normalisation cannot occur unless there are appropriate opportunities for the service-users. Any population that is deprived of the normal opportunities to engage in choice-making about where and how to live, which relationships to engage in, what to learn and what challenges to attempt is a population living outside the practices of normalisation. To deny these everyday rights and privileges to people with disabilities is to devalue them and exert power over them, no matter how benign it may be.

For normalisation to occur in practice, those responsible for it must ensure that there is an effective interaction between an appropriate value-base, a positive relationship with the clients and the provision of opportunities for them within the normal community. However, the parents to whom we have spoken indicate that this interaction fails on a depressingly frequent basis. As one parent put it,

> My son has never had a sense of self-worth; his teachers and ourselves have worked hard to try to build his self-esteem and make him feel that he is a valued member of our little community. It took many years to achieve some small steps towards this, but it took only months at the [adult provision] to brush all that aside. Unlike at school, where he was seen as having abilities, [at the adult provision] he was just seen as an individual with limited ability and not able to make use of the kinds of opportunities he has had before. It appals us that the effects of his autism have been enhanced by the opinions of those who were supposed to care for him; their prejudices have demoralised and defeated him.

The parents' responses to our survey presented a fairly depressing picture in which ignorance of the nature of autism and its particular impact on individuals gave rise to low expectations of these individuals on the part of residential and day-centre staff. Their lack of experience and their inability to provide appropriate opportunities combined to reduce the achievements of their autistic clients. Not surprisingly, the parents expressed distress and confusion, and several of them asked why it was that their adult children seemed to them to move along the continuum of autism towards its most severe end:

> We honestly thought that autism was something that just got biologically worse in adulthood. We never realised until the last assessment that he was getting worse because his environment made him like that.

This sentiment is in direct contrast to those parents whose adult children attended residential and day facilities that were staffed by well-trained and experienced people. To these staff, the principle of normalisation did not simply mean that all clients should have the same experiences, no matter what their abilities or disabilities. The parents' description makes clear that individual programmes were tailor-made to meet the needs of the adults with autism and, more frequently than not, they were made with the parents having a significant input into the process. Consequently, there was a good to high level of understanding of the impact of autism on adult development, and an awareness that, with the right strategies in place, the expectations of individuals should be as 'normal' as possible. Having such expectations resulted in staff seeking to identify environmental opportunities for continued learning, and engaging with the autistic adults in making the best of these opportunities, such that their life experiences were of a much higher quality than was the case for the first group. As a result, parents expressed satisfaction with the continued achievement of their adult children.

This dichotomy is not so simple as might appear from the way in which we have represented it above. Significant misunderstandings had arisen both among the parents and among the professionals dealing with their adult children. One of the most common misconceptions arose from the parents themselves. They felt that since their school-aged children with autism had received segregated special educational treatments, then therefore their adult children with autism would also require segregation. Many found it difficult to conceive of the fact that their children were continuing to develop even though they had left school. Such a rigid view of the role and purpose of school is to be found throughout the normal population, and is not peculiar to those parents whose children have autism. This viewpoint made it difficult for many parents to understand that their adult children needed a wider range of experiences, unlike those they had had at school, if they were to continue to develop and move further towards independence. As one parent said, 'He's never going to be normal, why should we try to pretend that we can make him normal?' In making this statement, he revealed another common misunderstanding, that the principle of normalisation is not just concerned with making people with special needs 'normal', or with fitting them to the cheapest possible provision on the grounds that such provision was more 'normal' than expensive specialist provision.

It helped many parents labouring under this misunderstanding to realise that, even within the so-called 'normal' population, there is a tremendous range of needs and capacity for independence. Within this range there are some people with high levels of skill who are able to access many more resources within the community than others. This may simply result from them having more money. However, despite this variation it is still possible for all members of society, be they disabled or non-disabled, to exercise such autonomy as they are capable of and to be shown the respect of other members of society. Brechin and Walmsey (1989) expand on Wolfensberger's concept of social role valorisation, which emphasises the need and rights of all disabled people to have appropriate and valued social roles. These are dependent on them having as much autonomy as possible, and for whatever restrictions may be imposed on the degree of autonomy they can utilise, to be imposed by the nature of their disability rather than by any cultural or resource-driven external factors. Not surprisingly, many parents were uncomfortable with the idea that their adult child with autism should be given personal autonomy. They argued strongly that their child needed protection, not only from the rigours of everyday life in the community, but also from his or her own vulnerability. They saw their roles as parents protecting their child, and making choices on behalf of him or her, being eroded by a concept that stylises the degree of protection they had offered as excessive and contributing to the devaluation of their adult child within the context of normalisation.

Although developing sexuality and the working practices that many residential and day facilities had for dealing with it confronted many parents with distressing thoughts and feelings, the majority of parents who were distressed by well-practised normalisation considered the issue of choice-making to be the most problematic. Given that the majority of these parents had adult children with extremely poor communication skills, they argued that they were the ones who were best able to tell and most experienced in determining what needs their child was communicating. Often they found their interpretations being gently challenged by staff who put forward alternatives and wanted to test these out by removing restrictions on opportunities that the parents had unwittingly used to inhibit the enskilling of their child on the grounds that he or she was too vulnerable to acquire such skills. One parent vocalised these fears in a simple question: 'All her life, we've known that she's not capable of making sensible choices; how do they (residential care staff) think that they can help her to make safe choices now?' The vexed question of choice-making as a central facet of normalisation set against the need to keep vulnerable individuals safe will be examined in a later section.

Often the parents' fears first find a focus when adult services become involved in drawing up an Individual Programme Plan (IPP) for their adult children with autism. Such plans are a vital component of the normalisation process, and are considered to be the most flexible and efficient way of ensuring that service-users work towards agreed skills using specified resources and engaging in a wide variety of opportunities for learning. Ideally, the derivation of the IPP involves everyone with a professional, family or social contact with the individual. Wherever possible, they should be drawn up in consultation with the autistic adult and the immediate family members. Parents have a vital role to play not only in the implementation of the plan, but also in the provision of information and the decision-making process itself. Unfortunately, problems often develop when protective parents do not agree on what is desirable or achievable, and shrink back from aims and objectives that would appear to leave their adult children in a vulnerable position.

The whole process can be fraught with anxiety for some parents and, as may be deduced from the comments which follow, each stage brings with it particular fears.

Assessment stage

Ideally all IPPs are based on an assessment designed to highlight particular strengths and needs. Given that social work, including residential social work, is heavily engaged in bringing its practice into line with an empowering *strengths approach*, the process of determining what strengths an individual adult with autism may have is of vital importance not only to that individual, but also to the professional development of those who provide the service. More will be said of this strengths approach in a later section, but essentially strengths are identified, defined and exploited as a means of helping the individual service-user to progress. Strengths are generally to be found in:

- what each individual can do;
- what each individual likes to do; and
- the important relationships that are recognised by that individual.

Many parents found the identification of strengths very stressful, generally because they felt the need to be over-protective of their adult child, and they sought to minimise what had already been achieved.

> They kept at us to say what Jerry could already do. We kept saying that he couldn't do very much but they weren't satisfied with that; 'Everybody can do something, no matter how little it might seem to us', they kept telling us. They didn't seem to realise that the only way he can communicate is by dragging us around to everything he wants—what sort of a strength is that?

Parents also felt vulnerable when determining which relationships were important to their adult child with autism. Many thought that some relationships were bad for their child, and sought to minimise the importance of them when discussing the assessment:

> They keep coming back to Sam's liking for a young man called Michael. We didn't want to encourage this; he comes from a dirty family and often smells. We know they get on well together but what would happen if as she gets older she got romantically inclined towards him?

In both examples the parents are unwittingly continuing to treat their adult child as though he or she was still a child. In doing so the first set of parents could not understand how the 'dragging' communication of Jerry could be built up into much more 'normal' forms of communication. The second set of parents were rightly anxious to maintain high standards for their daughter, but failed to see that at times the greater need is to prioritise strong and adaptive relationships over these standards. The process of allowing their children to grow away from them is difficult for many parents, and we noted that none of them had received any significant counselling or other intervention which would make the process easier.

Most parents had little difficulty in agreeing on the list of needs that are commonly associated with IPPs. In general, these needs are:

- educational (developing new skills);
- emotional (developing fulfilling relationships);
- intellectual (gaining and making use of new skills and knowledge);
- physical (exercise, monitoring body parts, diet and health);
- spiritual (developing self-esteem, feeling valued, developing a religious or other faith if possible);
- social (being exposed to a wide range of leisure activities).

To accomplish the fulfilment of these needs through the use of the individual's own strengths, most IPPs aim to:

- provide work or other goal-directed activity from which new skills may be developed;
- provide new experiences;
- develop the individual's response to familiar experiences;
- develop and reinforce positive self-esteem;
- ameliorate any challenging behaviours that prevent the service-user from accessing the opportunities provided as thoroughly as possible;
- ensure that all necessary services are co-ordinated;
- ensure that service-users are assisted in determining their own future.

As has been described above, some parents have difficulty in allowing their adult children to sample new experiences that they feel may leave them vulnerable, and they also have difficulty in allowing choice-making to the fullest possible extent. These parents told us that they often feel thwarted because the only time when they can vent their fears and describe their anxieties is at the regular review meetings. Some complained that their views were never taken account of in any case:

> There's no point in us talking about what Megan needs. They don't listen, we've had her for 21 years but they still think they know better than we do what she wants and needs. It's ridiculous, the way they try to get her to make choices. For example, we know that she is capable of choosing what colour sweater she wants to put on, but so what, where's that going to get her? And what happens if she wants to put on a yellow sweater which is thick and heavy on a scorchingly hot day, surely they couldn't let her do that?

Of course, that is precisely what the staff allowed Megan to do, whereupon she soon discovered that choosing her heavy yellow sweater on a hot day led to her feeling uncomfortable. As a result, she quickly learned other reasons for making choices in addition to those to do with colour.

Strengths approach

There are six basic principles to the strengths perspectives (Saleeby, 1996). Of these, the first, namely empowerment, will be considered in the next section, but in general terms it is about encouraging service-users to discover their skills and resources and then to use them regularly. The second principle concerns membership, ensuring that service-users are treated as members of their day centre or residential facility and external community. Thirdly, the strengths perspective is about regeneration and processes of change from within through the gradual relaxation of external controls. The fourth basic principle concerns synergy, i.e. the recognition that service-users and their professional workers can obtain a better result by working together than would be possible if there was no such partnership. It is also clear that parents should be an important part of any synergic relationship. The fifth principle concerns dialogue and collaboration. This can be particularly important for adults who are high-functioning such that they can be encouraged to consult with staff rather than expect the staff continually to provide them with answers and guidance. The final basic principle of the strengths perspective concerns the suspension of disbelief, i.e. a freeing from the negative self-opinions which effectively prevent the client from moving forward.

Making choices

The issue of autonomy in choice-making is inextricably linked to concepts concerning the quality of life. This also involves fundamental human needs such as autonomy, fulfilment and the right to respect. These core factors are embodied in guidance on the provision of services for disabled people (Department of Health and Social Security Inspectorate, 1989). Choice-making is an aspect of autonomous functioning which defines the individuality of another person (Wilson, 1992), being able to make choices and act on them to provide learning opportunities for individuals who profit from the resulting experiences. Independent choice-making involves the provision of opportunities to think, plan and perform under self-direction and, whether the individual is aware of it or not, also involves a degree of risk-taking when deciding to make one or more choices from a range of possible options (Department of Health and Social Security Inspectorate, 1989). It is the aspect of risk-taking that most frightens parents as they worry about the possible impact of bad choices on their adult children with autism. They cannot readily put aside their protective role as parents to allow their children to make mistakes and suffer the consequences simply on the grounds that these mistakes create an opportunity for learning. From the professional viewpoint, there is often a misunderstanding that autonomy in choice-making means that the service-provider is there merely to support the service-user's choices (Hughson and Brown, 1992).

> Sally has enjoyed pouring water from one jug to another for most of her life; if she is ever allowed to make a choice about what she does, then that is all she will do. In the past her teachers would only allow her that activity in exchange for work they wanted her to do, and this proved to be a very suitable reward at home as well as at school. When she moved into the Local Authority provision at the age of 19, we were told by the social worker that using that as a reward was unethical, that Sally was using that repetitive behaviour as a means of communication and it shouldn't be turned into a bribe. The social worker had a lot to say about her being able to make

choices from a range of appropriate options. This sounded all very well and good, but what we discovered was that, although the options were there for Sally to make a choice, she had no desire to do so and instead went on endlessly pouring water.

As is often the case, good intentions are not backed by sufficient skills to make a reality of them. The practice of Sally's schoolteachers had been to discourage the repetitive and stereotyped autistic behaviours that Sally showed and to help her to replace them with more adaptive ones. Far from being an incursion on her right to make choices, this actually enabled her to sample a range of activities and learn from them. The use of the activity reward not only positively reinforced the skilled behaviour that Sally had shown, but indeed did act as a form of communication in that it confirmed for her that she had functioned appropriately. Far from extending her autonomy of choice-making, the social work staff of the adult provision had unwittingly created a restricted environment for her.

This provision was generic in the sense that it was established for a wide variety of disabilities. The difficulties encountered by Sally, the staff and her parents would not have occurred in a specialist setting where the professionals involved would have developed gradual 'small-step' approaches to wean Sally on to a variety of appropriate activities. Once sampled, she would be in a better position to choose between them and, if necessary, to return to her repetitive behaviour of water-pouring at times of stress. The professionals involved would also have helped her parents to understand the process that was being undertaken, and they would doubtless have seen many parallels with what they had experienced while Sally was still at school.

One of the most telling arguments in support of specialist provision for adults with autism is that it is more likely to promote a process of normalisation than generic provision, where the needs of the adults are not understood and where teaching strategies are not properly targeted to the core deficits of autism. If opportunities are carefully presented and teaching strategies are carefully designed, there is a greater likelihood of maximisation of the potential of autistic individuals than if they are dealt with in a standard manner as part of a homogeneous group of people with disabilities. Clearly, if the right to make choices is interpreted simply as supporting the individual's choice whenever possible, then there is little opportunity for that individual to learn how to bring choice-making under his or her own internal control. Careful teaching is required to help service-users with autism to become less dependent on external controls provided by others and more able to function according to internal controls that have been fostered by careful teaching and efficient learning. This argument is apparently paradoxical in that it is making a case for normalisation through specialist provision. Yet there is support for this, and not just from the parents of autistic adults. Jordan and Powell (1995) have cautioned against a universal concept of quality of life in favour of a system of appropriate and specialist teaching strategies which enable people with disabilities to find consistent ways of expressing their needs and communicating their choices. Mesibov's (1990) opinion of normalisation was critical. He argued that global values purporting to cover all disabilities would distract attention away from the levels and types of support that were required by people with disabilities. It may also be that unplanned and uncritical normalisation processes may bring about the opposite of that which is intended, namely the erosion of skills and a reduction in autonomy. It is well known that the attitudes of society, including professional workers, have a profound influence on the functional performance of people with learning difficulties, and this is a reflection of the fact that societal expectations and attitudes may well create barriers to efficient learning by individuals with disability (Brown and Hughson, 1987).

> They (the day-centre staff) worked almost feverishly to make George fit in so that he could enjoy all the lovely opportunities that were on offer. But he couldn't fit in, he has never been able to fit in and without the structure and support that he had been given in previous teaching he just broke down under stress. They kept talking about his rights and choices, but it seemed like political correctness gone mad.

Some of the parents that we spoke to felt that they did not understand what was meant by 'the right to make choices'. They thought deeply about the way in which they made choices and realised that there was little similarity with the choice-making strategies, where they existed, of their adult children with autism. Many of them found that their own puzzlement was shared by some of the professionals dealing with their adult children. The situation is much improved if there is a satisfactory operational definition of choice-making which professionals can work to and parents can understand. One definition, as given by Morgan (1996), is that it is an ability to think abstractly when weighing up the advantages and disadvantages of particular options before making a particular selection. Many people with autism are perhaps unable to perceive that options exist in given situations, and may as a consequence display stereotypic behaviour.

Jordan and Powell (1996) have reasoned that choice can only be meaningful if an individual has sufficient understanding to realise and act upon alternatives, relate these to existing knowledge and skills, and know how to use them in specific situations. All of these attributes of choice-making may need to be taught to adults with autism if they are to develop an understanding of what making a choice may mean in terms of selecting between options and 'being responsible' for outcomes.

Parents are aware that their adult children with autism have very different memory-processing to their own, and are conscious of the fact that, without a variety of different cues, mainly visual but some behavioural, their young adults function as though little of themselves was involved in the process. Difficulties at the level of understanding self are likely to contribute to a situation whereby an individual with autism will experience difficulties in remembering his or her own participation in activities, and so will seek out familiar cues to help to guide his or her behaviour (Frith, 1989; Happe, 1994). A major definition of learning is that it brings about relatively permanent changes in an individual's behaviour. It may be argued that learning in this sense promotes a more developed sense of identity, which is reflected in the changing perceptions of the individual about his or her place and role in society. It is not surprising, therefore, that adults with autism, even in familiar situations, may appear to be lacking in spontaneity and seem poorly motivated. They may provide a set response to a question or other form of enquiry which is not a true reflection of their wishes. It is therefore very difficult at times to know whether the adult with autism does or does not choose to do something, as opposed to responding automatically and with no real involvement with self. Patterns of expectation give rise to standard responses from adults with autism, such that even 'Yes' and 'No' answers might be more geared to the environment in which they find themselves than to their own internal checking of their wants and needs. High-functioning people with autism (e.g. Williams, 1996) have described how they experienced difficulty in interpreting which behaviours were their own and which they had learned were expected by others. This need not be a particularly autistic trait, as there are many people without disabilities who have learned to suppress their own 'I want' statements in order to take account of other people's needs. The likely difference between such people and those with autism is that the former are able to understand why they are suppressing their own needs, and can understand that this will lead to some kind of social exchange which is ultimately preferable to making their own choice and adhering to it.

As may be seen, the whole theoretical position concerning autonomy with regard to choice-making is extremely complex, and it is made more so by the introduction of another concept of 'empowerment', which Meade and Carter (1990) define as an 'ability to make effective decisions'. This concept appears alongside others such as partnership, advocacy and enablement in much of the language of policy relating to social care and its values. In general terms, empowerment is used when those individuals who are to be empowered have the intellectual capacity to take power back for themselves. Most parents of adult children with autism would agree that this could be extremely dangerous if applied freely to their sons and daughters. Jack (1995) argues that the concept of empowerment is probably inappropriate for use in relation to individuals who lack the cognitive and other functional skills necessary to take back power. A distinction is made between empowerment and enablement, the latter being the use of professional skills and strategies to develop the capabilities of other individuals. That, of course, is a process which parents would recognise in the specialist teaching and training of their children with autism. This is a helpful distinction and one which permits a compromise position between 'hard-line' normalisation and 'knowing what is best for people'. Indeed, Atkins et al. (1996) have pointed out that enablement may be the foundation upon which later empowerment may hinge.

At times in our conversations with them, parents have expressed surprise that less emphasis is placed on the completion of tasks in specialist centres than on the development of an understanding by their adult children of the processes involved and the subsequent benefits. Although outside the realm of autism, it is relevant to consider the statement of Harris (1991), who suggested that some practitioners can work according to a mistaken belief that they are being professional and objective, when in fact, they are simply making assessments and decisions based on their own beliefs. Those who understand that processes are perhaps more important than outcomes to the development of an individual's autonomy know that these processes will ultimately enable the individual client to take back some power from the professional worker. This can be particularly helpful to those adults with autism who show no particular signs of wanting to take control of their own lives.

Those parents who felt most satisfied with the provision that their adult children were receiving understood a philosophy of care that made explicit the goals of developing autonomy and choice whilst acknowledging the specific difficulties of service-users with autism. In practice, this involves constructing learning environments in such a way that learning can take place and that meaningful choice-making will be taught and encouraged.

Sexuality

After provision, the next major concern represented in our survey was associated with the development of sexuality among adolescents and young adults with autism, not only with regard to the behaviour that arises during this development, but also in relation to the way in which it is handled both within the home and within the day or residential centre. Certainly of all the many challenges that confront carers of adolescent and adult people with autism, the problem of defending the rights of these young people to explore their sexuality without putting themselves or others at risk is one of the greatest. Many unqualified residential care staff, no matter how experienced they are, have told us how they have chosen to ignore this problem in every way except to acknowledge it. From her survey of parents, DeMyer (1979) found that those with adolescent boys with autism believed that their child was not particularly interested in intercourse, whereas the parents of girls were concerned that their daughters might become 'passively' engaged in intercourse at the instigation of a male. Her survey also revealed that a high proportion of the parents of adolescent males reported that they showed inappropriate behaviour in public places; this included masturbation and rubbing their genitals against other people. At that time there appeared to be little interest in finding ways of dealing with their sexuality appropriately, and the focus appeared to be more on the suppression of sexual behaviour on the grounds that it could lead to significant problems and embarrassment. More recently, however, parents have expressed a need to know how to help their adolescent and adult children with autism to learn appropriate sexual behaviours (e.g. Torisky and Torisky, 1985). This includes the teaching of normal sexual preferences and the acceptable social interactions that go with these based on the values held by the parents themselves (e.g. Akerly, 1984). Ruble and Dalrymple (1993) suggest that this significant change in parental attitude may be associated with the increased numbers of adults with autism who live within the community.

The latter researchers also state that typically the caregivers (usually the parents) are responsible for deciding whether information on sexuality in the context of autism should be provided for their adolescent and adult children. That decision may depend entirely on what they understand by sexuality in this context. Dewey and Everard (1974), who are themselves parents of people with autism, make the point that the absence of expressed concerns about sexuality and sexual behaviour does not mean that all is well. Specifically, it does not mean that the individual with autism is content with his or her sexual experiences or that there is no wish for fulfilment through sexual experience. The parents of many adolescent children with autism to whom we have spoken have expressed concern that they simply did not know enough about the development of sexuality to help them to decide whether there was a problem or not. They were much less confident about their ability to predict problems that might occurr in the future, and felt insufficiently informed to recognise the antecedents of such problems. As one mother told us, 'I really worried about Jane as she got further into adolescence. I could see all the usual physical changes occurring, but they didn't seem to mean much to her. I worried that she would suddenly wake up to her sexuality and could be hurt and confused by it. I didn't know what to do for the best because I didn't know in what way autism might affect normal sexual experiences anyway.'

Those parents whose adolescent children with autism also had severe learning difficulties as well as the core deficits in social communication, social imagination and social behaviour felt particularly 'at sea'. It is perhaps useful to review what is regarded as normal development for sexuality and to examine where there are particular areas of concern in the context of autism.

Physical development

The rapid changes occurring at puberty that create the secondary sexual characteristics such as body and facial hair can be distressing even for young people without disabilities. As well as these physical changes, there may be anxiety about the increasingly sensitive areas (erogenous zones) throughout the body. These changes typically occur between 10 and 14 years of age, but many young people find that they occur rapidly within that time span and are therefore difficult to accommodate without anxiety. It is thought that there may be some delay in the onset of puberty in people with autism, but the effects are very much the same.

> I remember seeing James standing in front of his full-length mirror trying to pluck out pubic hairs. He was crying with the pain, but his desperation to go back to what he thought was normal was greater. It was only after his older brother took him into the rugby team's changing-room that he realised he didn't have some horrible disease.

Intellectual changes

The onset of adolescence usually brings with it a significant advance in the way in which young people think and reason, often referred to as formal operational thinking, when young people progress from their very concrete intellectual patterns and become able to handle abstractions and abstract ideas. Not only does this mean that they become more able to tackle abstract concepts, such as those which occur in the maths curriculum, but they also become more able to formulate hypotheses about social interactions and the way in which other people think and feel. This is a powerful and beneficial factor enabling the more complex social interactions that adult sexual behaviour requires. However, young people with autism seldom enter this higher phase of intellectual development. Their thinking and reasoning remain locked into the concrete operational thinking of childhood, and this in turn augments their already defective social communication.

Social development

Allied to this important change in intellectual processes is the normal social development of adolescents which is focused on two particular factors. First of all there is a tendency for adolescents to identify strongly with people outside the family group. These may include pop idols, important sporting figures and also young people within their peer group. This identification, which is usually accompanied by a heightened sense of self, leads to an apparent moving away from the family group. The word 'apparent' is valid here because most adolescents still acknowledge the family group as being very important to them. It is perhaps fairer to say that their range of social interactions increases without necessarily excluding those groups which have been important to them from the earliest days of childhood.

Naturally this phase of development is more likely to progress smoothly if the young person has always had significant relationships within a peer group. This is unlikely to have been the case for many children with autism, because the core deficits in social understanding and communication will have largely ruled out the development of normal peer relationships. Even those who may be described as 'high-functioning' may at best have been participants within peer relationships on the fringe of a group, with little or no understanding of the group dynamics. Those children who have additional severe learning difficulties may not even have had this level of peer group experience, and so may only have observed, without understanding, normal patterns of interactions.

All my friends agreed that Robert was one of the most handsome boys they had seen. He was tall, slim and good-looking; when he smiled it was like the sun coming out. It broke my heart to see him standing on the edge of the school disco, occasionally hopping from one foot to another in a parody of the dancing that was going on in front of him. He seemed so cut off from it all; even those pupils who were much less able than he but without autism showed more understanding and more ability to have fun. Some of them were Down's children and others that had very severe learning difficulties, but there was that social spark about them that Robert never had and never would have. There he was, the best-looking boy in the room and the only one not joining in. I think that's when I really began to understand what autism would mean to Robert; no matter what happened, no matter how good his education, he was always going to be a wallflower.

Sexual behaviour

These strong sexual urges that are characteristic of adolescents can become intrusive if the young person is unable to control them properly or is upset by them. Hopefully their parents and/or school will be able to provide vital information about what these urges mean and what the purpose of sexual behaviour is in terms of reproduction. Secure and loving families are often able to give young people the support they need during this time, and so enable them to manage their developing sexual tendencies effectively.

This is, of course, far more difficult if the young person concerned is autistic and complex communication with him or her is difficult or impossible.

In normal terms, the age at which sexual behaviour commences seems to be getting younger. By the end of their adolescence, more than 50% of all girls and 75% of all boys will have engaged in sexual intercourse. A variety of forces interact to cause young people to seek their sexual expression through cross-gender sexual interaction. Again these forces are associated with their understanding of and familiarity with peer relationships and the way in which those are experienced, both directly and indirectly, through the media.

Little is known about the frequency with which people with autism engage in interactive sexual behaviour. Parents report little interest in sexual intercourse among their older adolescent or early adult children with autism, but masturbation is very common and, in the experience of many parents, can become compulsive.

Many parents who witness a rapid increase in the frequency with which their young people with autism masturbate become anxious that the provision of information to these young people about the appropriateness of sexual behaviour may stimulate direct sexual advances towards others with all that this would entail in terms of conflict and embarrassment. They recall their own experiences of their children touching their genital areas and breasts as evidence that this prediction might come horribly true. In fact there is little evidence to support this hypothesis. Certainly among the population of non-disabled adolescents there is no indication that information about sexuality actually promotes a desire to engage in it. Clearly the provision of information must be done sensitively and with due regard for the fact that people with autism do not pick up on inhibiting social cues as well as people without autism. Nevertheless, there is certainly no direct evidence that improving the understanding of sexual behaviour does provoke such behaviour in people with autism.

CASE STUDY 9.1

I had argued furiously with the Centre Manager that James should not be encouraged to masturbate in his room or anywhere else for that matter. I have had 3 years of him rubbing his crutch against me whenever he could and I thought that allowing him to masturbate would just set him off against other women. His Dad and I couldn't stand the thought of that.

Actually the Centre Manager was right; James was a lot less frustrated after he had been shown how to masturbate, and now we respect his privacy to do this when he is home with us.

Sexuality and autism

Returning now to the discourse on what is understood about sexuality in the context of autism, Ford (1987) suggested that issues concerning sexuality are taught too late, and often at the point when inappropriate sexual behaviour has already become problematic (e.g. masturbation in public). Menstrual hygiene also seems to be a powerful stimulus for parents to provide appropriate information. The way in which that information is given depends entirely upon the way in which the parent or other caregiver understands both the effects of autism and the effects of adolescence. Parents have told us that they find it difficult to reconcile the normal development of their adolescent with autism in terms of physical changes, in contrast to the abnormal aspects of development they have experienced for years. Cairns (1986) had heard similar confusions and acknowledged that many parents find it difficult to reconcile the normal physical development of their child with autism with the child they had known for so long who has consistently displayed impaired development and faulty social behaviour.

Ford (1987) believes that programmes should be established for individuals with autism on the assumption that they can learn relationship skills. This is contrary to other views, which either discourage sexuality for people with autism (e.g. Lieberman and Melone, 1979) or suggest that it is an irrelevance given the characteristics of autism (e.g. Elgar, 1985). Such conflicting viewpoints among professionals do nothing to help to resolve the bad experiences and confusion of parents and other caregivers, and are probably a legacy of the fact that, for the most part, the history of people with autism is that they have lived in segregated provisions (e.g. Sullivan, 1977, unpublished manuscript cited by Ruble and Dalrymple, 1993) where sexuality was either ignored or repressed.

Increasingly, however, there is a trend to assert the rights of individuals with disabilities. Thus over the past 20 years people with learning difficulties have been 'given' sexual rights (e.g. Craft, 1987), and gradually society is coming to accept that there are moral reasons why appropriate sexual experiences should not be limited by the wishes of the non-disabled population. At the very least, therefore, parents and other caregivers must acknowledge the sexual behaviour of people with autism, even if that is only at the level of solitary masturbation in private. As a consequence of such an acknowledgement, it is clear that however difficult and embarrassing it may be, it is necessary to teach where masturbation is and is not acceptable behaviour in order that people with autism do not further alienate themselves from society as a result of inappropriate sexual behaviour.

In one notable study, Ruble and Dalrymple (1993) analysed survey responses from the parents of people with autism. Their sampling resulted in an analysis of responses from 32 females and 68 males between the ages of 9.1 and 38.9 years (average age 19.5 years).

This wide-ranging survey of parental concerns and sexual awareness made use of the Sexuality Awareness Survey (SAS) instrument developed by the authors. This consisted of 15 open-ended questions covering the following:

1. social/sexual awareness;
2. sex education;
3. sexual behaviours;
4. parental concerns;
5. interest in receiving more information about sexuality.

The results were presented for each of the five issues addressed by the questionnaire.

Social/sexual awareness

The results showed that individuals with more verbal skills were more likely to demonstrate knowledge and understanding of sexuality, and to show an ability to be taught rules. Such individuals expressed a desire for privacy during toileting, by being alone during bathtime and when dressing. Of the sample, 33% showed an understanding of the need for privacy when masturbating, and a small minority also wanted to be alone when carrying out other activities such as eating or listening to music. People with autism who had more verbal skills were also more likely to want privacy.

In total, 94% of the parents claimed to have taught their children with autism specific rules governing sex-related behaviour:

- undressing only in the bathroom/bedroom (76%);
- touching private body parts only in private places (75%);
- closing the bathroom door (71%);
- walking around the home and outside only with clothes on (71%);
- taking underwear off (specifically) only in the bathroom/bedroom (64%);
- 'safety' rules about being touched by others, knocking on doors, etc. (8%).

Those parents who had taught such rules had used several methods, including the following:

- constant repetition (68%);
- redirecting (55%);
- rewarding appropriate behaviours (49%);
- modelling (44%);
- scolding/punishment (28%);
- other (8%).

Interestingly, a gender difference was found in that males were more likely to be taught rules than females.

Sex education
Only the parents of verbal offspring with autism reported attempts at sex education and thought that their sons/daughters would benefit from it. Of these parents, 45% used one-to-one discussion with a particular person (not necessarily a parent), whereas of the remainder the largest single group (55%) allowed their son/daughter to receive their sex education at school.

Sexual behaviours
The survey revealed that people with autism engage in a wide variety of sexual behaviours, including the following:

- touching their own private parts in public (65%);
- masturbation in public (23%);
- removal of clothes in public (28%);
- touching other people of the opposite sex inappropriately (18%);
- a wide variety of other behaviour was reported, including looking up or down the clothing of others, touching parents inappropriately, talking about sex-related subjects at inappropriate times and places, etc. (18%);

- masturbation involving inappropriate objects, such as (quoted by the authors of the survey) 'a pair of socks' (14%).

Ruble and Dalrymple (1993) also reported that some of the sex behaviours of the sons and daughters of the parents surveyed caused particular problems other than embarrassment in public. These difficulties ranged from males who refused to touch their penis while urinating, to compulsive masturbation.

Penile erection causes great concern among many adolescent males with autism. Ruble and Dalrymple (1993) report the case of one son who apologised for wetting the bed after he had ejaculated, and another who thought his penis had broken.

About 50% of the parents of girls reported that menstruation and the changing sensitivity of sex organs worried their daughters, and one parent reported problems with mood swings.

Although the proportions varied considerably, our own survey material supports all of these concerns, or variations on them. The following case studies clearly demonstrate the severity of problems that parents can face with regard to developing sexual behaviour.

CASE STUDY 9.2

Kenneth was one of the easiest autistic boys in our group. He had never developed any severe challenging behaviours, and for much of the time we never really thought about his autism.

But by the age of 14 he had discovered masturbation and he wouldn't stop. It was horrible to see him anywhere in the house or garden pulling at himself and getting it all over his hands and clothes.

We got to the point where we couldn't take him out—even to the shops and pubs that used to accept him happily. People were sympathetic but firmly rejected him. He wasn't our Ken anymore.

CASE STUDY 9.3

Michelle got obsessive about the way her body started changing. She spent ages each day in front of the mirror, stroking her breasts and pulling at her pubic hair.

Soon she wanted to do this wherever she saw her own reflection. We found her one day in Tescos in front of the reflective steel side of a refrigerator taking her top off and rubbing her breasts.

Parental concerns
A major concern shared by many parents in both surveys was that their child's behaviour would be misinterpreted and thought to be sexual when

in fact it was motivated by something completely different. These concerns were independent of the gender of their child, unlike those concerning pregnancy. For example, Ruble and Dalrymple estimated that 61% of the responding parents of girls in their study were concerned that their daughter would become pregnant, whereas only 19% of the parents of boys were concerned that their son would get a girl pregnant. Following the trends of the general population, the parents of boys were more likely to be concerned that their sons would be used sexually by a person of the same sex, whereas parents of girls were not unnaturally concerned about abuse by a person of the opposite sex.

Other parents expressed a different kind of concern. They knew that it was their parental responsibility to try to ensure the safety of their adolescents or young adults with autism, and also of those people whom their sons and daughters might encounter. Where those sons and daughters lacked verbal communication skills the main worry was how to teach them appropriate behaviour.

In many ways this concern was related to possible misinterpretation of behaviour by people outside the family, such that the son or daughter might be accused of doing something that was construed as a sexual invitation or as sexual abuse by an observer.

Information-seeking
Many of the concerns outlined above were linked by the parents in our survey to a requirement for detailed information. Many parents felt that they were not coping as well as they should be. This was often a consequence of their lack of knowledge about the relevance of sexual relationships to their growing son and daughter, or whether specific behaviour such as masturbation should be allowed, controlled or discouraged. Ruble and Dalrymple (1993) discovered that information about masturbation was significantly more frequently asked for by the parents of male adolescents than of females. However, our survey did not show quite such a marked gender difference. This suggests that 3 to 4 years on from the Ruble and Dalrymple survey, the parents of daughters with autism had perhaps become more aware of sexual satisfaction being obtained by masturbation.

In both surveys the parents of daughters had sought or would seek information on birth control and whether or not the latter should be practised. Inevitably that request for information was accompanied by another concerning who should introduce the use of birth control and the reasons for it, and how this should be done. Once again, the parents of higher functioning, verbally communicating sons and daughters with autism were more likely to require information.

Sexuality policies and the delivery of services

The attitude of parents to sexual matters is a powerful and important influence with regard to people with learning disabilities. According to Rose and Jones (1994), there are four levels of interaction between parents and professionals relating to sexuality that need to be addressed. These are:

- no interaction;
- reacting to incidents;
- receiving information;
- dialogue: development and education.

1. *No interaction*. Sexuality is dismissed and ignored because of the fear that raising issues will lead to promiscuity and over-sexualised behaviour. Another reason for no interaction taking place is that sexuality and sexual matters are located exclusively with either parents or professionals and conveniently forgotten by the other group.
2. *Reacting to incidents*. Sex is often seen as a problem regardless of its appropriateness or otherwise. When any sexual expression is labelled as problematic, the response is generally to minimise the risk and thereby curtail the freedom and potential for development of the individual concerned.
3. *Receiving information*. The then Department of Education and Science (1987) expected all schools to develop 'appropriate and responsible sex education'. This applies to children and young people with learning disabilities, and these curriculum developments are open to parental scrutiny at governors' meetings.
4. *Dialogue: development and education*. Dialogue between parents and professionals is the keystone of success. There is debate as whether individual or group approaches work best.

Policy guidelines can be invaluable in developing professional/parent co-operation, and can protect staff from the inevitable stresses that arise from issues of sexuality and sexual expression. A policy may also promote the rights of individuals with autism to be accepted as sexual beings, and provide a protective framework. Guidelines should be proactive, supportive and professional. They provide acceptable boundaries for the professional and the individual (Craft and Brown, 1994), and as such should be an important part of the 'life' of any organisation that provides care and training for young adults with autism. As unpalatable as the issue of sexuality may be to parents, it will not go away, so an overt policy that is carefully practical and closely monitored is ultimately reassuring to parents.

REFERENCES

Aarons, M. and Gittens, T. (1991) Autism as a context. *Special Children*, **September**, 14–17.

Aarons, M. and Gittens, T. (1992) *The Handbook of Autism*. London: Routledge.

Aiken, J. M. and Saltzberg, C. L. (1984) The effects of a sensory extinction procedure on stereotypic sounds of two autistic children. *Journal of Autism and Developmental Disorders*, **14**, 291–9.

Akerly, M. (1984) Developmental changes in families with autistic children: a parent's perspective. In E. Schopler and G. Mesibov (Eds), *The Effects of Autism on the Family* (pp. 85–98). New York: Plenum Press.

American Psychiatric Association (1994) *Diagnostic and Statistical Manual of Mental Disorders* (4th Edn). Washington, DC: American Psychiatric Association.

Apolloni, A. and Triest, G. (1983) Respite services in California: status and recommendations for improvement. *Mental Retardation*, **21**, 240–3.

Arbelle, S., Sigman, M. D. and Kasari, C. (1994) Compliance with parental prohibition in autistic children. *Journal of Autism and Developmental Disorders*, **24**, 693–702.

Asperger, H. (1944) Autistic psychopathy in childhood. In U. Frith (Ed.), *Autism and Asperger Syndrome* (pp. 37–92). Cambridge: Cambridge University Press.

Atkins, C., Burrows, T., Reynolds, B. and Shattock, P. (1996) *Promoting Social, Emotional and Physical Well-being*. Module 1, Unit 1, Distance Learning. Birmingham: Adults with Autism, School of Education, University of Birmingham.

Attwood, T. (1993) *Why Does Chris Do That?* London: The National Autistic Society.

August, G., Stewart, M. and Tsai, L. (1981) The incidence of cognitive disabilities in the siblings of autistic children. *British Journal of Psychiatry*, **138**, 416–22.

Ayer, S. and Alaszewski, A. (1986) *Community Care and the Mentally Handicapped: Services for Mothers and Their Mentally Handicapped Children* (2nd Edn). London: Croom Helm.

Bagenholm, A. and Gillberg, C. (1991) Psychosocial effects on siblings of children with autism and mental retardation: a population-based study. *Journal of Mental Deficiency Research*, **35**, 291–307.

Bailey, D. B., Simeonsson, R. J., Winton, P. J., Huntington, G. S., Comfort, M., Isbell, P., O'Donnell, K. J. and Helm, J. M. (1986) Family-focused intervention: a functional model for planning, implementing, and evaluating individual family services in early intervention. *Journal of the Division of Early Childhood*, **10**, 156–71.

Baird, T. D. and August, G. J. (1985) Familial heterogeneity in infantile autism. *Journal of Autism and Developmental Disorders*, **15**, 315–21.

Baltaxe, C. (1977) Pragmatic deficits in the language of autistic adolescents. *Journal of Paediatric Psychology*, **2**, 176–80.

Baron-Cohen, S. (1988) Social and pragmatic deficits in autism: cognitive or affective? *Journal of Autism and Developmental Disorders*, **18**, 379–402.

Baron-Cohen, S. (1989) The autistic child's theory of mind: a case of specific developmental delay. *Journal of Child Psychology and Psychiatry*, **30**, 285–97.

Baron-Cohen, S. (1991) Do people with autism understand what causes emotion? *Child Development*, **62**, 385–95.

Baron-Cohen, S., Leslie, A. M. and Frith, U. (1985) Does the autistic child have a 'theory of mind'? *Cognition*, **21**, 37–46.

Bauman, M. L., Courchesne, E., Denckla, M. B., Folstein, S. E., James, L. S., Minshew, N. J., Nelson, K. B., Piven, J. and Rapin, I. (1991) An update on autism: a developmental disorder. *Paediatrics*, **87 (Suppl.)**, v–vi.

Bernal, M. E. (1984) Consumer issues in parent training. In R. F. Dangel and R. A. Polster (Eds), *Parent Training: Foundations of Research and Practice* (pp. 477–503). New York: Guilford Press.

Bettelheim, B. (1967) *The Empty Fortress*. New York: Free Press.

Bolton, P., Macdonald, H., Pickles, A., Rios, P., Goode, S., Crowson, M., Bailey, A. and Rutter, M. (1994) A case-control family study of autism. *Journal of Child Psychology and Psychiatry*.

Bouma, R. and Schweitzer, R. (1990) The impact of chronic childhood illness on family stress: a comparison between autism and cystic fibrosis. *Journal of Clinical Psychology*, **46**, 722–30.

Bowers, T. (1995) Parents, partnership and education officers—a study in attributions. *Child Care Health and Development*, **21**, 135–48.

Boxill, E. H. (1985) *Music Therapy for the Developmentally Disabled*. Austin, TX: Pro-Ed, Inc.

Bradshaw, Y. W. (1993) The political economy of human needs. *Contemporary Sociology*, **22**, 77–88.

Brechin, A. and Walmsey, J. (1989) *Making Connections: Reflecting on the Lives and Experiences of People with Learning Difficulties*. London: Hodder & Stoughton/Open University.

Bristol, M. M. (1984) Family resources and successful adaptation to autistic children. In E. Schopler and G. B. Mesibov (Eds), *The Effects of Autism on the Family* (pp. 91–141). London: Plenum Press.

Bristol, M. (1987) Mothers of children with autism or communication disorders: successful adaptation and the double ABCX model. *Journal of Autism and Developmental Disorders*, **17**, 469–86.

Bristol, M. M. and Schopler, E. (1983) Coping and stress in families of autistic adolescents. In E. Schopler and G. B. Mesibov (Eds), *Autism in Adolescents and Adults* (pp. 251–78). New York: Plenum Press.

Bristol, M. M. and Schopler, E. (1984) A developmental perspective on stress and coping in families of autistic children. In J. Blacher (Ed.), *Severely Handicapped Young Children and Their Families: Research in Review* (pp. 91–141). Orlando, FL: Academic Press.

Bristol, M. M., Gallagher, J. J. and Holt, K. D. (1993) Maternal depressive symptoms in autism: response to psychoeducational intervention. *Rehabilitation Psychology*, **38**, 3–10.

Brown, R. and Hughson, E. A. (1987) *Behavioural and Social Rehabilitation and Training*. Chichester: John Wiley.

Burke, P. and Cigno, K. (1996) *Support for Families: Helping Children with Learning Disabilities*. Aldershot: Avebury.

Byrne, E. and Cunningham, C. (1985) The effects of mentally handicapped children on families—a conceptual review. *Journal of Child Psychology and Psychiatry*, **26**, 847–64.

Cairns, R. (1986) Social development: recent theoretical trends and relevance for autism. In E. Schopler and G. Mesibov (Eds), *Social Behavior in Autism* (pp. 15–33). New York: Plenum Press.

Campbell, M. (1975) Pharmacotherapy in early infantile autism. *Biological Psychiatry*, **10**, 399–423.

Cantwell, D., Baker, L. and Rutter, M. (1976) Family factors. In M. Rutter and E. Schopler (Eds), *Autism: A Reappraisal of Concepts and Treatment* (pp. 269–96). Plenum Press: New York.

Cantwell, D., Baker, L. and Rutter, M. (1979) Families of autistic and dysphasic children. I. Family life and interaction patterns. *Archives of General Psychiatry*, **36**, 682–8.

Capps, L., Yirmiya, N. and Sigman, M. (1992) Understanding of simple and complex emotions in non-retarded children with autism. *Journal of Child Psychology and Psychiatry*, **33**, 1169–82.

Carlberg, C. and Kavale, K. (1980) The efficacy of special versus regular class placement for exceptional children: a meta-analysis. *Journal of Special Education*, **14**, 295–309.

Cicirelli, V. G. (1985) Sibling relationships throughout the life cycle. In L. L'Abate (Ed.), *The Handbook of Family Psychology and Therapy. Vol. 1* (pp. 177–214). Homewood, IL: Dorsey.

Clark, P. and Rutter, M. (1981) Autistic children's responses to structure and to interpersonal demands. *Journal of Autism and Developmental Disorders*, **11**, 201–17.

Cohen, S. (1982) Supporting families through respite care. *Rehabilitation Literature*, **43**, 7–11.

Cohen, S., Mermelstein, R., Kamarck, T. and Hoberman, H. (1985) Measuring the functional components of social support. In I. G. Sarason and B. Sarason (Eds), *Social Support: Theory, Research and Application* (pp. 73–94). The Hague, The Netherlands: Martinus Nijhoff.

Courchesne, E. (1989) Neuroanatomical systems involved in infantile autism: the implications of cerebellar abnormalities. In G. Dawson (Ed.), *Autism: Nature, Diagnosis and Treatment* (pp. 119–43). New York: Guilford Press.

Cox, A., Rutter, M., Newman, S. and Bartak, L. (1975) A comparative study of infantile autism and specific developmental receptive language disorder. II. Parental characteristics. *British Journal of Psychiatry*, **126**, 146–59.

Craft, A. (1987) *Mental Handicap and Sexuality*. London: Costello.

Craft, A. and Brown, H. (1994) Personal relationships and sexuality. In A. Craft (Ed.), *Practice Issues in Learning Disabilities* I (pp. 1–22) London: Routledge.

Crynic, K. A. and Leconte, J. M. (1986) Understanding sibling needs and influences. In R. R. Fewell and P. F. Vadasy (Eds), *Families of Handicapped Children: Needs and Supports across the Life Span* (pp. 56–72). Austin, TX: Pro-Ed, Inc.

Cunningham, C. E., Reuler, E., Blackwell, J. and Deck, J. (1981) Behavioral and linguistic developments in the interactions of normal and retarded children with their mother. *Child Development*, **52**, 62–70.

Cutler, B. C. and Kozloff, M. A. (1987) Living with autism: effects on families and family needs. In D. J. Cohen and A. M. Donnellan (Eds), *Handbook of Autism and Pervasive Developmental Disorders* (pp. 513–27). New York: John Wiley.

Dangel, R. F. and Polster, R. A. (Eds) (1984) *Parent Training: Foundations of Research and Practice*. New York: Guilford Press.

DeMyer, M. K. (1979) *Parents and Children with Autism*. New York: John Wiley.

DeMyer, M. K. and Goldberg, P. (1983) Family needs of the autistic adolescent. In E. Schopler and G. B. Mesibov (Eds), *Autism in Adolescents and Adults* (pp. 225–50). London: Plenum Press.

Department of Health and Social Security Inspectorate (1989) *Homes Are For Living In*. London: HMSO.

Department of Health/Social Services Inspectorate (1991) *Care Management and Assessment: Manager's Guide*. Milton Keynes: HMSO.

Dewey, M. and Everard, M. (1974) The near normal autistic adolescent. *Journal of Autism and Childhood Schizophrenia*, **4**, 348–56.

Donenberg, G. and Baker, B. L. (1993) The impact of young children with externalising behaviors on their families. *Journal of Abnormal Child Psychology*, **21**, 179–98.

Dumas, J. E. and Wahler, R. G. (1983) Predictors of treatment outcome in parent training: mother insularity and socioeconomic disadvantage. *Behavioral Assessment*, **5**, 301–13.

Dunlap, G. and Robbins, F. R. (1991) Current perspectives in service delivery for young children with autism. *Comprehensive Mental Health Care*, **1**, 177–94.

Dunlap, G., Robbins, F. R. and Darrow, M. A. (1994) Parents' reports of their children's challenging behaviors: results of a statewide survey. *Mental Retardation*, **32**, 206–12.

Dunn, J. and Kendrick, C. (1982) Siblings and their mothers: developing relationships within the family. In M. E. Lamb and B. Sutton-Smith (Eds), *Sibling Relationships: Their Nature and Significance Across the Life Span* (pp. 39–60). Hillsdale, NJ: Erlbaum.

Dyson, L. L. (1989) Adjustment of siblings of handicapped children: a comparison. *Journal of Pediatric Psychology*, **14**, 215–29.

Elgar, S. (1985) Sex education and sexual awareness building for autistic children and youth: some viewpoints and considerations. *Journal of Autism and Developmental Disorders*, **15**, 214–6.

Ell, K. (1996) Social networks, social support and coping with serious illness: the family connection. *Social Science and Medicine*, **42**, 173–83.

Emerson, E., Barrett, S., Bell, C., Cummings, R., McTool, C., Toogood, A. and Mansell, J. (1987) *Developing Services for People with Severe Learning Difficulties and Challenging Behaviours*. Canterbury: Institute of Social and Applied Psychology, University of Kent.

Estrada, A. U. and Pinsof, W. M. (1995) The effectiveness of family therapies for selected behavioral disorders in childhood. *Journal of Marital and Family Therapy*, **21**, 403–40.

Factor, D. C., Perry, A. and Freeman, N. (1990) Brief report: stress, social support, and respite care use in families with autistic children. *Journal of Autism and Developmental Disorders*, **20**, 139–46.

Farber, B. (1963) Some effects of retarded children on the mother. In M. Sussman (Ed.), *Sourcebook on Marriage and the Family* (pp. 324–33). Boston, MA: Houghton-Mifflin.

Favell, J. E., McGimsey, J. F. and Schnell, R. M. (1982) Treatment of self-injury by providing alternate sensory activities. *Analysis and Intervention in Developmental Disabilities*, **2**, 83–104.

Featherstone, H. (1980) *A Difference in the Family*. New York: Basic Books.

Ferrari, M. (1987) The diabetic child and well sibling: risks to the well child's self-concept. *Children's Health Care*, **15**, 141–7.

Fisman, S. and Wolf, L. (1991) The handicapped child: psychological effects of parental, marital and sibling relationships. *Psychiatric Clinics of North America,* **14**, 199–217.

Folstein, S. and Rutter, M. (1998) Infantile autism: a genetic study of 21 twin pairs. *Journal of Autism and Developmental Disorders,* **18**, 3–30.

Ford, A. (1987) Sex education for individuals with autism: structuring information and opportunities. In D. Cohen and A. Donnellan (Eds), *Handbook of Autism and Developmental Pervasive Disorders* (pp. 430–9). New York: John Wiley.

Foxx, R. M. and Azrin, N. H. (1973) The elimination of autistic self-stimulatory behaviour by over-correction. *Journal of Applied Behaviour Analysis,* **6**, 1–14.

Franco, E. (1985) Unusual histories: clinical studies of autism. *Revue Freudienne,* **15**, 67–87.

Frith, U. (1989) *Autism: Explaining the Enigma.* Oxford: Basil Blackwell.

Frude, N. (1992) *Understanding Family Problems: A Psychological Approach.* Chichester: John Wiley.

Gallagher, J., Beckman, P. and Cross, I. (1983) Families of handicapped children: sources of stress and its amelioration. *Exceptional Children,* **50**, 10–19.

Gath, A. (1972) The mental health of siblings of congenitally abnormal children. *Journal of Child Psychology and Psychiatry,* **13**, 211–18.

Gibb, C. and Randall, P. E. (1989a) *Parents and Professionals.* London: Macmillan.

Gibb, C. and Randall, P. E. (1989b) Structured management and autism. *British Journal of Special Education,* **14**, 68–70.

Gillberg, C. (Ed.) (1989) *Diagnosis and Treatment of Autism.* London: Plenum Press.

Gillberg, C. (1993) Autism and related behaviours. *Journal of Intellectual Disability Research,* **37**, 343–72.

Gillberg, C., Steffenberg, S. and Schaumann, H. (1991) Is autism more common now than ten years ago? *British Journal of Psychiatry,* **158**, 403–9.

Goodman, R. (1989) Infantile autism: a syndrome of multiple primary deficits. *Journal of Autism and Developmental Disorders,* **19**, 409–24.

Gray, D. E. (1993) Perceptions of stigma: the parents of autistic children. *Sociology of Health and Illness,* **15**, 102–20.

Grossman, G. K. (1972) *Brothers and Sisters of Retarded Children: An Exploratory Study.* Syracuse: Syracuse University Press.

Gualtieri, C. T. (1991) The functional neuroanatomy of psychiatric disorders. In M. M. Konstantareas and J. H. Beitchman (Eds), *Pervasive Developmental Disorders* (pp. 113–24). Philadelphia, PA: W. B. Saunders.

Gurman, A. S., Kniskern, D. P. and Pinsof, W. M. (1986) Research on the process and outcome of marital and family therapy. In S. L. Garfield and A. E. Bergin (Eds), *Handbook of Psychotherapy and Behavior Change* (3rd Edn) (pp. 565–624). New York: John Wiley.

Handleman, J. S. (1990) Providing effective consultation to students with severe developmental difficulties and their families. *Journal of Educational and Psychological Consultation,* **1**, 137–47.

Hanson, C. L., Henggeler, S. W., Harris, M. A., Cigrang, J. A., Schinkel, A. M., Rodrigue, J. R. and Klesges, R. C. (1992) Contributions of sibling relations to the adaptation of youths with insulin-dependent diabetes mellitus. *Journal of Consulting and Clinical Psychology,* **60**, 104–12.

Happe, G. (1994) *Autism: An Introduction to Psychological Theory,* London: UCL Press.

Harris, P. (1989) *Children and Emotion: the Development of Psychological Understanding.* Oxford: Basil Blackwell.

Harris, S., Handleman, J., Kristoff, B., Bass, L. and Gordon, R. (1990) Changes in language development among autistic and peer children in segregated and integrated preschool settings. *Journal of Autism and Developmental Disorders*, **20**, 23–31.

Harris, S. L. (1982) A family systems approach to behavioral training with parents of autisic children. *Child and Family Behavior Therapy*, **4**, 21–35.

Harris, S. L. (1983) *Families of the Developmentally Disabled: A Guide to Behavioral Intervention*. New York: Pergamon Press.

Harris, S. L. (1984a) The family and the autistic child: a behavioral perspective. *Family Practice*, **33**, 127–34.

Harris, S. L. (1984b) Intervention planning for the family of the autistic child: a multilevel assessment of the family system. *Journal of Marital and Family Therapy*, **10**, 157–66.

Harris, S. L. (1984c) The family of the autistic child: a behavioral-systems view. *Clinical Psychology Review*, **4**, 227–39.

Harris, S. L. and Powers, M. D. (1984) Behavior therapists look at the impact of an autistic child on the family system. In E. Schopler and G. B. Mesibov (Eds), *The Effects of Autism on the Family*. London: Plenum Press.

Harris, S. L., Wolchik, S. A. and Weitz, S. (1981) The acquisition of language skills by autistic children: can parents do the job? *Journal of Autism and Developmental Disorders*, **11**, 373–84.

Harris, S. L., Wolchik, S. A. and Milch, R. E. (1982) Changing the speech of autistic children and their parents. *Child and Family Behaviour Therapy*, **4**, 151–73.

Harris, S. L., Gill, M. J. and Alessandri, M. (1991) The family with an autistic child. In M. Seligman (Ed.), *The Family with a Handicapped Child* (pp. 316–23). London: Allyn & Bacon.

Harris, V. (1991) Values of social work in the context of British society in conflict with anti-racism. In CCETSW (Ed.), *Setting the Context for Change: Anti-Racist Social Work Education*. Leeds: CCETSW Northern Curriculum Development Project.

Harrold, C., Boucher, J. and Smith, P. (1993) Symbolic play in autism: a review. *Journal of Autism and Developmental Disorders*, **23**, 281–307.

Henggeler, S. W. and Borduin, C. M. (1990) *Family Therapy and Beyond: A Multisystematic Approach to Treating the Behavior Problems of Children and Adolescents*. Pacific Grove, CA: Brooks/Cole.

Hermelin, B. and O'Connor, M. (1970) *Psychological Experiments with Autistic Children*. London: Pergamon Press.

Hobson, R. P. (1986a) The autistic child's appraisal of expressions of emotion. *Journal of Child Psychology and Psychiatry*, **27**, 321–42.

Hobson, R. P. (1986b) The autistic child's appraisal of expressions of emotion: a further study. *Journal of Child Psychology and Psychiatry*, **27**, 671–80.

Hobson, R. P. (1989) Beyond cognition: a theory of autism. In G. Dawson (Ed.), *Autism: Nature, Diagnosis and Treatment* (pp. 22–48). New York: Guilford Press.

Hobson, R. P. (1993) *Autism and the Development of Mind*. Hove/Hillsdale: Lawrence Erlbaum.

Hobson, R. P., Ouston, J. and Lee, T. (1988) Emotion recognition in autism: coordinating faces and voices. *Journal of Psychological Medicine*, **18**, 911–23.

Hockey, V. (1991) Carved in stone. *Special Children*, **March**, 22–3.

Holroyd, J. and McArthur, D. (1976) Mental retardation and stress on the parents: a contrast between Down's syndrome and childhood autism. *American Journal of Mental Deficiency*, **80**, 431–6.

Hoppes, K. and Harris, S. L. (1990) Perceptions of child attachment and maternal gratification in mothers of children with autism and Down syndrome. *Journal of Clinical Child Psychology*, 19, 365–70.

Hornby, G. (1992) A review of fathers' accounts of their experiences of parenting children with disabilities. *Disability, Handicap and Society*, 7, 363–74.

Horner, R. H., Dunlop, G., Koegel, R. L., Carr, E. G., Sailor, W., Anderson, J., Albin, R. W. and O'Neill, R. E. (1990) Toward a technology of 'nonaversive' behavioural support. *Journal of the Association for Persons with Severe Handicaps*, 15, 125–32.

Howlin, P. (1988) Living with impairment: the effects on children having an autistic sibling. *Child: Care, Health and Development*, 14, 395–408.

Howlin, P. and Rutter, M. (1987) *The Treatment of Autistic Children*. Chichester: John Wiley.

Hoyson, M., Jamieson, B. and Strain, P. (1984) Individualized group instruction of normally developing and autistic-like children: the LEAP curriculum model. *Journal of the Division for Early Childhood*, 8, 157–72.

Hughson, E. A. and Brown, R. I. (1992) Learning difficulties in the context of social change: a challenge for professional action. In T. Thompson and P. Mathias (Eds), *Standards in Mental Handicap: Keys to Competence*. London: Baillière & Tindall.

Intagliata, J. and Doyle, N. (1984) Enhancing social support for parents of developmentally disabled children: training in interpersonal problem-solving skills. *Mental Retardation*, 22, 4–11.

Jack, R. (Ed.) (1995) *Empowerment in Community Care*. London: Chapman & Hall.

Jordan, R. and Powell, S. D. (1995) *Understanding and Teaching Children with Autism*. Chichester: John Wiley.

Jordan, R. and Powell, S. D. (1996) Encouraging flexibility in adults with autism. In H. Morgan (Ed.), *Adults with Autism: A Guide to Theory and Practice* (pp. 74–88). Cambridge: Cambridge University Press.

Kanner, L. (1943) Autistic disturbances of affective contact. *Nervous Child*, 2, 217–50.

Kanner, L. (1949) Problems of nosology and psychodynamics of early infantile autism. *American Journal of Orthopsychiatry*, 19, 416–26.

Kanner, L. and Lesser, L. (1958) *Early Infantile Autism: The Paediatric Clinics of North America*. Philadelphia, PA: W.B. Saunders Co.

Kasari, C., Sigman, M. D., Baumgartner, P. and Stipek, D. J. (1993) Pride and mastery in children with autism. *Journal of Child Psychology and Psychiatry*, 34, 353–62.

Kazak, A. (1987) Families with disabled children: stress and social networks in three samples. *Journal of Abnormal Child Psychology*, 25, 137–46.

Kazak, A. (1989) Family functioning in families with older institutionalised retarded offspring. *Journal of Autism and Developmental Disorders*, 19, 501–9.

Kazdin, A. E. (1993) Treatment of conduct disorder. Progress and directions in psychotherapy research. *Development and Psychopathology*, 5, 277–310.

Keeling, D. I., Price, P. E., Jones, E. and Harding, K. G. (1996) Social support: some pragmatic implications for health care professionals. *Journal of Advanced Nursing*, 223, 76–81.

Kern, L., Koegel, R. L. and Dunlap, G. (1984) The influence of vigorous versus mild exercise on autistic stereotyped behaviours. *Journal of Autism and Developmental Disorders*, 14, 57–67.

Konstantareas, M. (1990) A psychoeducational model for working with families of autistic children. *Journal of Marital and Family Therapy*, 16, 59–70.

Konstantareas, M. (1991) Autistic, learning disabled and delayed children's impact on their parents. *Canadian Journal of Behavioral Science*, **23**, 358–75.

Konstantareas, M. and Homatidis, S. (1991) Effects of developmental disorders on parents: theoretical and applied considerations. *Psychiatric Clinics of North America*, **14**, 183–98.

Konstantareas, M., Homatidis, S. and Cesaroni, L. (1995) Brief report: variables related to parental choice to medicate their autistic children. *Journal of Autism and Developmental Disorders*, **25**, 443–52.

Landa, R., Isaacs, C. and Folstein, S. E. (1991) Spontaneous narrative discourse performance of parents of autistic individuals. *Journal of Speech and Hearing Research*, **34**, 1339–45.

Landa, R., Piven, J., Wzorekj, M. M., Gayle, J. O., Chase, G. A. and Folstein, S. E. (1992) Social language use in parents of autistic individuals. *Psychological Medicine*, **22**, 245–54.

Lavigne, J. V. and Ryan, M. (1979) Psychological adjustment of siblings of children with chronic illness. *Pediatrics*, **63**, 616–27.

Le Couteur, A. (1990) Autism: current understanding and management. *British Journal of Hospital Medicine*, **43**, 448–52.

Le Couteur, A., Rutter, M., Lord, C. *et al.* (1989) Autism diagnostic interview: a standardized investigator-based instrument. *Journal of Autism and Developmental Disorders*, **19**, 363–87.

LeLaurin, K. (1992) Infant and toddler models of service delivery: are they detrimental for some children and families? *Topics in Early Childhood Special Education*, **12**, 82–105.

Lemanek, K. L., Stone, W. L. and Fishel, P. T. (1993) Parent–child interactions in handicapped preschoolers: the relation between parent behaviors and compliance. *Journal of Clinical Child Psychology*, **22**, 68–77.

Leslie, A. M. (1987) Pretence and representation: the origins of 'theory of mind'. *Psychological Review*, **94**, 412–26.

Leslie, A. M. and Frith, U. (1988) Autistic children's understanding of seeing, knowing and believing. *British Journal of Developmental Psychology*, **6**, 315–24.

Lemert, E. (1967) *Human Deviance, Social Problems and Social Control*. Englewood Cliffs, NJ: Prentice Hall.

Levy-Shiff, R. (1986) Mother–father–child interaction in families with a mentally retarded young child. *American Journal of Mental Deficiency*, **91**, 141–9.

Lieberman, D. and Melone, M. (1979) *Sexuality and Sexual Awareness*. New Haven, CT: Benhaven.

Liu, C., Robin, A. L., Brenner, S. and Eastman, J. (1991) Social acceptability of methylphenidate and behavior modification for treating attention deficit hyperactivity disorder. *Pediatrics*, **88**, 560–65.

Liwag, M. E. (1989) Mothers and fathers of autistic children: an exploratory study of family stress and coping. *Philippine Journal of Psychology*, **22**, 3–16.

Lobato, D. (1983) Siblings of handicapped children: a review. *Journal of Autism and Developmental Disorders*, **13**, 347–64.

Lonsdale, G. (1978) Family life with a handicapped child: the parents speak. *Child Health, Care and Development*, **4**, 99–120.

Lord, C. (1991) Methods and measures of behaviour in the diagnosis of autism and related disorders. *Psychiatric Clinics of North America*, **14**, 69–80.

Lord, C. and Venter, A. (1992) Outcome and follow-up studies of high functioning autistic individuals. In E. Schopler and G. B. Mesibov (Eds), *High-Functioning Individuals with Autism* (pp. 187–99). New York: Plenum Press.

Lord, C., Rutter, M., Goode, S. et al. (1989) Autism diagnostic observation schedule: a standardized observation of communicative and social behaviour. *Journal of Autism and Developmental Disorders*, **19**, 185–212.

Lovaas, I., Calouri, K. and Jada, J. (1989) The nature of behavioural treatment and research with young autistic persons. In C. Gillberg (Ed.), *Diagnosis and Treatment of Autism* (pp. 285–305). New York: Plenum Press.

Madden, N. and Slavin, R. (1983) Mainstreaming students with mild handicaps: academic and social outcomes. *Review of Educational Research*, **53**, 519–69.

Marc, D. L. and MacDonald, L. (1988) Respite care—who uses it? *Mental Retardation*, **26**, 93–6.

Marcus, L. M. (1984) Coping with burnout. In E. Schopler and G. B. Mesibov (Eds), *The Effects of Autism on the Family* (pp. 311–26). New York: Plenum Press.

Mash, E. J. (1989) Treatment of child and family disturbances: a behavioral-systems perspective. In E. J. Mash and R. A. Barkley (Eds), *Treatment of Childhood Disorders* (pp. 3–36). New York: Guilford Press.

Maslow, A. H. (1954) *Motivation and Personality*. New York: Harper & Row.

Mates, T. E. (1990) Siblings of autistic children: their adjustment and performance at home and in school. *Journal of Autism and Developmental Disorders*, **20**, 545–53.

Maurer, H. and Sherrod, K. B. (1987) Context of derivatives given to young children and nonretarded children: development over two years. *American Journal of Mental Deficiency*, **91**, 579–90.

McAdoo, W. G. and DeMyer, M. K. (1978) Personality characteristics of parents. In M. Rutter and E. Schopler (Eds), *Autism: A Reappraisal of Concepts and Treatment* (pp. 251–67). London: Plenum Press.

McHale, S. M. and Pawletko, T. M. (1992) Differential treatment of siblings in two family contexts. *Child Development*, **63**, 68–81.

McHale, S. M., Simeonsson, R. J. and Sloan, J. L. (1984) Children with handicapped brothers and sisters. In E. Schopler and G. B. Mesibov (Eds), *The Effects of Autism on the Family* (pp. 399–413). London: Plenum Press.

McHale, S. M., Sloan, J. L. and Simeonsson, R. J. (1986) Sibling relationships of children with autistic, mentally retarded, and nonhandicapped brothers and sisters. *Journal of Autism and Developmental Disorders*, **16**, 399–413.

Meade, K. and Carter, T. (1990) Empowering older users: some starting points. In L. Win (Ed.), *Power to the People: The Key to Responsive Services in Health and Social Care*. London: The King's Fund Centre.

Mealia, W. L. (1976) Conjoint-behavior therapy: the modification of family constellations. In E. J. Mash, L. C. Handy and L. A. Hamerlynck (Eds), *Behavior Modification Approaches to Parenting* (pp. 121–33). New York: Brunner/Mazel.

Mesibov, G. B. (1990) Normalisation and its relevance today. *Journal of Autism and Developmental Disorders*, **20**, 379–90.

Mesibov, G. B. and Shea, V. (1996) Full inclusion and students with autism. *Journal of Autism and Developmental Disorders*, **26**, 337–46.

Meyer, D. J. (1986) Fathers of handicapped children. In R. R. Fewell and P. F. Vadasy (Eds), *Families of Handicapped Children*. Austin, TX: Pro-Ed, Inc.

Morgan, H. (1996) *Adults with Autism: A Guide to Theory and Practice*. Cambridge: Cambridge University Press.

Morgan, S. B. (1988) The autistic child and family functioning: a developmental family systems perspective. *Journal of Autism and Developmental Disorders*, **18**, 263–80.

Myles, B., Simpson, R., Ormsbee, C. and Erickson, C. (1993) Integrating preschool children with autism with their normally developing peers: research findings and best practices recommendations. *FOCUS on Autistic Behavior*, **8**, 1–20.

Narayan, S., Moyes, B. and Wolff, S. (1990) Family characteristics of autistic children: a further report. *Journal of Autism and Developmental Disorders*, **20**, 523–35.

Newson, E. and Hipgrave, T. (1982) *Getting Through to Your Handicapped Child*. Cambridge: Cambridge University Press.

Newson, E., Dawson, M. and Everard, P. (1982) *The Natural History of the Able Autistic People: Their Management and Functioning in Social Context (Report to the Department of Social Security)*. Nottingham: The University of Nottingham.

Nirje, B. (1976) The normalization principle: implications and comments. *Journal of Mental Subnormality*, **16**, 62–76.

Nolan, M., Grant, C. and Keady, J. (1996) *Understanding Family Care. A Multidimensional Model of Caring and Coping*. Buckingham: Open University Press.

O'Gorman, G. (1967) *The Nature of Childhood Autism*. London: Butterworth.

Olsson, I., Steffenburg, S. and Gillberg, C. (1988) Epilepsy in autism and autistic-like conditions: a population-based study. *Archives of Neurology*, **45**, 666–8.

Ottensbacher, K. and Cooper, H. (1984) The effect of class placement on the social adjustment of mentally retarded children. *Journal of Research and Development in Education*, **17**, 1–14.

Parker, J. and Randall, P. E. (1997) Factitious disorder by proxy and the abuse of a child with autism. *Educational Psychology in Practice*, **13**, 46–53.

Patterson, G. R. and Fleischman, M. J. (1979) Maintenance of treatment effects: some considerations concerning family systems and follow-up data. *Behavior Therapy*, **10**, 168–85.

Patterson, G. R., Reid, J. B., Jones, R. R. and Conger, R. E. (1975) *A Social Learning Approach to Family Intervention. Families with Aggressive Children*. Eugene, OR: Castalia Publishing Co.

Piven, J., Gayle, J., Chase, G., Fink, B., Landa, R., Wzorek, M. and Folstein, S. (1989) A family history study of neuropsychiatric disorders in autistic individuals. *Journal of the American Academy of Child and Adolescent Psychiatry*, **29**, 177–84.

Piven, J., Wzorek, M., Landa, R. *et al.* (1994) Personality characteristics of the parents of autistic individuals. *Psychological Medicine*, **24**, 783–95.

Potasznik, H. and Nelson, G. (1984) Stress and social support: the burden experienced by the family of a mentally ill person. *American Journal of Community Psychology*, **12**, 589–607.

Powers, M. D. (1991) Interviewing with families of young children with severe handicaps: contributions of a family systems approach. *School Psychology Quarterly*, **6**, 131–46.

Prizant, B. M. and Wetherby, A. M. (1988) Providing services to children with autism (ages 0–2 years) and their families. *Topics in Language Disorders*, **9**, 1–23.

Ramsey, J. M., Rapoport, J. L. and Sceery, W. R. (1985) Autistic children as adults. Psychiatric, social and behavioural outcomes. *Journal of the American Academy of Child Psychiatry*, **24**, 465–73.

Randall, P. E. (1995a) Autism: support work with families. *Behavioural Social Work Review*, **16**, 31–9.

Randall, P. E. (1995b) Autism, families and the behaviourist intensive approach. *Behavioural Social Work Review*, **16**, 7–16.

Randall, P. E. and Gibb, C. (1988) Concepts of the curriculum: why INSET fails. *Educational Psychology in Practice*, **4**, 29–35.

Randall, P. E. and Gibb, C. (1992) To throw a little light. *Special Children*, **February**, 26–7.

Richman, N. (1988) Autism: making an early diagnosis. *The Practitioner*, **232**, 601–5.

Riguet, C., Taylor, N., Benaroya, S. and Klein, L. (1981) Symbolic play in autistic, Down and normal children of equivalent mental age. *Journal of Autism and Developmental Disorders*, **11**, 439–43.

Robbins, F. R. and Dunlap, G. (1992) Effects of task difficulty on parent teaching skills and behaviour. *American Journal of Mental Retardation*, **96**, 631–43.

Robbins, F. R., Dunlap, G. and Plienis, A. J. (1991) Family characteristics, family training, and the progress of young children with autism. *Journal of Early Intervention*, **15**, 173–84.

Rodrigue, J. R., Morgan, S. B. and Geffken, G. (1990) Families of autistic children: psychological functioning of mothers. *Journal of Clinical Child Psychology*, **19**, 371–9.

Rodrigue, J. R., Morgan, S. B. and Geffken, G. (1992a) Psychological adaptation of fathers of children with autism, Down syndrome, and normal development. *Journal of Autism and Developmental Disorders*, **22**, 249–64.

Rodrigue, J. R., Geffken, G. and Morgan, S. B. (1992b) Perceived competence and behavioral adjustment of siblings of children with autism. *Journal of Autism and Developmental Disorders*, **23**, 665–74.

Rose, J. and Jones, C. (1994) Working with parents. In A. Craft (Ed.), *Practice Issues in Learning Disabilities* (pp. 23–49). London: Routledge.

Rostain, A. L., Power, T. J. and Atkins, M. S. (1993) Assessing parents' willingness to pursue treatment for children with attention-deficit hyperactivity disorder. *Journal of the American Academy of Child Adolescent Psychiatry*, **32**, 175–81.

Roth, F. P. and Spekman, N. J. (1984) Assessing the pragmatic abilities of children learning language. 2. Guidelines, considerations and specific evaluation procedures. *Journal of Speech and Hearing Disorders*, **49**, 12–17.

Ruble, L. S. and Dalrymple, N. J. (1993) Social/sexual awareness of persons with autism: a parental perspective. *Archives of Sexual Behaviour*, **22**, 229–40.

Rutter, M. (1983) Cognitive deficits in the pathogenesis of autism. *Journal of Child Psychology and Psychiatry*, **24**, 513–31.

Rutter, M. and Schopler, E. (1987) Autism and pervasive developmental disorders: concepts and diagnostic issues. *Journal of Autism and Developmental Disorders*, **17**, 159–86.

Rutter, N. (1978) Diagnosis and definition. In M. Rutter and E. Schopler (Eds), *Autism: A Reappraisal of Concepts and Treatment* (pp. 1–25). London: Plenum Press.

Saleeby, D. (1996) The strengths perspective in social work practice: extensions and cautions. *Social Work*, **41**, 296–305.

Salisbury, C. L. and Intagliata, J. (Eds) (1986) *Respite Care: Support for Persons With Developmental Disabilities and Their Families*. Baltimore, MD: Paul H. Brookes.

Sarason, S. and Doris, J. (1979) *Educational Handicap, Public Policy and Social History*. New York: Free Press.

Scheff, T. (1974) The labelling theory of mental illness. *American Sociological Review*, **39**, 444–52.

Schopler, E. (1995) *Parent Survival Manual*. New York: Plenum Press.

Schopler, E. and Mesibov, G. (Eds) (1984) *The Effects of Autism on the Family*. New York: Plenum Press.

Seligman, M. (Ed.) (1991) *The Family With a Handicapped Child*. London: Allyn & Bacon.

Sharp, S. and Smith, P. K. (1994) *Tackling Bullying in Your School: a Practical Handbook for Teachers*. London: Routledge.

Sheldon, B. (1995) *Cognitive Behavioural Therapy. Research, Practice and Philosophy*. London: Routledge.

Sigman, M. and Mundy, P. (1989) Social attachments in autistic children. *Journal of the American Academy of Child and Adolescent Psychiatry*, **28**, 74–81.

Sigman, M., Mundy, P., Sherman, T. and Ungerer, J. (1986) Social interactions of autistic, mentally retarded and normal children and their caregivers. *Journal of Child Psychology and Psychiatry*, **27**, 647–56.

Sigman, M., Kasari, C., Kwon, J. and Yirmiya, N. (1992) Responses to the negative emotions of others by autistic, mentally retarded and normal children. *Child Development*, **63**, 796–807.

Simeonsson, R. J. and McHale, S. M. (1981) Review: research on handicapped sibling relationships. *Child Care, Health and Development*, **7**, 153–71.

Simpson, R. L. (1995) Individualized education programs for students with autism: including parents in the process. *Focus on Autistic Behavior*, **10**, 11–15.

Sloman, L. (1991) Use of medication in pervasive developmental disorders. *Psychiatric Clinics of North America*, **14**, 165–81.

Smalley, S. L., Asarnow, R. F. and Spence, M. A. (1988) Autism and genetics: a decade of research. *Archives of General Psychiatry*, **45**, 953–61.

Snow, C. (1972) Mothers' speech to children learning language. *Child Development*, **49**, 549–65.

Steffenburg, S. (1991) Neuropsychiatric assessment of children with autism—a population-based study. *Developmental Medicine and Child Neurology*, **33**, 495–511.

Steffenburg, S. and Gillberg, C. (1986) Autism and autistic-like conditions in Swedish rural and urban areas: a population study. *British Journal of Psychiatry*, **149**, 81–7.

Steffenburg, S. and Gillberg, C. (1989) The etiology of autism. In C. Gillberg (Ed.), *Diagnosis and Treatment of Autism*. London: Plenum Press.

Strain, P. S. and Kerr, M. M. (1981) *Mainstreaming of Children in Schools*. New York: Academic Press.

Strain, P. S. and Danko, C. D. (1995) Caregiver encouragement of positive interaction between preschoolers with autism and their siblings. *Journal of Emotional and Behaviour Disorders*, **3**, 2–12.

Strain, P. S., Hoyson, M. and Jamieson, B. (1985) Normally developing preschoolers as intervention agents for autistic-like children: effect of class deportment and social interaction. *Journal of the Division of Early Childhood*, **9**, 105–19.

Suelzele, M. and Keenan, V. (1981) Changes in family support network over the life cycle of mentally retarded persons. *American Journal of Mental Deficiency*, **86**, 526–32.

Tantum, D. (1993) *A Mind of One's Own: a Guide to the Special Difficulties and Needs of the More Able Person with Autism or Asperger Syndrome* (2nd Edn). London: The National Autistic Society.

Tew, B. J. and Laurence, K. M. (1973) Mothers, brothers and sisters of patients with spina bifida. *Developmental Medicine and Child Neurology*, **15 (Suppl. 29)**, 69–76.

Tew, B. J., Payne, J. and Laurence, K. M. (1974) Must a family with a handicapped child be a handicapped family? *Developmental Medicine and Child Neurology*, **16 (Suppl. 32)**, 95–8.

Torisky, D. and Torisky, C. (1985) Sex-education and sexual awareness building for autistic children and youth: some viewpoints and considerations. *Journal of Autism and Developmental Disorders*, **15**, 213.

Trevarthen, C. D., Aitken, K., Papoudi, D. and Robarts, J. (1996) *Children With Autism: Diagnosis and Interventions to Meet Their Needs*. London: Jessica Kingsley Publishers.

Trillingsgaard, A. and Sorensen, E. U. (1994) School integration of high-functioning children with autism. A qualitative clinical interview study. *European Child and Adolescent Psychiatry*, **3**, 187–96.

Tritt, S. G. and Essess, L. M. (1988) Psychosocial adaptation of siblings of children with chronic medical illness. *American Journal of Orthopsychiatry*, **58**, 211–20.

Trute, B. and Hauch, C. (1988) Social network attributes of families with positive adaptation to the birth of a developmentally disabled child. *Canadian Journal of Community Mental Health*, **7**, 5–11.

Tsai, L. Y. (1992) Diagnostic issues in high-functioning autism. In E. Schopler and G. B. Mesibov (Eds), *High-Functioning Individuals with Autism* (pp. 11–40). New York: Plenum Press.

Turnbull, A. P., Turnbull, H. R., Summers, J. A., Brotherson, M. J. and Benson, H. A. (1986) *Families, Professionals and Exceptionality: A Special Partnership*. Columbus, OH: Merrill.

Unger, D. G., Jacobs, S. B. and Cannon, C. (1996) Social support and marital satisfaction among couples coping with chronic obstructive airway disease. *Journal of Personal and Social Relationships*, **13**, 123–42.

Volkmar, F. R. and Mayes, L. (1990) Gaze behavior in autism. *Development and Psychopathology*, **2**, 61–9.

Volkmar, F. R. and Nelson, D. S. (1990) Seizure disorders in autism. *Journal of the American Academy of Child and Adolescent Psychiatry*, **29**, 127–9.

Wang, M. and Baker, E. (1985–1986) Mainstreaming programs: design features and effects. *Journal of Special Education*, **19**, 503–21.

Watters R. and Watters, W. (1980) Decreasing self-stimulatory behaviour with physical exercise in a group of autistic boys. *Journal of Autism and Developmental Disorders*, **10**, 379–87.

Wells, M. and Smith, D. W. (1983) Reduction of self-injurious behavior of mentally retarded persons using sensory integrative techniques. *American Journal of Mental Deficiency*, **87**, 664–6.

Wigham, S. and Tovey, C. (1994) Sweet success. *Care Weekly*, **3 March**, 12.

Williams, D. (1996) *Like Color to the Blind*. New York: Times Books.

Wilson, E. (1992) Contemporary issues in choice-making for people with a learning disability. Part 1. Underlying issues in choice. *Mental Handicap*, **20**, 31–3.

Wimpory, D. (1991) Autism: breaking through the barriers. *Nursing Times*, **87**, 58–61.

Wing, L. (Ed.) (1976) *Early Childhood Autism* (2nd Edn). Oxford: Pergamon Press.

Wing, L. (1988) The continuum of autistic characteristics. In E. Schopler and G. B. Mesibov (Eds), *Diagnosis and Assessment in Autism* (pp. 91–110). London: Plenum Press.

Wing, L. (1995) *Autistic Spectrum Disorders: An Aid to Diagnosis* (3rd Edn). London: The National Autistic Society.

Wing, L. (1996) *The Autistic Spectrum: A Guide for Parents and Professionals*. London: Constable.

Wing, L. and Gould, J. (1979) Severe impairments of social interaction and associated abnormalities in children: epidemiology and classification. *Journal of Autism and Development Disorders*, **9**, 11–29.

Wing, L., Gould, J., Yeates, S. and Brierly, L. (1977) Symbolic play in severely mentally retarded and in autistic children. *Journal of Child Psychology and Psychiatry*, **18**, 167–78.

Wolfensberger, W. (1972) *The Principle of Normalisation in Human Services*. Toronto: National Institute on Mental Retardation.

Wolff, S., Narayan, S. and Moyes, B. (1988) Personality characteristics of parents of autistic children. *Journal of Child Psychology and Psychiatry*, **29**, 143–53.

World Health Organisation (1993) *The ICD-10 Classification of Mental and Behavioural Disorders*, Geneva: World Health Organisation.

Zappella, M. Y. (1990) Young autistic children treated with ethologically oriented family therapy. *Family Systems Medicine*, **8**, 14–27.

Zarkowska, M. and Clements, J. (1989) *Problem Behaviour in People with Severe Learning Difficulties*. London: Croom Helm.

INDEX

Index compiled by Alan Whittle

Related titles of interest..

Teaching Children with Autism to Mind-Read
PATRICIA HOWLIN, SIMON BARON-COHEN and JULIE HADWIN
0471 976237 November 1998 302pp Paperback

Children with Autism and Asperger Syndrome
A Guide for Practitioners and Carers
PATRICIA HOWLIN
0471 983284 October 1998 342pp Paperback

Understanding and Teaching Children with Autism
RITA JORDAN and STUART D. POWELL
0471 958883 1995 188pp Hardback
0471 957143 1995 188pp Paperback

Dyslexia
2nd Edition
A Practitioner's Handbook
GAVIN REID
0471 973912 March 1998 264pp Paperback

WILEY

ST. PATRICKS
COLLEGE
LIBRARY